The Syntax of Verb Initial Languages

OXFORD STUDIES IN COMPARATIVE SYNTAX
Richard Kayne, General Editor

The Syntax of Verb Initial Languages

Edited by
Andrew Carnie and Eithne Guilfoyle

OXFORD
UNIVERSITY PRESS
2000

OXFORD
UNIVERSITY PRESS

Oxford New York
Athens Auckland Bangkok Bogotá Buenos Aires Calcutta
Cape Town Chennai Dar es Salaam Delhi Florence Hong Kong Istanbul
Karachi Kuala Lumpur Madrid Melbourne Mexico City Mumbai
Nairobi Paris São Paulo Singapore Taipei Tokyo Toronto Warsaw

and associated companies in
Berlin Ibadan

Copyright © 2000 by Oxford University Press

Published by Oxford University Press, Inc.
198 Madison Avenue, New York, New York 10016

Oxford is a registered trademark of Oxford University Press

Library of Congress Cataloging-in-Publication Data

The syntax of verb initial languages / edited by Andrew Carnie and Eithne Guilfoyle.
    p. cm. — (Oxford studies in comparative syntax)
    Includes bibliographical references and index.
    ISBN 0-19-513222-X. — ISBN 0-19-513223-8 (pbk.)
  1. Grammar, Comparative and general—Syntax.   2. Grammar, Comparative and
general—Verb.   3. Grammar, Comparative and general—Word order.   I. Carnie,
    Andrew.   II. Guilfoyle, Eithne.   III. Series.
        P295.S94   2000
        415—dc21   99-40359

1 3 5 7 9 8 6 4 2

Printed in the United States of America
on acid-free paper

Contents

Contributors

Judith Aissen
University of California, Santa Cruz

Andrew Carnie
University of Arizona

Edit Doron
Hebrew University of Jerusalem

Ray Freeze
University of Utah

Carol Georgopoulos
University of Utah

Eithne Guilfoyle
Dun Laoghaire Institute of Art Design and Technology
and University of Calgary

Heidi Harley
University of Arizona

Randall Hendrick
University of North Carolina

Eloise Jelinek
University of Arizona

Felicia Lee
University of California, Los Angeles

Diane Massam
University of Toronto

Seth Minkoff
New Mexico State University

Elizabeth Pyatt
Harvard University

Andrea Rackowski
Massachusetts Institute of Technology

Lisa Travis
McGill University

The Syntax of Verb Initial Languages

1

Introduction

Andrew Carnie and Eithne Guilfoyle

Until quite recently, the study of basic word order and correlates of 'basic' word order was limited to typological studies of language. The issue was either ignored by generative grammar or assumed to have no theoretical basis. Recent work in the minimalist approaches to principles and parameter syntax, however, has opened up the study of word orders, their derivations, and the correlates of those orders. Influential papers by Pollock (1989) and Chomsky (1991) provided a framework in which to develop a constrained view of phrase structure and predicate-argument placement. Kayne's (1994) antisymmetric approach to phrase structure further constrains the possible word orders of language. In his view, the only underlying word order is subject-verb-object; all other word orders are derived from this order by one means or another. In this volume, we consider one subset of word orders—those that are verb initial; whether these orders are derived or not; whether there is a uniform derivation of the word orders; and whether there are any putative universal correlates of these orders.

Languages that have as their "basic" or "default" word order an order that puts the verb first in the sentence (verb-subject-object, VSO, and verb-object-subject, VOS) make up about 10% of the world's languages, yet they are relatively untreated in the generative grammar literature.[1] These languages bring their own special problems to the discipline. As will be seen in section 1, the basic derivation of one of these word orders (VSO) is itself highly problematic and a matter of great debate. With the advent of restrictive theories of phrase structure, such as Kayne (1994), even the simpler VOS order is also problematic. Despite the fact they come from a variety of language families and from a great variety of geographical locales, all verb initial languages seem to have certain properties in common, such as preverbal particles and special types of locative constructions. Questions as to the nature of the derivation of verb initial order and its correlates are the focus of this volume. We have compiled here a collection of essays by a variety of authors about a number of verb initial languages. Even though many of these essays are about diverse and unrelated languages, the results show a remarkable uniformity in a number of domains.

3

Below, we consider some of the major themes that emerge throughout these articles. We start by considering the derivations of verb initial order, looking first at VSO and then at VOS. Then we turn to the question of word order correlations.

1. The Problem of VSO Languages

Verb-subject-object order has long been problematic for theories of grammar that assume a universal VP constituent containing both the verbal predicate and its complements. Take, for example, the typical sentence in (1) from Modern Irish:

(1) **Irish**
Leanann   an t-ainmní an briathar i nGaeilge.
follow.PRES the subject the verb   in Irish
'The subject follows the verb in Irish.'

In this sentence, the verb *leanann* is separated from the object *an briathar* and other complements by the subject *an t-ainmní*. A contiguous constituent of the verb and its complements is clearly impossible, at least on the surface.

A number of theories of VSO structure have been proposed to account for this apparent anomaly. The earliest researchers on VSO languages proposed simply that these languages lacked a VP constituent (Schwartz 1972, Anderson 1984, Awbery 1976, Tallerman 1990, Stenson 1981, McCloskey 1979, 1980, Chung 1983). These theorists lacked VP phrase structure rules (2), in an approach we refer to as *flat structure* (3):

(2) S → V NP NP

(3)

This theory, while appealingly simple, runs into many problems cross-linguistically. Such a structure makes very clear predictions about the behavior of the subject and object arguments which are not borne out by the data. As noted by Berman (1974), it predicts that subject and object NPs, since they are both postverbal, should not be distinguishable in contexts where only one NP argument appears. In other words, verb-object sequences and verb-subject sequences should behave identically with respect to various syntactic processes. Anderson and Chung (1977) argue that this is not true for many languages that are clearly VSO. Samoan and Tongan show demonstrable differences between VO and VS sequences in the interaction of Equi-NP Deletion and Subject to Object Raising—two rules of the Extended Standard Theory that make reference to subjects and not to objects. If the VO and VS sequences are structurally indistinguishable, then verbs that allow both Equi and Subject to Object Raising to apply should allow Subject to Object Raising to apply to objects, provided Equi has applied to delete the subject in an embedded context. This prediction is false.

In this volume, Minkoff discusses a well-known "argument" or "animacy" hierarchy pattern in Mam. The argument, which is interpreted as a "subject" in Mam, must be more animate than the object argument. This pattern emerges in an environment much like the one described above. He shows that this phenomenon occurs as a result of the complex interaction of parsing/processing principles and the fact that the language is both *pro*-drop and verb initial.

A great body of empirical evidence has surfaced showing that many VSO languages have VP-like constituents which consist of a non-finite verb and object but exclude the subject. In many VSO languages, sequences of untensed verbs or participles and objects appear that function as syntactic constituents, reminiscent of verb phrases. McCloskey (1983) shows that participles and objects obey several standard tests for constituency. For instance, a participle plus object sequence functions as a constituent with respect to such tests as clefting. Similar facts are found in Breton (Anderson and Chung 1977) and in Welsh (Sproat 1985). This lends strong support to the idea that VSO order is derived from an underlying structure that has a VP constituent. These facts are discussed in detail by Hendrick in this volume.

Similarly, there is evidence concerning the relative prominence of subjects and objects in VSO languages. In flat structure, subjects and objects are sisters to one another. Given this, we expect that there will be no structure dependent subject/object asymmetries in VSO languages. Once again, this prediction is proven false (Speas 1990). For example, in Niuean, as discussed by Woolford (1991), the subject is not c-commanded by the object; thus the following sentence is not a violation of Principle B:

(4) **Niuean** (Seiter 1980:78)
Fana n-e ia a ia ni neafi.
shoot EMPH-ERG he ABS him REFL yesterday
'He shot himself yesterday.'

Fassi Fehri (1993) and Choe (1987) discuss similar data in Arabic and Berber, respectively. Related evidence from parasitic gaps in Welsh (Sproat 1985), violations of the ECP in Chamorro (Chung 1983), superiority effects in Welsh and Breton (Hendrick 1988), and relativization in Kwakwala (or Kwakiutl) (Anderson 1984) show similar subject-object asymmetries in other VSO languages.

Woolford (1991) discusses a set of facts from Jakaltek, originally presented by Craig (1977), which seem to go against this analysis. She notes that R-expressions embedded in the subject NP cannot be co-referent with an object pronoun:

(5)   **Jakaltek**
      Xil [smam$_i$ naj   pel]   Ø$_{j/*i}$
      Saw POSS.father CL   Peter him
      'Peter$_i$'s father saw him$_j$'
      *'Peter$_i$'s father saw him$_i$'

She interprets this as a condition C effect (Chomsky 1981) where the object c-commands the R-expression in the subject NP. She claims this is only possible with a flat structure approach. While not looking directly at the facts discussed by Woolford, Aissen in this volume takes a careful look at the distribution of binding in Jakaltek. She claims that the relevant criteria for binding of pronouns in Jakaltek is not c-command, but rather a prosodic domain. By extension, then, Woolford's arguments for flat structure disappear.

A number of different derivational approaches have also been proposed for VSO languages. One early theory is that of *subject lowering* proposed in Choe (1987) for Berber, Chung (1990) for Chamorro, and Shlonsky (1987) for Arabic. Choe (1987) argues that a language like Berber derives VSO when the subject NP lowers for Case reasons from its base position in the specifier of IP to a position adjoined to the verb:

(6)

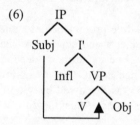

For Choe, Case assignment in VSO languages may only apply to the right, so in order for Case to be assigned, the subject must lower to a position immediately following the verb. Chung (1990) also argues for a subject lowering approach to VSO order for Chamorro. Her evidence comes from the fact that the subject can appear after any projection of V. Chung also notes that Chamorro requires that coordinated elements be identical constituents. Interestingly, it appears that the subject of two coordinated VPs can appear between the verb and the object of the second conjunct:

(7)   **Chamorro**
      [Tumohgi]   ya   [ni-rekuknisa   si **Maria** ni gubietnu].
      INFL.stand   and.then INFL.PASS.recognize   Maria   OBL governor
      'Maria stood and was recognized by the governor.'

Chungs claims that such sentences can follow only from an analysis according to which the subject starts in the specifier of IP, where it discharges its function as "subject" of both of the conjoined VPs, then lowers and adjoins to the V2.

Another analysis of VSO that makes use of argument movement is the *object postposing approach*, proposed by England (1991) to account for the diachronic shift from VOS to VSO languages in the Mayan family. She claims that the ancestor of most Mayan languages was VOS. Many of the languages are now VSO or VOS/VSO alternating. On this basis, she argues that VSO order was derived by shifting the object to the right from an underlying VOS order. Based on evidence from non-verbal predicates in Maori, which show predicate complement subject order, Chung (1996) claims that Maori is underlyingly VOS, and has an object postposing derivation for VSO order.

A more common class of analyses of VSO involves the *raising of verbal predicates* from the VP around the subject argument to some inflectional head (8). Among the authors who have proposed such analyses in various forms are Emonds (1980), Sproat (1983, 1985), Sadler (1988), Mohammed (1988), Ouhalla (1994), Duffield (1991, 1995), Guilfoyle (1993), Noonan (1994), McCloskey (1991, 1996a, 1996b, 1997), Chung and McCloskey (1987), Kaplan (1991), Fassi Fehri (1993), and Carnie (1995).

(8)

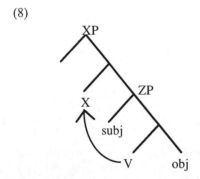

Authors in this volume who take this approach include Hendrick, Doron, Carnie, Pyatt and Harley, and Guilfoyle.

McCloskey (1991) provides strong evidence in favor of a general verb-raising approach to VSO order for Modern Irish. McCloskey notes that in a structure like (8), once the verb has raised, there exists a constituent which consists of the subject, the trace of the verb, and the object (represented by ZP in (8)). Again, this is true independently of the surface location of the verb and its arguments, as long as the verb has raised around the subject. The claim here is that if such a grouping passes tests for constituency separate from the verb, then we have evidence for the verb raising analysis. McCloskey's prediction is borne out. Irish has a process of VP ellipsis which parallels English VP ellipsis in many ways. It differs from English VP ellipsis, however, in what is deleted. In English, the subject obligatorily remains, but the verb and the object (and any other VP-internal material) are elided and replaced with *did (too)*. In Irish, on the other hand, the verb is the one element that is not elided; rather, it is the ZP constituent that is elided:

(9)   English: S V O and S ~~V O~~
        Irish: V S O and V ~~S O~~

(10)   Duirt mé go gceannódh sí é agus cheannaigh ~~subj object~~.
        said I that would.buy she it and bought
        'I said that she would buy it and she did.'

As McCloskey notes "the almost unanimous view in the literature is that the elided material in VP ellipsis forms a syntactic constituent." The raising analysis, with a ZP constituent, provides us with an elegant account of these facts. The verb has raised outside of the domain of the ellipsis process, whereas the subject and object remain within the ZP constituent, which is elided.

Perhaps the earliest raising analysis of VSO order involves the raising of the verb to the complementizer head, in a manner familiar from V2 languages and from question formation in SVO languages like English:

(11)

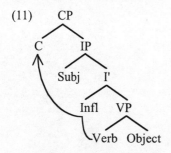

This approach, frequently called the *weak-V2 approach* to VSO order was first proposed by Emonds (1980), who suggested that all verb fronting was motivated by "attraction to the complementizer." This approach was also popular in the early work in the Government and Binding framework (Stowell 1989, Déprez and Hale 1986, Hale 1989). More recently it has been proposed to account for the change from V2 in Middle Welsh to VSO in Modern Welsh by Clack (1994) and Sáinz (1994), and for Pembrokeshire Welsh by Watanabe (1993). In this volume, Carnie, Harley and Pyatt propose that this is exactly the derivation of VSO in Old Irish. Arguments against the weak V2 approach for Modern Irish are presented by McCloskey (1996a). McCloskey argues, on the basis of IP adjoined adverbs, that verbs in Modern Irish are no higher than the left edge of IP. Massam's article in this volume argues extensively against a raising to C approach for Niuean.

The class of analyses that hold that the verb in VSO languages is in the highest inflectional projection can be called the *Left-Edge of IP* group. Innumerable variations of this approach are found in the literature on VSO. The first to present this view was Sproat (1985). With the advent of the VP-internal subject hypothesis (Koopman and Sportiche 1991), a simple formulation of this group was proposed (see, for example, McCloskey 1991): Verbs raise to Infl, while subjects stay *in situ* in the specifier of VP. With minor variations, this is the view adopted by, among many others, Guilfoyle (1990), Noonan (1994), and McCloskey (1991) for Irish; Mohammed (1988) and Fassi Fehri (1989) for Arabic; Sadler (1988) for Welsh; Schafer (1994, 1995) for Breton; Woolford

(1991) for Chamorro and Niuean; Guilfoyle, Hung, and Travis (1992) for Tagalog and Cebuano; Massam (1996) for Niuean; Kaplan (1991) for Welsh, Breton, Berber, and Biblical Hebrew; Koopman and Sportiche (1991) for Irish, Welsh, and postverbal subjects in Italian and Kilega; Borer (1995) for stylistic inversion structures in Modern Hebrew; and Chomsky (1991) for VSO languages in general.

With the advent of Pollock's (1989) split Infl hypothesis, the possibilities for what might constitute the left edge of Infl greatly expanded. The arguments no longer have to be VP-internal. Bobaljik and Carnie (1996), McCloskey (1996a), Fassi Fehri (1993), Aoun, Benmamoun, and Sportiche (1994), and Rouveret (1991) have all argued this to be true for various VSO languages. Other authors, such as Ouhalla (1994) and Carnie (1995), have argued that the relative order of inflectional heads differs in VSO languages, such that Tense dominates Agreement. In this volume, Hendrick attempts a characterization survey of such approaches to the Celtic literature.

Many of the articles in this volume attempt to motivate the postverbal positioning of subjects in verb initial languages from very different perspectives. Doron's article builds upon work by McCloskey (1996a) in deriving the postverbal nature of the subject from EPP properties of the language; she adduces evidence for this proposal from left conjunct agreement phenomena in Biblical Hebrew. Massam, by contrast, claims that the verb satisfies EPP features, thus explaining its initial position. Guilfoyle's article links this positioning to the semantics of tense and initiation point.

An interesting and exciting variation on the verb raising approach emerges for the first time in three articles in this volume. Quite independently, Lee, Massam, and Travis and Rackowski have proposed, for widely divergent languages (Malagasy, Niuean, Zapotec), that verb initial order does not arise from head movement of the verb to some initial position, but instead via fronting of the verb phrase (or predicate phrase) to some specifier position. We call this proposal the *VP raising approach*. The fact that variants on this analysis are presented by independent researchers and for a wide variety of languages is quite provocative. This new alternative is likely to arouse great controversy among researchers in verb initial languages.

Another alternative within the verb-raising family is discussed by Jelinek in this volume. She argues that verb (or more precisely predicate) raising in Lummi, Straits Salish, is due to information structure effects. She claims that Lummi, a pronominal argument language, shows a strict mapping between topic-focus structure and the surface syntax. She links initial position to focus; for her, predicates are usually new information and thus move to this initial position.

2. The Problem of VOS Order

The question of the derivation of VOS order has been paid less attention in the generative literature (notable exceptions include Guilfoyle, Hung, and Travis

1991 and Pearson 1996). The question of whether VOS order is a base-generated or derived order is especially important in light of the recent proposals of Kayne (1994), who claims that specifier-head-complement order is the universal order. Under this conception, the origins of VOS order become mysterious, because the order does not lend itself as readily as VSO to verb raising analyses. This puzzle is relevant to the discussion here for two reasons. First, many languages, in particular Austronesian and Mayan languages, show alternations between VSO and VOS order. The nature of these alternations is of course important to understanding how both VSO and VOS order are derived. Second, from a typological perspective, there is the problem that many of the properties associated with VSO order (see below) are also found in VOS languages. Why this should be the case requires explanation. This question is dealt with most extensively in this volume by the articles by Travis and Rackowski, Massam, and Freeze and Georgopoulos. Massam and Travis and Rackowski claim that VSO and VOS order are tightly linked. The differences between the two lie only in the degree to which objects shift out of the VP before VP remnant movement. Freeze and Georgopoulos take a very different view. In looking at the locative paradigm, they observe that certain patterns emerge only if VOS and VSO are underlying or base orders. They argue against a Kaynean antisymmetic approach to underlying word order.

3. A Fundamental Tension

With these numerous ways of deriving verb initial order all present in the literature, the obvious question arises as to whether different verb initial languages derive the basic order in different ways (as is suggested by McCloskey 1996a), or whether one of these approaches to deriving the order is universal. Balanced against this question we have another issue: If the derivation of verb initial order is not homogenous, then why are there a number of syntactic phenomena common to many or most VSO languages?

Many VSO languages (although by no means all) share the following traits, all of which have been claimed to be correlates of VSO order. Some of these are Greenbergian (1963); others are correlates that have surfaced in other work.

1. Head initiality (Greenberg)
2. Prepositional (Greenberg)
3. Post-nominal adjectives (Greenberg)
4. Preverbal tense, mood/aspect, question, and negation particles
5. Inflected prepositions (Kayne 1994)
6. Left-conjunct agreement (Doron, this volume)
7. Lack of a verb "have" (Freeze and Georgopoulos, this volume)
8. Copular constructions without verbs (Carnie 1995)
9. "Verbal noun" infinitives (Myhill 1985)

Although not all verb initial languages have all these characteristics, a striking number of them have at least some subset of them; in contrast, SVO and SOV languages rarely show a large range of these phenomena. We thus pose the question of why this should be the case if these languages have different derivations for their order. Is it a fact about Universal Grammar, about diachronic syntax (see, for example, Gensler 1991), or merely coincidence? All the papers in this volume make some attempt at explaining a few of these properties. Freeze and Georgopoulos link certain behaviors to the typological properties of verb initial languages. In particular, they consider the differences between a parametric approach to word order and one which assumes a universal base order. Hendrick attacks the question of how tightly linked these properties are to word order, by examining the differences among the Celtic languages. He argues against a unified approach to verb initial order and deals in particular with the question of whether synthetic agreement is a property of the word order type.

A number of chapters in this volume deal with the issue of preverbal particles, which seem prevalent in the syntax of verb initial languages. These include Hendrick, Carnie, Harley and Pyatt, Lee, Massam, and Rackowski and Travis.

Acknowledgments

A great number of people helped in the development of this volume. We would like to thank Tom Bever, Ray Freeze, Carol Georgopoulos, Heidi Harley, Eloise Jelinek, Simin Karimi, Richard Kayne, Jim McCloskey, Martha McGinnis, Janet Nicol, Gillian Ramchand, Betsy Ritter, and an anonymous OUP reviewer, all of whom either provided extensive comments on the contents or helped us with reviewing the papers. Peter Ohlin and MaryBeth Branigan of OUP provided extremely helpful editorial advice throughout the process. Sarah Corlett Longstaff and Caterine Hicks Kennard help enormously in the preparation of the finished product. Work on this project was partially supported by a grant from the Vice President for Research at the University of Arizona and by separate grants to the editors from the Social Sciences and Humanities Research Council of Canada.

Notes

1. A notable exception is the special edition of *Lingua* (volume 85), edited by James McCloskey (1991).

2

Celtic Initials

Randall Hendrick

The modern Celtic languages are comprised of Irish, (Scots) Gaelic, Welsh, and Breton.[1] These languages pose the fundamental problem for linguistic thought: How can we best explain overlapping patterns of similarity and dissimilarity between languages? One interesting line of explanation is to historicize these patterns.[2] The Celtic languages share a common historical source, and a variety of historical forces have operated to make each one distinct with rich dialectal variety. While the historical perspective has proven productive elsewhere, it is not seriously appealed to as an explanation for the commonalities of word order among the Celtic languages; there is no "Celtic syntax" that correlates syntactic properties with specific non-linguistic aspects of Celtic history. Most linguists see the syntactic similarities as reflections of some "universal" principles or tendencies operative in language more generally. Some of the characteristics of each language might still be given a historical explanation, but the common historical source of the languages is displaced as an explanation for their syntactic similarities. In this way, the pattern of similarity and dissimilarity mentioned above is taken to bear on the question of what is the best way to understand the universal principles or tendencies that languages exhibit. It is in this light that the syntax of the Celtic languages is currently investigated.

There is, of course, a plethora of proposed universal principles that regiment the commonality and variation among natural languages. One view of how we might explain the overlapping patterns of similarity and difference among languages is to hold that the lexical elements are ordered in a more or less constant way from language to language, with variation from that constant base being the consequence of the functional items and the various morphological requirements they must satisfy.[3] On this view, lexical items are universally ordered (perhaps to facilitate semantic interpretation, which would also be constant), and variation between languages is morphosyntactic.[4]

This chapter examines the clause initial syntax of the Celtic languages from this broad perspective. I will concentrate on those syntactic elements that appear to the left of the non-finite verb. They include the subject, some adverbials, and the rather complex pattern of preverbal particles. In the course of this exploration, I will emphasize how little the positioning of these elements is dependent on the specifically verb initial character of the languages involved.

1. Derived VSO Clausal Structure

Each of the modern Celtic languages exhibits constructions in which the verb is initial relative to the subject and object. It is this fact that leads to the common observation that these languages are VSO languages:

(1)   **Irish**   (Bobaljik and Carnie 1996)
       Chonaic   Seán   an   madra.
       see-PAST   John   the   dog
       'John saw the dog.'

(2)   **Gaelic**   (Gillies 1993)
       Chunnaic   mi   Iain   an dé.
       see-PAST   I   John   yesterday
       'I saw John yesterday.'

(3)   **Welsh**   (T. Watkins 1993)
       Gwelodd   y   bachgen y   dyn.
       see-PAST   the   boy   the   man
       'The boy saw the man.'

(4)   **Breton**
       Gwelet   an deus   Yann   an   den   e kêr.
       see   have-3S   Yann   the   man   in town
       'Yann saw the man in town.'

Although early work on the Celtic languages treated the subject and object as structural sisters, substantial evidence has accumulated that these languages contain a constituent comprised of the verb and its object, to the exclusion of the subject.[5] Much of this evidence concerns periphrastic constructions in which an auxiliary verb carries tense inflection and the verb and its object form a phrase by standard constituency tests.[6] Infinitives in some of the Celtic languages also provide some evidence for the existence of a VP. In these structures, the verb appears between the subject and object, making it possible to claim that the verb and object form a constituent. Welsh, Breton, and a southern dialect of Irish have infinitives that pattern in this fashion:[7]

(5)   **Welsh**
       Mi ddisgwyliodd   John   i   Gwyn   weld   Mair.
       PRT expect-PAST   John   to   Gwyn   see   Mair
       'John expected Gwyn to see Mair.'

(6) **Breton**

Ret   e   oa   da Yann deskiñ   brezhoneg.
necessary PRT   be-IMPERF to Yann study   Breton
'It was necessary for Yann to study Breton.'

(7) **Munster Irish**   (Bobaljik and Carnie 1996)
Ba   mhaith   liom   Seán   a   scriobh   na   habairte.
COP   good   with.1S John   PRT write   the   sentence
'I want John to write the sentence.'

Infinitives in other dialects of Irish and Gaelic do not provide similar evidence of a subject-verb-object order because they contain an operation that shifts an object to the left of non-finite verbs.[8]

The issue is how the facts in (1)–(4) can be reconciled with the evidence that the verb and its object might form a constituent. One way of achieving this reconciliation is to posit a position on the left edge of the clause that attracts the tensed verb.[9] To make this idea more concrete we could specify that the tense inflection appears on the left edge of the clause, as in (8), and that the verb raises to that position. This makes the claim that there is a class of grammars that show verb initial structures only for tensed verbs, and gives the pattern in (1)–(4). When tense is absent or otherwise supported by auxiliary verbs, the verb remains with the direct object with which it forms a constituent (as in (5)–(7)).

(8) a. $[_\alpha$ Tense $\ldots [_\beta$ NP $\ldots [_\chi \ldots$ V $\ldots$ NP $\ldots$]]]
    b. $[_\alpha$ V$_i$+Tense $\ldots [_\beta$ NP $\ldots [_\chi \ldots$ V$_i \ldots$ NP $\ldots$]]]

Other realizations of the same broad intuition are of course possible. One might say, for example, that the tensed verb raises to a complementizer position (C) on the left edge of the sentence, as in Emonds (1980). This assimilates the verb initial status to the V→C movement common in analyses of German and Dutch (cf. den Besten 1983, Platzack 1986c).

(9)   [C... [$_{IP}$ NP... [... V...NP....]]] → [V$_i$+C...[$_{IP}$NP...[...V$_i$...NP...]]]

This approach has not found much favor among Celtic scholars, in part because the finite verb and overt complementizers are usually not in complementary distribution—as they are in the Germanic languages. In addition, the finite verb and the subject cannot easily be separated by adverbials, as one might expect if the finite verb is outside IP and IP is a level for adverbial adjunction. However, Schafer (1995) argues convincingly that finite verbs in Breton are able to raise to C precisely because one finds the finite verb replacing an overt complementizer *ma* 'if' in (10).

(10)	**Breton**					(Schafer 1995)
	a. M' am bije	echuet	ar	labour, e	vefen	aet	raok.
	   if	haveCOND1S finished the work	PRT	beCOND1S gone	away
	   'If I had finished the work I would have gone.'

	b. Am bije	echuet	ar	labour, e	vefen	aet raok.
	   haveCOND1S finished	the work	PRT	beCOND1S gone	away
	   'If I had finished the work I would have gone.'

Carnie, Harley, and Pyatt (this volume) adduce related evidence for raising to C in Old Irish.

The approach to sentences like (1)–(4), which raises a verb to some clause initial position, asserts that the subjects and objects in these sentences occupy hierarchically distinct positions in the sentence structure, both before and after the tensed verb is moved to clause initial position (i.e., the subject and object are not distinguished by linear order alone). Several arguments have been constructed to bolster this claim. One of the stronger arguments to this effect is built on the distribution of pronouns. Principle A of the Binding theory (cf. Chomsky 1981, 1986) identifies a class of pronouns, the anaphors (e.g., a reflexive or reciprocal pronoun), that are referentially incomplete and require a co-referential NP to fix their reference. This co-referential NP must furthermore c-command the anaphor. If the structure of the Celtic sentence was "flat," treating both subject and object as sisters, we would expect that an anaphor could appear in subject position and its antecedent could appear in object position. This expectation follows from the fact that the object would c-command the subject. The distribution of anaphors parallels that in English, with the anaphor disfavored in subject position.

(11)	**Irish**						(Carnie 1995)
	Chonaic Seán agus	Máire lena	chéile.
	Saw	John and	Mary with3P	other
	'John and Mary saw each other.'

(12)	*Chonaic lena	chéile Seán agus	Máire.
	  Saw	with3P	other John	and	Mary
	*'Each other saw John and Mary.'

(13)	**Welsh**						(Awbery 1976)
	Rhybuddiodd	Wyn ac Ifor ei	gilydd.
	Warned		Wyn and Ifor each	other
	'Wyn and Ifor warned each other.'

(14)	*Rhybuddiodd ei	gilydd Wyn ac Ifor.
	  Warned	each	other	Wyn	and Ifor
	*'Each other warned Wyn and Ifor.'

Similar arguments can be built appealing to principles B and C of the Binding theory.

Other phenomena also exhibit significant asymmetries between subject and object that can be interpreted as a reflex of a structural asymmetry between these two kinds of NPs. Expletives appear to a limited extent in these languages; they are restricted to subjects of weather verbs and extraposed sentential subjects. We also find asymmetries between subject and object with respect to multiple questions in languages where those are possible.

2. Where is the Subject?

Many researchers accept some version of the VP Internal Subject hypothesis (Koopman and Sportiche 1991). Under this view, subjects are generated as the specifier of a VP, where they receive their thematic role from the verb. In English, the subject must then raise to a higher structural position (such as specifier of IP or one of its decomposed projections such as AgrP) to satisfy other grammatical requirements (e.g., the Case filter). In this sense there are at least two subject positions, and the notion "subject" is decomposed in such a way that its properties (having a privileged thematic role, or playing a special morphological role) are distributed among distinct structural positions.[10]

If we grant that subjects originate within the VP where they receive a semantic role, and if we adopt some operation that raises the verb out of the VP in Celtic finite clauses, it is not obvious whether the subject ever needs to move in a derivation out of the position where it receives its semantic role. Chung and McCloskey (1987) and McCloskey (1991) argue that the clausal structure of Irish contains a head Infl that embeds a small clause. The subject in this analysis never needs to raise and satisfies its morphosyntactic requirements (e.g., Case theory) in place. A similar analysis of Welsh is suggested by Koopman and Sportiche (1991). The subject of at least some verb initial languages, in this view, is special because it avoids raising from its original position. Important evidence from the distribution of adverbs, however, undermines this view and suggests that subjects raise out of the VP even in these verb initial languages.

Pollock (1989) has used the positioning of adverbs as a useful diagnostic for clausal structure. Assuming that adverbs are adjoined to non-argument maximal projections and are immobile, Pollock argues that finite verbs in French and English occupy distinct structural positions because they stand in different orders relative to adverbs. This is illustrated in (15) where the adverb *à peine* 'hardly' must stand after the finite verb in French but before it in the English gloss.

(15) **French**
　　　J' embrassai à peine　Marie.
　　　I kiss.PAST　hardly　Marie
　　　'I hardly kissed Marie.'

Extending a proposal of Emonds (1978), Pollock argues that the French verb raises out of VP to a higher inflectional head of phrase, while the English verb remains within VP. This explains why the French finite verb is separated from its direct object by an adverb, but the English verb is not. McCloskey (1997) uses the distribution of adverbs to argue that the subject in Irish must ultimately be positioned outside the VP. This conclusion is motivated by the observation that the subject appears to the left of adverbs, as in (16):

(16)   **Irish**
       Chuala Róise go   minic roimhe   an t-amhrán sin.
       heard   Róise ADV   often before-it   the song that
       'Róise had often heard that song before.'

The same argument can be constructed in the other Celtic languages:

(17)   **Breton**   (Press 1986)
       Gallout a   ran   testeniañ e   vije   bet   aet
       Can   PRT do1S   testify   PRT beCOND   been gone

       houmañ [vp kuit, a-bell zo,   diwar douar hor bro...
       this one   away long since from earth our country
       'I can testify that this one would have gone (away), long since, from
       the earth of our country. . . '

(18)   **Welsh**   (Thorne 1993)
       Ni   wnaethai'r   un ohonynt erioed [vp osgo   at
       NEG make.PAST'the one of-them ever   attempt toward

       roi   unrhw help ariannol iddi].
       give any   help financial to.her
       'Not one of them had ever attempted to assist her financially.'

(19)   **Gaelic**   (Robertson and Taylor 1993)
       Bha   mi gu   [vp tuiteam nam   chadal].
       be.PAST I   almost   falling in1S sleep
       'I was almost falling asleep.'

The adverbial evidence seems to argue that the subject in the Celtic languages generally appears outside of the lowest VP. We can capture this generalization either by raising the subject outside of the lowest VP to satisfy some morphosyntactic requirement like the Case filter, or by generating the subject outside of the lowest VP to begin with for semantic reasons.

The adverbial evidence that I have just used to argue that the subject is outside the VP in the Celtic languages conflicts with an argument about the position of subjects in Breton that is developed by Schafer (1995). Breton employs an inflected preposition to express an object pronoun.

(20) **Breton** (Desbordes 1983)
    a. Gwelet am eus da   vreur.
       seen   have-I your brother
       'I have seen your brother.'

    b. Gwelet am eus anezhañ.
       seen   have-I of-3SM
       'I have seen him.'

Schafer claims that these pronouns undergo object shift to appear on the left edge of a VP, a process that has been studied extensively in the Scandinavian languages. This allows her to explain the contrast between (21) and (22):

(21)   Bremañ e   wel anezhañ Maia.
        Now   PRT sees it   Maia.
        'Maia sees it now.'

(22)   *Bremañ e   wel Maia anezhañ.
        now   PRT see Maia it
        *'Maia sees it now.'

The subject *Maia* remains within the VP in (21), presumably in the position of specifier of VP, where it receives its thematic role. This conclusion follows from the claim that the pronoun *anezhañ* marks the edge of the VP, and the subject is on its right. At the time of its writing Schafer (1995) made the position of subjects in Breton and Irish look rather similar because Chung and McCloskey had argued that the Irish subject remained internal to the VP. In the wake of the argument by Bobaljik and Carnie (1996) and Duffield (1995) that the object is raised out of the VP in infinitival structures like (23), Irish and Breton look quite different, as pointed out by McCloskey (1997):

(23)   **Irish**   (Bobaljik and Carnie 1996)
        Ba   mhaith liom   [(e) an teach$_i$ a   thógáil t$_i$].
        COP good   with1S he the house TRANS build
        'I would like him to build the house.'

The point is that if the object is outside the VP in (23), then the subject must be as well. The Irish is apparently different from the Breton in (21), where the subject is to the right of the raised object.

    Schafer's conclusion is at odds with the direction of the adverbial evidence and should give us pause. We need either to re-evaluate adverbs as a diagnostic for the position of subject or to reconsider the force of the argument based on the Breton object pronouns. Because of the general utility of the adverbial diagnostic, I believe that the Breton pronominals should be analyzed differently. Schafer's claim that (22) is unacceptable conflicts with other surveys of Breton that report sentences like (24) to be acceptable:

(24) **Breton**   (Stephens 1993)
E   kêr   e   welas   Yannig   anezho.
in town PRT see-PAST   Yannig   them
'Yannig saw them in town.'

Moreover, there is some reason to doubt the claim that the object shifts to the left edge of the VP in this construction. This Breton construction does not in fact parallel the object shift construction in Scandinavian. Holmberg (1997) argues that object shift is blocked when any other phonologically overt constituent appears within the VP. Yet the analysis of Breton would require object shift even over a phonologically overt subject. It seems more likely that the pronominal form *anezhañ* is treated as a pronoun that undergoes head raising to adjoin to the verb in the dialect of Breton that Schafer describes.[11] The verb+*anezhañ* complex will then be positioned clause initially like other tensed verbs. This operation will cause the pronoun to raise with the verb outside the VP, and we expect that pronoun to appear to the left of VP-adjoined adverbs. This expectation is confirmed in (25):

(25) **Breton**   (Press 1986)
Ne   zisoñje   anezhañ morse pa veze   an   disterañ feson   glav.
NEG forgetPAST it   never if was   the smallest chance rain
'She would never forget it if there was the slightest chance of rain.'

3. Preverbal Particles

We have observed that the Celtic languages are verb initial in the sense that the finite verb is positioned before the subject and object. A more careful examination of the languages concerned reveals that a range of other elements can appear to the left of the verb, although it is still true that the subject and the object remain to the verb's right. This section examines the syntax of these other clause initial elements, with particular emphasis on the system of preverbal particles so characteristic of the Celtic languages.

Since Bresnan (1974), syntactic analyses of English and a host of other languages have made use of a complementizer position to class functional elements such as *that, if,* and *for*. Four functions of complementizers have been identified. Complementizers have a subordinating function: They introduce embedded clauses. They can also cross-classify sentence types: They distinguish indicatives from interrogatives and conditionals as well as positives from negatives. They carry some rudimentary temporal information, often contrasting finite and non-finite clauses. And when *wh*-phrases move, they position themselves relative to complementizers. Let us provisionally identify all the particles that appear clause initially in the Celtic languages as complementizers. Later we will find some reason to refine this gross classification.[12]

The Celtic languages all have complementizers that introduce embedded clauses, as in (26–29). In these examples the complementizer has been italicized:

(26) **Irish** (Carnie 1995)
Ceapaim [*go* bhfaca sé an madra].
think1S [that saw he the dog]
'I think that he saw the dog.'

(27) **Gaelic** (Robertson and Taylor 1993)
Thuirt i [*gun* robh iad glè laghach].
Said she that were they very nice
'She said that they were very nice.'

(28) **Welsh** (T. Watkins 1993)
Dywedodd [*y* deuai y bachgen].
said3S that comeCOND the boy
'He said that the boy would come.'

(29) **Breton** (Desbordes 1983)
Gouzout a ran mat [*e* responto din diouzhtu].
know PRT do1S well that answered3S to1S immediately
'I know that he answered me immediately.'

One also finds complementizers that do not have an exclusive subordinating function. These are often particles that express distinctions of sentence type (or "mood"). The question particle, for example, introduces both direct and indirect questions:

(30) **Irish** (McCloskey 1979)
a. *An* bpósfadh duine ar bith í?
Q marryCOND anyone her
'Would anyone marry her?'

b. Níl fhios agam [*an* bpósfadh duine ar bith í].
NEG.be know at1S Q marryCOND anyone her
'I don't know if anyone would marry her.'

(31) **Gaelic** (Robertson and Taylor 1993)
a. *An* robh sibh anns an achadh an diugh?
Q were you.PL in the field today
'Were you in the fields today?'

b. Dh'fhaighnich e	dhomh *an* robh	sibh	anns an
   asked	he	of1S	Q	was	you.PL	in	the

   achadh	an diugh
   field	today.
   'He asked me whether you were in the fields today.'

(32)	**Welsh**	(Thorne 1993 and *Gramadeg* 1976)

   a. *A* wyf yn	euog	o	gamliwio?
     Q am PRT guilty	of	misrepresentation
     'Am I guilty of misrepresentation?'

   b. Tybed	[*a* ydy John	yn	dod].
     wonder	Q	is	John	PROG coming
     'I wonder whether John is coming.'

(33)	**Breton**	(Gregor 1980 and Stephens 1993)

   a. *Ha* te	a	glevas?
     Q	you PRT hearPAST
     'Did you hear?'

   b. Gwelet	e	vo	[*ha* brav	e	vo	an	amzer].
     see	PRT beFUT Q	nice	PRT beFUT the	weather
     'We shall see whether the weather is nice.'

Negative particles also precede the finite verb in the Celtic languages in both main and subordinate clauses. They are often classed as complementizers.

(34)	**Irish**	(Ó Siadhail 1980)

   a. *Ní* heo	é an	bord.
     NEG here	it the	table
     'This here is not the table.'

   b. Deir	sé [*nach* 'eo	é an	bord].
     say	he NEG here	it the	table
     'He says this here is not the table.'

(35)	**Gaelic**	(Robertson and Taylor 1993)

   a. *Nach* robh	còta	aice.
     NEG	was	coat	at3SF
     'She didn't have a coat.'

   b. Bha	Ceiteag ag	ràdh	[*nach* robh	còta	aice].
     Was	Katie	PROG say	NEG was	coat	at3SF
     'Katie was saying that she didn't have a coat.'

(36) **Welsh**   (T. Watkins 1993)

    a. *Ni* welodd   y   bachgen y   dyn.
       NEG saw   the boy   the man
      'The boy did not see the man.'

    b. Dywedodd   [*nad* oedd y   bachgen yn   dod].
       said   NEG was   the boy   PROG coming
      'He said the boy was not coming.'

(37) **Breton**

    a. *Ne* lennan   ket al   lizher.
       NEG read1S   NEG the   letter
      'I don't read the letter.'

    b. Gouzout a   ran   mat   *ne* lennan   ket al   lizher.
       know   PRT do1S   well   NEG read1S   NEG the   letter
      'I know I don't read the letter.'

It is common to claim that complementizers can be integrated into X-bar theory as heads of the phrase CP (Chomsky 1986). *Wh*-movement is movement to the specifier of CP, perhaps to satisfy a morphosyntactic requirement that the head C when it bears a feature [+*wh*] must have a *wh*-phrase in its specifier.[13] From this perspective, it is not surprising that *wh*-phrases move to the left of both the finite verbs and the kinds of elements we have classed as complementizers.

(38) **Irish**   (McCloskey 1979)

    Cén   fear   a   n-éisteann tú   leis?
    which man   C   listen   you with3S
    'Which man do you listen to?'

(39) **Gaelic**   (Mackinnon 1971)

    Cuin   a thogas   tu   e?
    when   C buildFUT   you it
    'When will you build it?'

(40) **Welsh**   (Thorne 1993)

    Sut   y gwyddoch chi hynny?
    How   C know   you that
    'How do you know that?'

(41) **Breton**   (Stephens 1993)

    Pegoulz e teuio   da   gêr?
    when   C comeFUT3S   to   home
    'When will he come home?'

While all the Celtic languages make use of preverbal elements that serve the typical syntactic functions of complementizers, they exhibit variation in whether these functions can be distributed between multiple particles. To appreciate this point let us briefly consider Welsh. Welsh has a particle, *mai/tau,* which simply introduces embedded clauses.[14] In addition it has two particles, *y* and *a,* which appear adjacent to the finite verb. There are also the negative particles *nid* or *dim,* which can appear between the two. Dislocated arguments appear between the negative particles and the preverbal particle just mentioned. This relative ordering can be observed in (42):

(42)   Roedd   e'n   gwybod [mai   [dim   [fi   (a)   [ddaeth   â'r
       Was   he'PRT know   PRT   NEG   I   PRT brought   with-the

anrheg]]].
present
'He knew it wasn't I who brought the present.'

These facts suggest that we posit a structure like (43), a structure that converges with the typological studies of Bhatt and Yoon (1991) and Rizzi (1997):

(43)   [subordinator [mood [finite [IP]]]]

The subordinate particles are *mai/tau.* Mood contains the negative *nid* or *dim.*[15] Finite is the locus of the particles *y* and *a* that co-occur with tensed clauses as well as of the prepositional complementizer *i* that co-occurs with infinitives. The specifier of finite is the target for operator movement.

While sentences like (42) assign three functions of complementizers to distinct particles, these particles do not appear in every sentence. In other sentences, more than one function can be assigned to a single particle. For example, (44) can also be expressed as (45), where the negative is carried by the finite complementizer rather than by the mood complementizer:

(44)   **Welsh**   (*Gramadeg* 1976)
       dim   fy   nhad   (a)   [brynodd   y   teledu lliw   yma].
       NEG   my   father PRT   bought   the TV   color   this
       'My father didn't buy this color TV.'

(45)   Fy   nhad   na   [brynodd   y   teledu lliw   yma].
       my   father NEG.PRT bought   the TV   color   this
       'My father didn't buy this color TV.'

The preverbal particle *y(r)* can introduce subordinate clauses. Here the function of signaling subordination and finiteness are expressed with only one particle:[16]

(46) **Welsh**   (Thorne 1993)
Ofnwn   [y byddai'n   anodd   cael   enillydd clir].
feared1S   PRT would-be difficult get   winner   clear
'I feared that it would be difficult to have a clear winner.'

Subordinators can also collapse two complementizer functions. Interrogative particles appear to occupy the position we have labeled "subordinate," alternating with *mai/tau*. They co-occur with the separate negative particle in questions like (47):

(47) **Welsh**   (Thorne 1993)
A   yw'n gyfreithlon   talu treth   i   Gaesar, *ai* *nid* yw?
Q   is-PRT legal   pay tax   to   Caesar Q   NEG is
'Is it legal to pay tax to Caesar, or is it not?'

In other negative yes-no questions, however, the functions of the question particle and the negative particle are assigned to a single particle.

(48) **Welsh**   (*Gramadeg* 1976)
 a. *A* brynodd hi'r   beic?
    Q bought   she-the bike
    'Did she buy the bike?'

 b. *Oni*   phrynodd hi'r   beic?
    Q.NEG bought   she-the bike
    'Didn't she buy the bike?'

I assume rather tentatively that these facts about Welsh complementizers can be explained in the following fashion. The complementizer system should be decomposed into three positions as in (49). Each of these complementizer positions in (49) is filled derivationally, either by insertion of distinct particles from the lexicon or by the syntactic raising of a complementizer that carries the relevant feature of that position.[17] The raising is the familiar head to head movement, and I assume that it is motivated by a morphosyntactic requirement either to check appropriate features on the functional items raising or to realize features on the target of the movement. Let us assume that adverbials adjoin to non-arguments: MP, FP, and IP in (49). SubP is not an adjunction site because it is an argument.

(49)

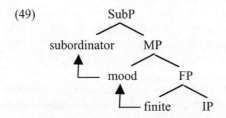

Now, Breton patterns like Welsh with a series of distinct particles that co-occur with one another, and we would advocate a similar analysis for those elements. Irish has the particles in the table in (50), taken from Chung and McCloskey (1987).

(50)

Irish	non-past	past
subordinating	go^N	gur^L
"direct" relative	a^L	a^L
"indirect" relative	a^N	ar^L
interrogative	an	ar
embedded negative	$nach^N$	$nár^L$

These particles show a close connection to tense, each having a past and non-past form, although the distinction might be more appropriately classed as a realis/irrealis opposition.[18] Irish also has distinct subordinating and matrix negative particles. In both respects Irish differs from Welsh and Breton, which use the same particles for past and non-past and for both matrix and embedded negatives. More important, the Irish particles do not co-occur in series. On this score Irish is more like English, where clauses appear with a single complementizer. The Irish conditional particle *má* cannot appear with other particles or topics and has a distinct negative form, *mura,* rather than *ma nach.* This is quite different from the Welsh conditional particle *os,* which can appear with negatives, as in (51), as well as with finite complementizers and dislocated topics, as in (52):

(51) **Welsh**   (Thorne 1993)
      Os na   chân nhw falu   a   dinistrio.
      if NEG allow they wreck and destroy
      'If they are not allowed to wreck and destroy.'

(52) Os chwychwi a   fedrwch roddi rhoddion da.
      if you   PRT able   give gifts   good
      'If you are able to give good gifts.'

We hypothesize that Irish involves the same hierarchical structure in its preverbal complementizer system as in (49). Its complementizers behave like Welsh *y* in (46), essentially controlling the several complementizer positions through movement.

There is some reason to think that this raising may occur covertly. Suppose that when an element α is moved to a target it is simply copied there. The resulting chain, (α_i, α_i), subsequently has two options: either the right member can be deleted, giving the typical appearance of movement, or the left member can be deleted, leaving the moved element in its original position. This second alternative is "covert" movement because the moved element α occupies the target but is not realized phonologically in that position. With this notion of covert movement in mind, the sentences in (53)–(54) are informative.[19]

(53) | Mae | he'n | siwr *mai* | heddiw | *y* | bydd | y | plant |
| | is | she-PRT | sure PRT | today | PRT | beFUT3SF | the | children |

yn swnllyd.
PRT noisy
'She's sure that it's today that the children will be noisy.'

(54) | Mae he'n | siwr | heddiw | *y* | bydd | y | plant |
| | is | she-PRT | sure | today | PRT | beFUT3SF | the | children |

yn swnllyd.
PRT noisy
'She's sure that it's today that the children will be noisy.'

The sentences (53)–(54) are significant because the complementizer *y* appears to the right of the adverbial in each example. No problem arises in (53) because there is an overt subordinator, *mai*. In (54), however, that position is unfilled. These facts are quite different from those in English, where the adverbial must position to the right of the complementizer *that,* as in (55). When the adverbial appears on the left of the complementizer, as in (56), it is no longer an adjunct of the embedded clause but modifies the main clause.

(55) She's sure that today the children will be noisy.
(56) #She's sure today that the children will be noisy.

We hypothesize that the movement we appealed to in (54) can apply covertly. This means that *y* occupies both the finite position and the subordinator position, but that ultimately it is deleted from the higher one. Evidently, the English complementizer occupies the highest complementizer position and, if it undergoes raising, that movement is overt rather than covert.

Irish adverbials interact with complementizers much as adverbials do in Welsh. McCloskey (1996b) reports that in (57) the complementizer *go* appears to the right of the adverbial *i lár an gheimhridh* 'in the middle of winter.'

(57) **Irish**   (McCloskey 1996b)
Tá a   fhios   agam
Is its knowledge   at3S

i lár   an gheimhridh ón   ngrinneal aníos
in middle-of the winter   from-the sea-bed   up

go gcaitear   ballaigh ar an dtráigh.
C   throwIMP   wrasse   on the beach
'I know that in the middle of winter wrasse are thrown up on the
beach from the seabed.'

Assuming that adverbs are adjoined to IP below the complementizer system,
McCloskey takes the Irish facts to argue that the complementizer has lowered to
the finite verb as a post-syntactic repositioning. The analysis suggested here
covertly raises the Celtic complementizers and assimilates these structures to
more familiar instances of raising driven to satisfy morphosyntactic features on
the functional categories.

The advantage of the covert raising analysis can be seen when negative
polarity items are examined. Ladusaw (1979) has argued that negative polarity
items must be c-commanded by a negative element.[20] McCloskey (1996b) shows
that in Irish negative polarity items may appear before the negative
complementizer, as in (58), in apparent violation of Ladusaw's licensing
requirement.

(58) **Irish**
Glór ar bith níor   chuala sé.
voice any   NEG.PST hear   he
'He didn't hear any voice.'

McCloskey solves this apparent contradiction in the following way: The
negative polarity item is adjoined to IP, and the negative complementizer c-
commands that item, putting the negative complementizer to the left of the
negative polarity item. In the derivation of phonological form, the negative
complementizer must then lower to the finite verb, giving the pattern in (58),
where the negative is to the right of the negative polarity item. Breton, as
described by Hendrick (1988), also has negative polarity items that appear in
clause initial position, as in (59).

(59) **Breton**
Den ebet ne   gar   ket   Mona.
any one   NEG love NEG Mona
'No one loves Mona.'

As we noted in section 2, Schafer (1995) argues that the Breton verb raises to C.
On this assumption, we are unable to generalize McCloskey's lowering analysis
to Breton. However, the covert raising of the negative complementizer to a

higher complementizer position would allow us to give a single explanation to both the Irish and the Breton facts. In both cases the raised negative complementizer satisfies Ladusaw's licensing requirement. The lower member of the movement chain is the one that survives at phonological form.[21]

Taking stock of our discussion, we have claimed that all languages have available the three-tiered complementizer system of (49). Adverbials adjoin to non-arguments IP, FiniteP, MoodP. The specifier of FiniteP is the target of operator movement.[22] The Celtic languages differ among one another in regard to whether they contain distinct particles that realize each of these positions, or whether the positions are combined by movement and instantiated by a single particle. In structures with a single complementizer particle, the Celtic languages seem to admit adverbials to the left of complementizers, unlike English. This difference between Celtic and English lies in whether the raising of the single complementizer particle to SubP is covert (as it is in Welsh and Irish) or overt (as in English).

4. Agreement

One of the most striking features of the Celtic languages is the pattern of subject-verb agreement. In essence, the languages have two paradigms: a synthetic agreement pattern that distinguishes person and number, and an analytic pattern (homophonous to the third singular form), which remains invariant despite the grammatical features of the subject. Overt NPs typically appear with the analytic agreement. The synthetic agreement form occurs with unexpressed subjects.[23] In the examples that follow, sentences (a) and (b) show that the verb does not change its morphological shape as the overt subject changes in number. Example (c) shows that null subjects do lead the verb to change shape.

(60) **Irish**   (McCloskey and Hale 1984)
   a. *Chuirfeadh* sé isteach ar an phost sin.
      putCOND he in on the job that
      'He would apply for that job.'

   b. *Chuirfeadh* siad isteach ar an phost sin.
      putCOND they in on the job that
      'They would apply for that job.'

   c. *Chuirfinn* isteach ar an phost sin.
      putCOND1S in on the job that
      'I would apply for that job.'

(61) **Gaelic**   (Mackinnon 1971)

    a. *Bhuaileadh*   e   an cù.
       strikeCOND   he   the dog
       'He would strike the dog.'

    b. *Bhuaileadh*   iad   an cù.
       strikeCOND   they   the dog
       'They would strike the dog.'

    c. *Bhuailinn*   an cù.
       strikeCOND1S the dog
       'I would strike the dog.'

(62) **Welsh**

    a. *Canodd*   Sion.
       singPAST   Sion
       'Sion sang.'

    b. *Canodd*   y   plant.
       singPAST   the   children
       'The children sang.'

    c. *Canon*   [pro].
       singPAST3PL
       'They sang.'

(63) **Breton**

    a. Bremañ e   *labour*   Yann.
       today   PRT workPRES Yann
       'Today, Yann works.'

    b. Bremañ e   *labour*   ar   vugale.
       today   PRT workPRES the   children
       'Today, the children work.'

    c. Bremañ e   *labouront.*
       today   PRT work3PL
       'Today, they work.'

Although all of the Celtic languages prohibit the co-occurrence of the synthetic agreement with overt nominals in most contexts, the languages present variations on this basic generalization. First, the languages vary as to whether they make available an analytic and synthetic form for each verb: Irish and Gaelic have many verbs and parts of verbal paradigms that lack synthetic forms; Breton has a verb *kaout* 'have' that lacks any analytic form. Second, there is variation regarding the co-occurrence of agreement and pronouns. In Irish and Gaelic, overt pronouns may appear with the analytic agreement, but this is not possible in Welsh or Breton. In Welsh, and to a lesser extent in Breton, the synthetic agreement can co-occur with a special set of pronominal forms that "double" the synthetic agreement. This doubling is unavailable in Irish or Gaelic.

Two lines of thought have been used to explain the complementary distribution of overt NPs and the synthetic agreement. One relates the synthetic agreement to movement to explain its preference for a gap in subject position. The synthetic agreement is a pronoun that incorporates or cliticizes onto the host verb. The second approach tries to explain these facts as an agreement phenomenon rather than as a result of movement; some aspect of the feature matrix of the agreement inflection interacts with the adjacent subject position to disfavor the rich synthetic agreement with an overt subject. The first approach has been extensively used in analyses of Welsh; the very regular morphological patterns presented in Welsh are conducive to the systematic movement approach (e.g., Rouveret 1990, 1994, Sadler 1988).[24] The second has appeared in studies that attempt to come to terms with the less regular morphological pattern found in the other Celtic languages (e.g., McCloskey and Hale 1984, Stump 1985, 1989, Hendrick 1988, 1994). More recently, analyses with the Minimalist Program combine movement and feature checking (e.g., Roberts and Shlonsky 1996). These two approaches differ in whether the pattern of agreement pointed out above is correlated to the verb initial syntax of finite clauses. The movement analyses typically hypothesize a correlation between the verb initial character of the clause and the presence of analytic agreement. See, for example, Roberts and Shlonsky (1996).

I am skeptical that the verb initial character of the finite clause is a necessary or sufficient criterion for the analytic agreement pattern. Other languages that are not verb initial exhibit similar patterns. Ouhalla (1993), citing Kornfilt (1985), reports that Turkish requires its verbs to agree in number with a null subject, as in (64a–b), but with an overt subject number agreement is not necessary, as in (64c).

(64)   **Turkish**
    a. Geldi-ler.
       came-PL
       'They arrived.'

    b. *Geldi.
       came
       'They arrived.'

    c. Öğrenciler geldi(-ler).
       students came-PL
       'The students have arrived.'

It thus seems that the alternation between synthetic and analytic agreement extends beyond verb initial languages. This fact, coupled with the observation made above that the complementary distribution of the synthetic and analytic agreement forms breaks down in several places, suggests that attributing the phenomena to movement is inappropriate: The phenomena seem to manifest a strategy of maximization of constraint satisfaction.

To capture this intuition, suppose that languages draw from the following principles.

(65) IDENTIFY
>   The grammatical features of an empty category must be morphologically identified by an overt head bearing those same grammatical features.

(66) AVOIDPRO
>   Delete the phonological matrix of an independent pronoun.

(67) AVOIDAGR
>   Delete the phonological matrix of agreement.

Suppose further that these principles can be organized on a hierarchy the order of which determines which principle applies when there is an ambiguity in their application. This ordering is a partial one. Structures may violate principles on the right of this hierarchy to satisfy more highly valued principles on the left. In this schema, if α is more highly valued then β, we say $\alpha > \beta$. If α and β are equally valued, we write $\{\alpha,\beta\}$. Let us assume that the deletion of (synthetic) agreement in (67) yields the analytic agreement.[25] We can describe the Celtic agreement patterns as in (68)–(69).

(68)   Welsh, Breton
>   IDENTIFY > AVOIDPRO > AVOIDAGR

(69)   Irish, Gaelic
>   IDENTIFY > {AVOIDPRO, AVOIDAGR}

The interaction of the principles in (65)–(67) can be observed in the following table:

(70)

	IDENTIFY	AVOIDPRO	AVOIDAGR
a. V [$_{AGR}$ ∅]$_i$ NP$_i$			
b. V [$_{AGR}$ α]$_i$ NP$_i$			*
c. V [$_{AGR}$ ∅]$_i$ NP$_k$	*		
d. V [$_{AGR}$ α]$_i$ NP$_k$	*		*
e. V [$_{AGR}$ ∅]$_i$ [$_{PRO}$ α]$_i$		*	
f. V [$_{AGR}$ α]$_i$ [$_{PRO}$ α]$_i$		*	*
g. V [$_{AGR}$ ∅]$_i$ [$_{PRO}$ α]$_k$	*	*	
h. V [$_{AGR}$ α]$_i$ [$_{PRO}$ ∅]$_k$	*		*
i. V [$_{AGR}$ ∅]$_i$ [$_{PRO}$ ∅]$_i$	*		
j. V [$_{AGR}$ α]$_i$ [$_{PRO}$ ∅]$_i$			*
k. V [$_{AGR}$ ∅]$_i$ [$_{PRO}$ ∅]$_k$	*		
l. V [$_{AGR}$ α]$_i$ [$_{PRO}$ ∅]$_k$	*		*

In (70) [$_{PRO}$ α] indicates an overt pronoun while [$_{PRO}$ ∅] represents a null pronoun. Similarly [$_{AGR}$ α] is the overt, synthetic agreement marker, while [$_{AGR}$ ∅] is the null, analytic marker. Matching of grammatical features is represented here as co-indexing, so that in (a), but not (c), the NP and the agreement marker have matching grammatical features.

In structures that have a full NP the null, analytic agreement is preferred, as can be seen by an inspection of (a–d), which will show that such combinations satisfy all three constraints. This is the aspect of the agreement pattern common to all the Celtic languages. When a pronoun is present, as in (e–l), we find that we have a violation of at least one of our principles governing the morphological realization of categories. We select the most highly valued combination. In Welsh and Breton, that means preferring (j) where we satisfy IDENTIFY and AVOIDPRO but violate the weaker AVOIDAGR. In Irish and Gaelic, since AVOIDPRO and AVOIDAGR are equally valued, both (j) and (e) are equally good combinations.[26] When the lexicon does not make available an appropriate analytic or synthetic form, we predict that the system will satisfy (65–67) in an optimal way. For example, the Breton verb *kaout*, which lacks any analytic form, will necessarily violate AVOIDAGR, but it still patterns in such a way as to satisfy IDENTIFY and AVOIDPRO. In this way the interaction of the principles models fairly closely the similarity and variation among the languages under consideration.

5. Conclusion

I have developed a view of Celtic clausal structure that takes the structure of the VP to be much as it is in English, hierarchically distinguishing subject and object. I have suggested that the verb raises at least to Tense and the subject raises outside the VP, although there may be some variation as to whether the verb continues to raise into the C system. I have explored the possibility that the preverbal particles are part of a universal three-tiered complementizer system that distinguishes three positions: subordinate, mood, and finite. These positions can be assigned distinct particles, or they can be united by head raising and realized as a single particle. Adverbial evidence suggested that this raising is covert in Celtic. We have treated the realization of subject verb agreement as a process that maximizes its congruence with competing principles and have thereby disassociated these facts from verb raising.

I began this chapter by cautioning against the search for a Celtic syntax. The progression of my inquiry has been equally deflationary towards the prospect of a verb initial syntax. The raising of the verb to clause initial position is the only special characteristic of these verb initial languages. The characteristic particles and agreement of the verb initial languages discussed here do not appear to correlate with this verb initial property. Instead, they seem to access other universal principles organizing natural languages.

There remains a residue of verb initial syntax, however, in the apparent parallel between the structure of the clause and the structure of the nominal. Just as the verb raises to a clause initial position, so does the noun raise to an initial position within its phrase:

(71) **Irish**
[doras an tí]
 door   the house.GEN
'the house's door'

(72) **Gaelic**   (Gregor 1980)
[dorus an tighe]
 door the house
'the house's door'

(73) **Welsh**   (Gregor 1980)
[drws y tŷ]
door the house
'the house's door'

(74) **Breton**   (Trépos 1980)
[dor an ti]
door the house
'the house's door'

This process has been studied with some care by Duffield (1996) and Rouveret (1994). Many have expressed the intuition that the same principle guides the construction of the finite clause and the nominal, yielding their initial character. It is significant, however, that this parallelism is not theoretically required to exist. Perhaps further research will reveal whether this is a fault of our theoretical understanding or of our intuition.

Notes

1. Manx and Cornish have sadly disappeared, although there are attempts to resurrect them. See George and Broderick (1993) on these efforts.

2. See, for example, Gregor (1980) for a careful treatment along these lines.

3. Syntactic elements naturally divide into a class of lexical items such as nouns, verbs, prepositions, and adjectives on the one hand, and functional items such as negatives, determiners, and particles on the other hand. The functional classes have few tokens, while the lexical classes are large. The lexical classes are semantically and morphologically complex, while the functional classes are morphologically and semantically simple.

4. A second view takes the position that the variation among languages is better modeled as differences in the positioning of lexical items themselves. Any generalizations among these differently positioned lexical items that emerge from comparing one language to another are expressed in some nonstructural way. These may be semantic generalizations or patterns based on grammatical relations such as subject and object, or ordering restrictions sensitive to morphological classes, but each shares the contention that the principle in question should not be expressed structurally. See work carried out in the family of theories established by Lexical Functional Grammar outlined in Bresnan (1982), and Generalized Phrase Structure Grammar in Gazdar et al. (1985) that eschew syntactic derivations. While these different approaches to the universal principles organizing sentence structure influence how descriptions of the Celtic languages are articulated, in practice there is considerable convergence: When detailed examinations are pursued, the variation in the Celtic languages is attributed to the distribution of morphosyntactic features, such as whether a verb carries a tense inflection or not. See, for example, Borsley (1990). There remain deep differences over whether such morphosyntactic features head syntactic constituents themselves, or whether they are syntactically inert.

5. For analyses that deny a structural asymmetry between subject and object, see Anderson (1981) on Breton, Awbery (1976) and Tallerman (1990) on Welsh, and Stenson (1981) and McCloskey (1979) on Irish.

6. See McCloskey (1983) on Irish, Harlow (1981), Sproat (1985) and Sadler (1988) on Welsh, and Stephens (1982) on Breton. Traditional grammars often treat the non finite verb in these constructions as "verbal nouns." Some researchers have formalized this intuition as claiming that these "verbs" are in fact "nouns" (Willis 1988, Anderson 1981). Others (e.g., Rouveret 1990) have analyzed them as "archicategories," similar to "archiphonemes" in phonology that do not have all their feature values specified.

7. Welsh has another construction in which the embedded verbs are not inflected for tense and in which the verb is situated between the subject and object.

(i) **Welsh** (T. Watkins 1993)
Dywedodd fod y bachgen yn dod.
said-he be the boy in coming
'He said that the boy comes/is coming/was coming/used to come.'

See Harlow (1992) for an analysis of this construction. In terms of the analysis outlined in section 4, the verb *fod* 'be' in this example must raise to the complementizer 'finite' where it replaces the otherwise expected complementizer *i* 'to'.

8. See Adger (1996) on Gaelic. Chung and McCloskey (1987), as well as Guilfoyle (1993) and Bobaljik and Carnie (1996), describe Irish.

9. Actually, other constituents besides verbs are attracted to this initial position: All types of predicates are. See Carnie (1995) and Doherty (1996) for a discussion of Irish. Hendrick (1994) and Rouveret (1996) treat Welsh and Breton, while Higginbotham and Ramchand (1996) analyze Gaelic.

10. Another view of how subjects receive their semantic role takes them to be external to the (lowest) VP. The idea is that the subject semantic role is assigned compositionally from the VP rather from the lexical structure of the verb alone (Chomsky 1981, Marantz 1984, Kratzer 1996, Harley 1995). On this view, however, the subject may still need to raise from its semantic position to satisfy morphosyntactic requirements.

11. In older and literary forms of the language, a preverbal monosyllabic clitic pronoun appears in these structures.

12. For a different view of how preverbal particles function in a verb initial language see Massam (this volume).

13. This is the *Wh*-criterion of May (1985).

14. Another set, *mi* or *fi*, introduce main clauses.

15. The mood category here resembles the functional projection Σ under CP employed by Carnie, Harley, and Pyatt (this volume), building on the work of Laka (1991).

16. The Welsh sentence in (i), noted in Awbery (1976), would provide a case in which the negative particle is assigned the mood and subordinator positions:

(i) Dwed Emyr nad yw Ifor yn dod   yno.
     says   Emyr NEG is   Ifor PRT come   there
     'Emyr says that Ifor is not coming there.'

Nad is also assigned the finite position since negatives complementizers only co-occur with tensed clauses, as we will see below.

17. Alternatively, we could create the distinct complementizer positions through the process of "fission" hypothesized by Nash and Rouveret (1996).

18. See Ó Sé (1987, 1990).

19. These examples are adapted from Tallerman (1996). She explains these facts through CP recursion.

20. Ladusaw (1979) formulates this requirement as an S-structure constraint. From my perspective, it is a diagnostic for covert movement. For example, English negative auxiliary verbs will need to be prevented from covertly raising into the complementizer system because negative polarity items are impossible in structures like (i).

(i) *Anyone can't leave.

Moreover, a reconsideration of how quantifier scope is represented will also be in order since standard LF phrasal movement accounts of quantifier scope, such as May (1985), do not interact with the licensing of negative polarity items.

21. Another advantage of the decomposed complementizer system concerns long head movement of participles in Breton, as described in Hendrick (1994) and Borsley, Rivero and Stephens (1996). In these structures both a finite verb and a participle appear clause initially, as in (i).

(i) **Breton**
   Gwelet en deus   Yann   Mona.
   seen   has   Yann   Mona
   Yann has seen Mona.

If the finite verb moves to C—as Schafer suggests—one needs another head position for the participle. The higher mood position provides such a target. On the assumption that the mood is the position of the negative feature, we will be able to explain why long head movement of the participle is disfavored with negative complementizers.

22. The specifier of MoodP is a position for topics not involving operator movement generally. See Rizzi (1997) for a detailed treatment of this aspect of the decomposition of the complementizer system.

23. In fact, this generalization extends beyond subject-verb agreement and also holds for prepositions that inflect to agree with their object and nouns that agree with their possessor. I limit my discussion here to the verbal morphology.

24. But see Hale (1990) on Irish and Anderson (1982) on Breton.

25. Perhaps AVOIDNUM (avoid number agreement) would be a more precise characterization of the agreement principle. Another principle requiring the preservation of agreement would also be needed. It would be highly valued in languages like Italian where synthetic agreement co-occurs with overt nominals. Turkish would rank equally the principle AVOIDAGR and the principle preserving it, giving its optional appearance with nominals.

26. If the identification principle were less highly valued than both the avoid overt pronoun principle and the avoid overt agreement principle, we would find a language that lacked both overt agreement and overt pronouns.

3

VSO Order as Raising Out of IP?
Some Evidence from Old Irish

Andrew Carnie, Heidi Harley, and Elizabeth Pyatt

In the generative paradigm, there are at least two schools of thought about the derivation of VSO order via verb raising. One holds that the verb raises to the highest complementizer position (C°) of the matrix clause, in a manner familiar from den Besten's (1981) analysis of verb second languages like German and Dutch. The other holds that the verb is not in C° at all; rather it appears on the highest head of the inflectional complex, with the subject in some lower structural position. The first of these approaches was popular in the early work in the Government and Binding framework (Stowell 1989, Déprez and Hale 1986, Hale 1989). The latter approach has gained popularity in more recent work (Chomsky 1993, Bobaljik and Carnie 1996, Carnie 1995, Chung and McCloskey 1987, McCloskey 1990, 1991, 1996a, 1996b, Rouveret 1991, Sadler 1988, Guilfoyle 1990, 1993, Duffield 1991, 1995, Pyatt 1992, Fassi Fehri 1993, among many others). In this chapter, we would like to reopen the question of whether V→C° movement is relevant to word order considerations in VSO languages. We will argue that both V→Infl and V→C° are present in the VSO language Old Irish. We will argue that Old Irish had a "filled C°" requirement (in a sense to be made more precise below), thus deriving its basic VSO order from V→C° movement. However, we will also assume that Old Irish derived VSO order from V→Infl movement in clauses with filled complementizers.

1. Two Approaches to VSO order

The earliest raising analysis of VSO order involved the movement of the verb to the complementizer head in a manner familiar from analyses of word order in verb second (V2) languages and from subject-auxiliary inversion in questions in languages like English. This approach to verb second order was first proposed by den Besten (1981). Emonds (1980) extended this approach to VSO languages by claiming that all verb fronting was motivated by "attraction to the complementizer." This approach was also popular in the early work on VSO in the Government and Binding framework (Stowell 1989, Déprez and Hale 1986, Hale 1989, Eska 1994, 1996). More recently, movement to C° has been proposed for Middle Welsh by both Clack (1994) and Sáinz (1994), and for Pembrokeshire Welsh by Watanabe (1993).

German and Dutch stand as typical examples of verb second languages. In tensed clauses without an overt complementizer, the verb must appear in "second position" in these languages. The first position in the sentence is occupied by any other XP constituent. In example (1) below (data from Haegeman 1991), the verb *kaufte* always appears in the second position; any of the other constituents (the subject *Karl*, the object *dieses Buch*, or the temporal adverb *gestern*) can appear in the first position. The remaining constituents follow the verb.

(1) a.   Karl   kaufte   gestern   dieses Buch.
          Karl   bought   yesterday this   book
          'Karl bought this book yesterday.'

    b.   Dieses Buch kaufte Karl gestern.
         'Karl bought this book yesterday.'

    c.   Gestern kaufte Karl dieses Buch.
         'Karl bought this book yesterday.'

In clauses with overt complementizers, by contrast, there is no verb second ordering. The verb appears in final position:

(2)   Ich dachte   daß Karl   gestern   das Buch gekauft hat.
      I   thought   that Karl yesterday   the book bought has
      'I thought that Karl had bought the book yesterday.'

The traditional analyses of verb second (e.g., den Besten 1981, McCloskey 1992, among many others[1]) hold that there is a requirement that the complementizer position be filled in tensed clauses.[2] The verb raises to the empty complementizer position in matrix clauses. There is then an additional requirement that the specifier of a matrix complementizer be filled by some element, giving the verb second orderings.

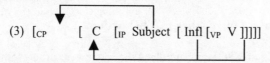

(3) [$_{CP}$ [C [$_{IP}$ Subject [Infl [$_{VP}$ V]]]]]

In embedded clauses, however, the complementizer position is filled, and the verb cannot raise to it; thus, verb second ordering is blocked.

An obvious extension of this approach is to posit a set of "verb first" (V1) languages where the requirement on filling the specifier of CP is not imposed, giving a VSO ordering.[3] In this analysis, a Modern Irish VSO sentence like (4a) would have a derivation as in (4b).

(4) a. Leanann   an t-ainmní an briathar i   nGaeilge.
        follow.PRES the subject   the verb   in   Irish
        'The subject follows the verb in Irish.' (Modern Irish)

b.

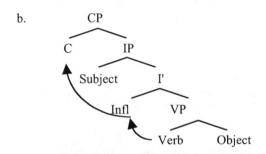

The verb raises through its inflectional complex to C° and all the other arguments stay in their canonical positions. VSO order, under this approach, is thus like a "weak verb second effect", in the sense that it is triggered by whatever triggers V→C° movement in verb second languages, but lacks actual verb second order.

(5) THE RAISING TO C HYPOTHESIS (V→ C°)
     VSO order is derived via head movement of the verb to C°.[4] There is a requirement in VSO languages that C°s be filled, but the specifier of CP need not be filled

An alternative approach to VSO order claims that the verb does not appear in C°, but rather appears at the left edge of the inflectional complex. In Sproat (1985), this is obtained by the adjunction of the verb to IP. In later work (e.g., McCloskey 1991, Duffield 1991, 1994, 1995, Guilfoyle 1993, Bobaljik and Carnie 1996, Pyatt 1992, Carnie 1995, etc.) this is achieved by head movement of the verb to the highest inflectional projection, in addition to shorter movement of the subject to some specifier of a lower inflectional head. In this chapter we will use Infl as shorthand for the inflectional complex, and leave the subject in the specifier of the VP, because the difference between positioning the subject in the specifier of VP or in some other specifier in the inflectional complex is irrelevant to the current discussion.

(6)   [CP C [IP   [Infl   [VP Subject [V object]]]]]

The exact details of how such an approach works are not crucial here, and we refer the reader to the above-mentioned works for more details. It is sufficient to note that in an expanded Infl syntax (Pollock 1989, Chomsky 1993), the verb need not raise to C° to be initial in its clause; instead, it can raise to the highest inflectional category, with its arguments in the specifiers of lower inflectional phrases. Even in a non-expanded Infl, provided one assumes the Internal Subject Hypothesis of Koopman and Sportiche (1991), the verb needs only to raise to Infl to derive VSO order. After McCloskey (1996a), we will call this class of approaches the "left edge of inflection hypothesis" (7). We argue that, in Old Irish at least, both the "Raising to C" system and the "left edge of Infl" system are present. First, however, we will briefly discuss the evidence that has led many researchers to abandon the Raising to C analysis for other VSO languages (such as Modern Irish.)

(7) THE LEFT EDGE OF INFLECTION HYPOTHESIS (V→ Infl)
VSO order is derived via head movement of the verb to the highest inflectional head (AgrS/T/Infl). Arguments appear in surface positions lower than this head. There is no (overt) raising to C°.

2. Against the Raising to C° Approach

McCloskey (1996a) has argued that a V → C analysis is unavailable for deriving basic VSO order in Modern Irish. First, as noted by Koopman and Sportiche (1991), there is the question of word order in embedded clauses with complementizers. Recall that in German, when the complementizer position is filled, verb second order does not arise. If Irish were analyzed similarly, then we would expect the order C°-SOV or C°-SVO in embedded clauses. In fact, we only see C°-VSO order. The verb still must raise:

(8) Ceapaim   [go   bhfaca   sé   an madra.]
     think.PRES.1s [that   see.PST he.NOM   the dog   ]
                   COMP   V   Subj   Obj
     'I think that he saw the dog.'

The motivation for this verb-first ordering in the embedded clause cannot be a V → C° movement requirement, since the complementizer position is filled.

McCloskey (1996a) makes a further argument against V-movement to C° in Modern Irish based on the interpretation of adjoined adverbials. McCloskey argues that elements like the italicized clausal adverbial in (9) are IP adjoined,[5] since they modify only the lower clause.

(9) Líonaim d'eagla *dá dtógfainn   mo radharc dóibh*   go dtitfinn.
     Fill.1s of-fear if   lift-1S.COND my sight   from.3.s that fall.1.s
     'I fill up with fear that, were I to take my eyes off, then I would fall.'

If McCloskey is correct in saying that these adverbial elements are IP adjoined material, it then follows directly that the verb cannot be higher than the left edge of the inflectional complex, since it appears to the right of the IP adjoined adverbials.

3. Old Irish: A Language with Two Kinds of Raising

There is some evidence that in most cases Old Irish only moves its verb to the left edge of IP, just like Modern Irish. This evidence comes from the complementizer system. Old Irish has VSO word order in declarative sentences like (10).[6]

 (10)   Beogidir   in   spirut   in   corp.
         vivifies.3S the   spirit   the   body
         'The spirit vivifies the body.'

As in Modern Irish, when C° is filled, the verb is still otherwise clause initial:

 (11)   As•berat   [co   mbeir   in   fer   in   claideb].
         Say-3P   that   carries-3S-CONJ   the   man   the   sword
         'They say that the man carries the sword.' [7]

 (12)   Ní   beir   in   fer   in   claideb.
         NEG-C°   carries-3s-CONJ   the   man   the   sword
         'The man does not carry the sword.'

In (11), we have a subordinate clause with the overt complementizer *co*, and VSO order is still maintained. In (12), we have a matrix clause with a negation marker. Following the tradition in Celtic (see for example Duffield 1991, Guilfoyle 1987), we will assume that these negative markers (and certain other preverbal particles) are generated in C°.[8] The fact that we still have VSO order even with an overt particle suggests that verb raising in Old Irish is not to C°, but rather to Infl. In this sense, then, Old Irish patterns with Modern Irish.

We claim, however, using evidence from the placement of enclitic pronouns and phonological behavior of certain verbal elements, that Old Irish also has a filled C° requirement[9] (see also Eska 1994, 1996). This requirement can be met by complementizers, by verbs, or by subparts of morphologically complex verbs. Thus Old Irish is a language that has both raising to C° and raising to the left edge of IP.

3.1 The Cast of Characters

A major difference between Old Irish and Modern Irish lies in the complexity of the verbal system. The morphology of the Old Irish verb includes verbal roots, inflectional endings, and a series of preverbal particles. The particles are of three types: conjunct particles (C), preverbs (P) and object enclitics (E). These particles, the verb, and its person/number endings form what is called the "verbal complex." Excluding the enclitics for the moment, there is a strict ordering to these forms (13b). An example of a maximal verbal complex is given in (14).

(13)   a.   *Conjunct Particles (C)*
                        negation, question marker, complementizers
                Preverbs (P)
                        alter verb meaning, add perfective aspect
                Verb (V)+Subject inflection (S)
                        the verb root itself and person agreement
                Enclitics (E)
                        object clitics and relative markers

        b.   C > P > V-S

(14)   Ní-m• accai.   (Ní +   m +   ad +   ci+3s)
        NEG-me•see.3s   C   (E)   P   V-S
        'he does not see me.'

Following Chung and McCloskey (1987), we assume the conjunct particle position (C) corresponds to the $C°$ position. This would explain why it must be ordered before the other preverbal particles (P). In Modern Irish, the conjunct particles form phonological units with overt complementizers (see Duffield 1991, 1995, for discussion and a slightly more elaborate view):

(15) a.   go 'that' + ní 'neg'   → nach 'neg.comp'
     b.   go 'that'+ níor 'neg-past'   → nár 'neg.past.comp'
     c.   a^L 'that [+wh]' + ní 'neg'   → nách 'neg.comp.[+wh]'

Similar facts are found in Old Irish

(16) a.   co^N 'that' +ní 'neg'   → coní 'neg comp'
     b.   Ø 'that[+wh]' + ní 'neg'   → nád 'neg.comp.[+wh]'

Thus for the moment, we assume that the conjunct particles correspond to $C°$ in the older form of the language as well.[10]

We now turn to our arguments that certain morphological, phonological, and syntactic processes show raising of the verb both to the left edge of IP and to $C°$.

3.2 Deriving Absolute vs. Conjunct Forms

In Old Irish, the verb and its inflection take two different forms[11] depending upon whether it is in absolute initial position. These two forms are traditionally called ABSOLUTE and CONJUNCT (17) (examples taken from Strachan 1949):

(17)   *Absolute*   *Conjunct*
        beirid   -beir   'he carries'
        berait   -berat   'they carry'
        marbfa   -marbub   'I will kill'
        midimmir   -midemmar   'we judge'

The absolute form is used when the inflected verb is not preceded by any conjunct particles, preverbs, or pronouns (18). The conjunct form is used when the verb is preceded by a conjunct particle (complementizer) or a preverb (19).

(18)   Beirid   in fer   in claideb.   (absolute)
        Carries.3s.ABS the man   the sword
        'The man carries the sword.'

(19)   Ní beir/*beirid   in fer   in claideb.   (conjunct)
        NEGcarries.3s.CONJ/*ABS   the man   the sword
        'The man does not carry the sword.'

Interestingly, the appearance of the conjunct verb form is not necessarily a function of the presence of the preverbs or conjunct particles. Rather, the conjunct form is found anywhere that the verb is not in absolute first position.[12] This is often called "Bergin's law"[13] (Bergin 1938). This is especially true in some poetic forms where strict VSO order is not obligatory. Take the following lines from the *Énna Labraid Luad Cáich,* as cited in Carney (1978):

(20)   ...srethaib   sluag   *soí*   Crimthan Coscrach   cing
        ...with-lines of-hosts won.CONJ   Crimthan Victorious hero

        cét   catha, ...
        hundred   battles

        'with lines of hosts, Crimthan the victorious hero, won a hundred battles'
                                        (absolute: **soid*)

In this fragment, the verb *soí* takes conjunct form, despite the fact that it does not appear with a conjunct particle or preverb. We can conclude, then, that conjunct verbal inflection is a feature of non-initial position.[14] We claim that this distribution is definable in a systematic way: When the verb has raised to C°, it takes the absolute morphology. We assume that the movement to this position is caused by a filled C° requirement. When the verb is in any other position (either at the left edge of IP or in verb medial order as in the poem fragment above), it takes the more basic conjunct form. Consider the case of (19) above, where the C° has been filled with the conjunct particle *ní* 'neg', thus blocking the raising of *beir* 'carries-3S-CONJ' to C°. The verb raises through the inflectional heads to the left edge of Infl just as it would in Modern Irish; the inflected verb is thus realized as *beir*. The resultant S-structure is seen in (21):

(21) [$_{CP}$ Ní[$_{IP}$beir$_i$+Infl [$_{IP}$ in fer [$_{VP}$ t$_i$ in claideb.]]]]

In (18), by contrast, there is no overt complementizer nor any other type of preverbal particle. The filled C° requirement forces the verb to raise to C° (22).

(22) [$_{CP}$ Beirid$_i$+C° [$_{IP}$t$_i$ [$_{VP}$ in fer [$_{V'}$ t$_i$ in claideb.]]]]

When the inflected verb *beir* 'carries' raises to C°, it actually is incorporating into a null C°. This C-Infl-V complex is then realized as absolute *beirid* instead of conjunct *beir*.[15]

    An important variation to this pattern occurs in relative clauses. If the null C° is [+wh], then a third form of the verb is used in lieu of the absolute form (23). For example, in the sentence below, the inflected verb of the relative clause: *gaibid* 'grabs.ABS' surfaces as *gaibes*, the relative form of the verb:

(23) Is   oinfer$_i$ [$_{CP}$ Ø$_i$ gaibes$_i$ [$_{IP}$ t$_i$ búaid.]]
      COP   one-man   OP. grabs-3S-REL   victory
      'It is one man who grabs victory.'

The differences between the relative form and the matrix absolute form show that the morphology of the absolute is used to signal which null C° ([±wh]) is present in the complementizer position. Since the verb forms in absolute initial position vary depending upon what type of complementizer is present in the clause, this data lends support to the theory that these verbs are in fact in C°.[16]

3.3 Compound Verbs and Preverbal Particles

Let us now consider alternations in the forms of preverbs and how they lend support to the analysis we have presented here. The preverbs are the prepositional components of Old Irish compound verbs. For example, given the basic verb *beirid* 'carries', the addition of a preverbal particle shifts the meaning in unpredictable ways: *as•beir* means 'says' (literally 'out-carry'). Similar forms, such as *shine/outshine* and *blow/blow up*, are occasionally found in English, and prepositional preverbs and separable prefixes are found in many Germanic and Slavic languages. Certain preverbs may also cause a shift in aspect, giving perfective force.[17] In Old Irish, the use of these particles is quite common, and they form a large class of Old Irish verbal morphology. We claim that depending upon what other elements appear in the complex, these preverbal particles can behave either as if they were in C° or as if they were combined with the verb in Infl. In particular, we propose that given a compound verb with no conjunct particle, a preverbal particle satisfies the filled C° requirement.

    Consider the following compound verb: *as•beir* 'says-3s'. This is composed of the preverbal particle *as-* 'out' and *beir* 'carries'. However, when this verb comes after a conjunct particle *ní* 'NEG', the form of the verb is radically changed. In the example below, the form for 'say-1s' is *as•biur* when there is no conjunct particle (24), but *epur* when it follows a conjunct particle like *ní* (25):

(24)   As•biur   in-so.
         say-1S   this
         'I say this.'

(25)   Ní epur/*as•biur   a   n-anman   sund.
         NEGsay-1S   their   names   here
         'I do not say their names here.'

Despite the obvious differences between these forms, there is no suppletion here. Instead, rules of stress shift, syncope, provection, reduplication, and lenition all interact to muddy the forms (see McCloskey 1978 and McCone 1987, 1994, for more detailed discussion of the actual phonological forms). The domain of application of these phonological rules provides evidence for our analysis. The entire verbal complex forms a single phonological unit that cannot be broken apart by adverbs and other intrusive material.[18] Following the phrasal phonology frameworks of Selkirk (1984), Hayes (1989), and Nespor and Vogel (1986), we will call this grouping the "clitic group"—(κ).[19] However, there is a smaller phonological unit, the word (ω), which is the domain of stress and syncope. Consistently, conjunct particles (C) and enclitic pronouns stand outside the phonological word (26a). Preverbal particles (P), on the other hand, vary in their position, depending upon what other material is in the clitic group (26b):

(26)   a.   [$_\kappa$ C [$_\omega$ P (P) (P) (P) V]]
         b.   [$_\kappa$ P [$_\omega$ P (P) (P) V]]

For concreteness, let us consider the example of stress. Stress in Old Irish is always on the leftmost syllable in the word. This is true of absolute verbs, nouns, and adjectives. When the verb is complex, however, either with a conjunct particle or with a preverb, the stress falls on the second non-enclitic morphological unit, indicated here in boldface:

(27)   a.   C • '**P** (P) (P) (P) V
         b.   C • '**V**
         c.   P • '**P** (P) (P) V
         d.   P • '**V**

There thus is a special "pretonic" slot in initial position for a preverb or conjunct particle, which does not participate in the metrical structure of the rest of the verbal complex. We will indicate the division between the pretonic position and the rest of the complex with the use of the symbol <•> (following Thurneysen 1946). Prosodically, this pretonic position corresponds to a form which is outside the domain of ω but is still within the domain of the clitic group (κ). Usually, the enclitic and any syllabic material it brings with it will be part of the pretonic. We can thus describe the distribution of the elements as follows:

(28) i.   Conjunct particles are always pretonic.
     ii. If there is no conjunct particle, then the first preverb is pretonic.

If we add a conjunct particle to a verb with preverbs, then the previously pretonic preverb joins the rest of the verbal complex and participates in its metrical structure, causing the stress pattern to change, as seen in (29):

(29) a.   as•biur   'say-1s'   /as.b**j**ur / (stress on the second syllable)
     b.   •epur   'say-1s'   /e.bur/ (stress on the first syllable)

The boldface syllable is the one that receives the stress. In (29a) the preverb *as* appears in pretonic position and does not participate in the metrical structure of the verb (stress falls on *biur*). When the conjunct particle is added, the preverb behaves as if it is part of the second element in the complex and takes main stress. The other phonological alternations, /a/~/e/ and /sb/~/b/ (orthographic <p>) follow from this shift in metrical structure.[20] See McCone (1987, 1994), Pyatt (1996), and McCloskey (1978) for more details.

As the conjunct particles always fall in the pretonic position, and these conjunct particles are C°s, we assume that the pretonic position is associated with the complementizer head. Since one preverb is required to be pretonic when there is no complementizer, it follows that a preverb can satisfy the filled C° requirement. When there is no overt complementizer, only the preverb, not the entire inflected verb, raises to C° to satisfy the filled C° requirement. When there is neither a preverb nor a complementizer, the verb itself raises to C°, taking absolute inflection as a result, to satisfy the filled C° requirement.

Supporting evidence for this approach to preverbs comes from their behavior in relative clauses. Recall that absolute verb forms in relative clauses varied in form depending upon the [±*wh*] content of the complementizer head, lending support to the notion that these forms represented incorporation of the verb to C°. The pretonic preverb can also show special marking in relative clauses. For instance, if the preverb is *im(m)* 'about', as in the sentence *imm•rádi* 'he thinks/meditates' (literally 'about-speak'[21]) in example (30a) below, then in a relative clause the suffixed form *imma* or *imme* appears (30b), as noted by Greene (1977:24). Let us emphasize that this form, with a pretonic preverb, only appears if there is no complementizer particle occupying the preverbal slot.

(30) a.   imm•rádi
          about•speak.CONJ.
          'he thinks/mediates'

     b.   imma•rádi
          about.REL•speak.CONJ.
          'who thinks/mediates'   (Thurneysen 1946:§841)

This provides further evidence that the pretonic slot is in fact the realization of the complementizer head, since the relative marking appears on the preverb—precisely what is predicted by the idea that these elements are in C°.

3.4 Moving Preverbs to C°: Long Head Movement

Let us consider a derivation of a compound verb, with a pretonic preverbal particle in C°. We will assume that the preverbal particles are reflexes of a Hale and Keyser (1991) type complex VP, or a Pesetsky (1995) style stacked PP structure. We will consider the sentence in (24) with the base form in (31):

(31) $[_{CP} [\emptyset] [_{IP} [Infl] [_{VP} pro [_{V'} as [_{V'} biur\ in\ so]]]]]$.

The preverb *as* raises to C° to satisfy the filled C° requirement. The root *biur* raises to Infl, as in Modern Irish, accounting for the difference in phonological domains. The two domains correspond to two syntactic heads: Infl and C°.

(32) $[_{CP} [as_i] [_{IP} [biur_j] [_{VP} pro [_{V'} t_i [_{V'} t_j\ in\ so]]]]]$.

When a conjunct particle complementizer like *ní* 'NEG' is present, however, the preverb remains in Infl with the rest of the verb, putting it into the same metrical unit with the root verb (33):

(33) $[_{CP}$ Ní $[_{IP}[_{Infl}$ epur ($\leftarrow$as +biur)]   a   n-anman sund]].
        NEG   say-1s   their   names   here
        'I do not say their names.'

The reader may have noticed that in allowing the two verbal heads (the preverb and the verbal root) to raise to separate functional categories, we may well have created a violation of the Head Movement Constraint (HMC) (Travis 1984), which prohibits moving X°s from skipping intermediate potential X° landing sites. Consider (32). It appears as if the verbal root skips the intermediate preverb on its way to Infl. Similarly, the preverb seems to skip the intermediate inflectional heads on its way to C°.

This problem is especially acute in the cases where more than one preverb appears, as in (34). In *ad•roilli* 'deserves' *(ad-ro-sli),* the first preverb moves to the C° head, but the other preverb is incorporated with the verbal root *(ro + sli → •roilli).*

(34) $[_{VP} [_{V'} $ ad $]$ $[_V $ ro $ [_{V'} $ slí $ . .]]]$
                to C   to Infl

When the C° head is filled with a complementizer, of course, both preverbs are incorporated with the verbal root, giving •*árilli* (Thurneysen 1946:§822).

One possible approach to this problem is to claim that (34) is in fact the correct representation of the phenomenon. In this illustration, the preverb moves to C° in one jump, skipping the intermediate Infl head(s) as it does so. Although such movement at first glance appears to violate the HMC, certain phenomena in other languages (including a Celtic language, Breton) have inspired a proposal which allows precisely this type of movement in cases which are at least superficially similar to the one presented here. We refer to Long Head Movement (LHM) of participle heads around auxiliaries to create a participle-auxiliary initial order, a phenomenon common to Bulgarian, Czech, Slovak, Serbo-Croatian, Rumanian, Old Spanish, and European Portuguese as well as Breton (Rivero 1991, 1994, Roberts 1994, Schafer 1994, Borsley et al. 1996, among others).

A typical example of a LHM proposal is seen for the Breton sentence in (35) below, with the structure and movement in (36) (Borsley et al. 1996:56):

(35)   Lennet   en   deus   Yann   al   levr.
        read   3SM   has   Yann   the book
        'Yann has read the book.'

(36)   [cp C [ip Infl [vp Yann   [v'[v en deus][v'[vlennet] [np al levr]]]]]]

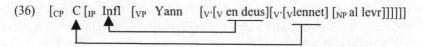

The above cited analyses provide convincing evidence that the phenomenon under discussion must in fact be head movement, rather than, for instance, remnant topicalization (for example, it can be blocked by other heads, such as negation). Without going into too much detail, the analysis of this phenomenon asserts that head positions, as well as XP positions, are subject to an A/A-bar distinction. Tense in the LHM-type languages requires syntactic licensing of some sort; one way in which such licensing can occur is by movement of a participle to the C° head. The C° head is an A-bar head position, while Infl (and members of the Infl complex) and V° are A head positions. Head movement is subject to Relativized Minimality (Rizzi 1990), which prevents the skipping of a potential landing site by a moving element. Participles moving to C°, however, are moving to an A-bar position, not an A position, and hence are not skipping any potential landing sites by moving past the Infl head position.

The extension to the present situation should be clear. Movement to C° is A-bar movement, not A movement; hence, a preverbal particle moving to the pretonic C° position in one long leap, as illustrated in (34) above, is not skipping any potential landing sites and is not in violation of the HMC as restated in terms of Relativized Minimality. This account also represents a satisfactory mechanical treatment of the phenomenon, and there are some interesting parallels which perhaps make it a desirable treatment. LHM is blocked in Breton by a negative element, which Borsley, et al. argue is in C°— precisely the effect a negative particle has in Old Irish. Movement of a preverbal prepositional particle is disallowed with a negative conjunct particle.[22]

3.5 Placement of Enclitics

The final piece of evidence we present in favor of our account comes from object enclitics. The somewhat convoluted facts of enclitic placement do not lend themselves obviously to a phonological analysis, but on the approach adduced here, a straightforward syntactic account is possible.

Old Irish has second position enclitics (E) which include object pronouns, relative pronouns, and conjunctions. Following the tradition in Celtic grammars we will call these "Wackernagelian clitics."[23] The enclitic pronouns[24] are always found after the first morphological element in the verbal complex (38). The following examples are taken from Strachan (1949):

(38) a. Ní-m• accai.   (Ní +   m +   ad +   cí-3s)
         NEG -me P.see.3s   C   E   P   V-S
         'She does not see me.'

    b.   At-on•cí.   (ad +   (do)n + cí -3s)
         P-1PL see.3s   P   E   V-S
         'She sees us.'

    c.   Bertaig-th-i.[25]   (bertaig -th +i)
         shake-3s.ABS-him   V-   S   E
         'he shakes him.'

The distribution of enclitics is somewhat puzzling from a syntactic perspective if no filled C° requirement is assumed; sometimes they precede the verb (when there is a preverb or conjunct particle); other times they follow the verb (when the verb is absolute). Similarly, there is no easy phonological characterization of their placement. Sometimes they precede the first phonological word, i.e., when there is a preverb or conjunct particle, as outlined above. When the verb is absolute, however, there is no pretonic slot in the phonological sense—the first syllable of the verb receives main stress, as usual. In these cases, the enclitic follows the first phonological word. Enclitics appear *within* the first prosodic unit when there is a pretonic slot ($[_\kappa$ C (E)$[_\omega$ P (P) (P) (P) V]]); otherwise, they follow the first prosodic unit. Thus, a Wackernagel-style analysis of this cliticization under which these enclitics attach after the first prosodic unit is *prima facie* untenable. An account of enclisis according to which the enclitic attaches either to the first phonological word or to the first prosodic unit (the clitic group κ) would predict that the enclitic would suffix to the verbal complex rather than appearing medially.[26] The enclitic only follows the first phonological word if there is no pretonic element; when there is a pretonic element, it precedes the first phonological word. While a phonological account would have to include a two-part rule to this effect, the syntactic account we present requires no such disjunctive rule. The distribution of enclitics is transparent when we assume that Old Irish had a filled C° requirement. Once we make this claim, the distribution of enclitics is straightforward. We express this in (41). This is true whether the C is filled by a conjunct particle, a preverb, or an absolute verb form:

(41) Enclitics (E) adjoin to C°.[27]

4. Complementizers, Verb Second, and Negation

In this section, we consider a few of the open questions remaining to our analysis. First, we examine in detail the assumption that the head we are looking at is indeed the complementizer head. Next, we consider some alternative analyses of V2 phenomena. Finally, we consider what the content of the "filled C° requirement" might be.

4.1 Is It Raising to C°?

The above discussion is aimed purely at establishing that Old Irish had what we have called up to this point a "filled C° requirement"; that is, that Old Irish C° was always filled by some element, whether it was a complementizer particle, preverb, or finite verb. In addition, finite verbs moved to Infl, giving CVSO order in all Old Irish clauses, both matrix and embedded.

Let us now briefly consider the possibility that the head involved is not C° but some lower inflectional head. An analysis of this kind has been proposed for Modern Irish by Duffield (1995). The vast majority of cases we have examined have negative particles serving as exemplars of complementizer particles. The claim that negation is in C° is perhaps problematic, since it is widely claimed that negation heads its own functional projection (either NegP or Laka's (1991) ΣP, generated between IP and CP). Other elements are found in Old Irish conjunct particles, including particles expressing [±Q] (such as *an*), particles expressing subordination, and the variety of suffixal elements expressing [±*wh*]. These, unlike Negation, are clear cases of elements we expect to find in complementizers. So let us consider the possibility that negative particles are generated in some position lower than C° but higher than Infl, corresponding to the positioning of Laka's ΣP:

(47)   [$_{CP}$ C [$_{ΣP}$ [$_Σ$ Ní] [$_{IP}$ Infl . . .]]]

This seems a likely locus of base-generation for negation in Old Irish, and nothing we have seen would preclude an analysis where negation was generated in this position, and the elements we have been identifying as C° in fact represent a combination of the Σ° and C° heads incorporated together.

First, let us consider whether there are any empirical differences between this proposal and the simpler one made in previous sections of this chapter. The primary difference between this analysis and one without ΣP lies in the number of heads above IP. Under this story, we predict that we should be able to have more than one particle preceding the verb. In essence, this is correct, since we get combinations of negation with the other complementizer material:

(48)   a.   coni (co + ní)   'that.neg'
        b.   arna (ar + ní)   'that.neg'
        c.   ná   (a + ní)   'rel.that.neg'

Notice, however, that these complex complementizers form a single phonological unit (either obviously decomposable like *coni*, or blended like *ná*). It seems to be a requirement of Old Irish that this class of elements forms a single head. A straightforward account of this fact follows if we assume with Laka that ΣP is an A-bar category (see also Schafer 1995 on the A/A-bar status of ΣP); assuming the A-bar equivalent of head movement, the negation head might raise and incorporate into the complementizer.[28] In the general case, for chain uniformity reasons, A-heads (like verbs) may not incorporate into these positions, except as a measure of last resort to satisfy our still unspecific "filled C° requirement." This explains why, when there is an overt complementizer of some kind, the verb is at the left edge of IP, and no higher. When there is no phonological content to any of the A-bar heads, the filled C° requirement (in a sense to be defined below in section 4.3) is not met, and either the verb or one of its preverbs moves through these A-bar heads.

Given this, there actually seems to be no empirical difference between the accounts where negation is generated in C° or in Σ°. The two analyses seem to be notational variants in that they both predict a strong complementarity between overt complementizers (the complex of Neg, [±Q], and subordinating C°s), and preverbal and verbal elements bearing special absolute ([-*wh*]) or relative ([+*wh*]) marking. For this reason we do not distinguish between the two approaches, and we claim that V→ C° can either mean "raising to a single head C°" or "raising to the class of A-bar heads constituting C°."[29]

4.2 What Drives Movement to C°?

The primary goal of this chapter has been to motivate a certain structural analysis of Old Irish clauses which can involve movement of the verb to C°. The possibility of this movement is in striking contrast to Modern Irish, where, it can be argued, such movement never occurs and the verb moves only to the left edge of the inflectional complex. This entails that a parametric change must have occurred by the time of Modern Irish which caused the disappearance of the filled C° requirement. The obvious question, then, is what originally drove the movement to C° in Old Irish, and what changed diachronically to produce the Modern Irish V→ I system.

A full treatment is obviously beyond the scope of this chapter. However, as we are drawing the parallel with verb second languages, it could be instructive to consider possible proposals for the motivation of V-to-C movement in such languages. Platzack (1995) provides an analysis of the loss of verb second phenomena in English and French which is of considerable relevance to the discussion here. He proposes (following Holmberg and Platzack 1988) that the finiteness feature [± F] is responsible for verb second, reducing the raising to C parameter to a parameter where [+F] is or is not located in C°. Finiteness (distinct from Tense) is responsible for the assignment of Nominative Case, argues Platzack; to assign Case, [+F] must be lexicalized[30] (that is, phonologically realized, or overtly checked, in a feature-driven theory of movement like that of Chomsky 1993). Hence, when the verb second parameter above is active, C° must be lexicalized to permit the assignment of Nominative Case and thus to trigger the appearance of V-to-C movement. When the V2 parameter is not activated, [+F] appears in Infl, and must be lexicalized there. Platzack argues that the deactivation of the V2 parameter in English and French resulted in the non-verb second nature of the modern languages. Crucially, Infl had differing properties in the two languages at the time of deactivation, resulting in the modern differences in the lexicalization of [+F]: *do*-support and Infl-lowering/affixation in English, but verb-raising to Infl in French. (It is not clear from the discussion in Platzack (1995) what drives movement of an XP to the specifier of CP in V2 languages. In the absence of anything less stipulative, and assuming a feature-checking account of movement, we can posit strong D-features on C°, requiring topicalization of an XP.

Evidently, the extension to Old Irish should be clear: Old Irish had the V2 parameter activated, such that C° needed to be lexicalized to permit the [+F] feature[31] to assign Case. (Evidently the requirement that the specifier of CP be filled was not operative in Old Irish; that is, C° had weak D-features.) The parameter is deactivated in Modern Irish, triggering only movement to Infl, as in Modern French; again, French and Irish differ in the requirement on overt movement of the subject to the specifier of IP.

It follows from this suggestion that the possibilities for legitimate lexicalization must differ cross-linguistically. Lexicalization in V2 languages always involves either movement of the finite V or phonological realization of the complementizer. Lexicalization in Old Irish can mean realization of the complementizer, movement of a preverbal particle, or as a last resort, movement of a finite verb. The difference between Old Irish on one hand and Middle English and Middle French on the other could rest either in the availability of items in the lexicon or in the type of element that qualifies as "lexical" enough to satisfy the requirement for [+F]. The first type of approach would argue that Middle English and French simply lacked the repertoire of separately realizable complementizer and preverbal particles that Old Irish has available, and which considerations of economy (move the least amount necessary) would dictate are preferred to the verb itself as candidates for movement to C°. This approach, however, has the drawback that it predicts that the forms which can satisfy the parameter will vary arbitrarily cross-linguistically, which is *prima facie* false. In the Germanic languages, it is always a full verbal form that satisfies the parameter; no particles of the Old Irish type ever appear. The second account might prove more principled, and could presumably be linked to the differences between the systems in the requirement on movement to the specifier of CP. Under this view, the weaker verb initial language requires a weaker type of lexicalization for [+F] in C°, perhaps connected to the fact that C does not have strong D-features (associated with XP topicalization) on top of the strong [+F] feature which motivates V → C movement. A fuller account will be left to future research.

5. Conclusion

In this paper, we have accounted for the complex and intricate behavior of verbs, preverbs, particles and clitics in the Old Irish verbal complex. We have argued that, contra most current theories of VSO ordering, Old Irish makes use of raising to C° due to a filled C° requirement, which in turn is due to the lexicalization of [+F]. The fact that the pretonic element and the rest of the verbal complex behave metrically like two words rather than one follows from the fact that the two elements are in different structural positions in the sentence, forming a "clitic group" rather than a single phonological word. The distribution of absolute inflection is now definable in a systematic way: The raising of the verb to C° is reflected morphologically as the absolute inflection. Finally, the position of enclitics is now uniformly accounted for. They always attach to C°, whether C° is filled by a preverb, conjunct particle, or the verb itself. The fact that this analysis provides a systematic account for these facts is a strong argument for the raising to C° analysis. Raising to the left edge of Infl is also still required to account for the fact that the verb still precedes its subject even when there is an overt complementizer. The filled-C° requirement, not active in Modern Irish, thus explains many facts about the Old Irish verbal complex that would otherwise remain mysterious.

Acknowledgments

Our thanks to David Adger, Cathal Doherty, Nigel Duffield, Joe Eska, Eithne Guilfoyle, Alec Marantz, Jim McCloskey, David Pesetsky, and Calvert Watkins for helpful comments; mistakes are without a doubt our own. Earlier versions of this work were presented to audiences at the Fifth Formal Linguistics Society of the Midwest annual meeting at the University of Illinois, Urbana-Champaign, at the Celtic Linguistics Conference in Dublin, and before audiences at MIT and Harvard.

1. See, for example, Schwartz and Vikner (1989, 1996), Koopman (1984), Holmberg and Platzack (1988), Platzack (1986a, 1986b, 1987, 1995), Taraldsen (1986), Roberts (1993) and Vikner (1994).

2. In section 4, we will consider the motivations for this requirement. For the moment, however, we simply discuss it in descriptive terms. We assume, following Platzack (1995), that the filled C° requirement holds in order to give lexical content to the contentful complementizer. See also Travis (1984), Zwart (1993b), de Haan and Weerman (1985), Rizzi and Roberts (1989), Vikner (1991), and Iatridou and Kroch (1992), among others, for more involved explanations of V→ C raising.

3. We are assuming here, of course (after McCloskey 1983, Sproat 1985, Duffield 1991, Bobaljik and Carnie 1996), that VSO order is a derived order and that the underlying order of Modern Irish is SVO.

4. In section 4 below, we consider a minor variant to this proposal, where the verb raising is not to C°, but simply to some head higher than the left edge of Inflection. For expository purposes, however, we will continue to use the simpler V→ C° terminology here, with the understanding that C° should be read as "some head position higher in the tree than the highest instantiation of Infl."

5. McCloskey claims this despite the fact they appear to the left of the complementizer marking the edge of the embedded clause. He presents extensive evidence from types of selectional restrictions to support the idea that these elements are IP rather than CP adjoined. McCloskey's solution to the relative ordering of the adverbial and complementizer is that in the PF component the complementizer lowers to and adjoins to the Infl head for phonological reasons.

6. Throughout this chapter we will use the traditional spelling system of Old Irish. We refer the reader to Thurneysen (1946) for the complete details of how Old Irish is pronounced. The Old Irish examples have been taken from Strachan (1949), McCone (1987), Greene (1977), and Thurneysen (1946) who take them from various primary sources.

7. Example (11) is not taken from an Old Irish text. It was constructed by us to simplify some of the irrelevant problems (e.g., *pro*-drop) found in many textual examples with subordinate clauses. A real example of an embedded VSO clause in Old Irish is given below. This example is taken from the Wurzburg Glosses (Wb2^{b}4) (Strachan 1949):

(i)	connách	moidea	nech	[ar	bed	áarillind	[nod•nicad]]
	so-that-NEG	boast	someone	[COMP	be	his-merit	[that-him-saved]]
		C	V	S			Complement

'so that no one may boast that his merit was that which saved him'

8. See the discussion in section 4 concerning this assumption.

9. We do not attempt here an account of how VSO order arose in Old Irish. For speculations thereon, see Watkins (1963), Eska (1994, 1996), and McCone (1994).

10. The issue of whether negation, questionhood, and other "conjunct particle" functions are base-generated in C° is of obvious concern here. We will return to this question below in section 4.

11. For a useful list of Old Irish verbal paradigms see Green (1995).

12. There are two exceptions to this claim. The first is imperative verbs (McCloskey 1978), where the verb is in absolute first position but takes conjunct form. We do not attempt an account of this fact here, but the solution may well lie in the presence of a null imperative complementizer which blocks raising of the verb to C°. The second is in the responsive system. Rather than answer "yes" or "no," the affirmative response to a yes/no

question is the verb, standing alone, copying the tense, mood, and agreement features of the verb of the question: *An mbeir in fer in claideb?* 'Does the man carry the sword' is answered simply with *beir*, 'carries', in conjunct form. In this case, it seems likely that either the verbal head is simply copied, without the associated clausal structure. (See McCloskey 1991 for a discussion of the related phenomenon in Modern Irish, claiming that the responsive is simply an ellipsis phenomenon where everything but the tensed verb and the elements adjoined to it are elided.) In such circumstances there is no C° present, so it is expected that only the conjunct form is found.

13. Bergin's Law is usually not phrased exactly this way. In Thurneysen (1946:§513), for example, it is articulated as "Simple and compound verbs may be placed at the end of the clause; . . . [they] then have conjunct flexion . . ." However, Carney (1978) argues that the formulation adopted in the text above is more accurate, since verbs can appear medially in some poetic registers. It is also a relatively rare and marked phenomenon.

14. A well-known fact about Modern Irish is that the conjunct/absolute distinction has some remaining reflexes in some irregular verbs; when a verb appears in a clause with certain clause initial particles, a conjunct (or dependent) form of the verb appears, apparently selected for by the particle:

(i)	*without particle*	*with particle*	
	chonaic	ní	fhaca
	saw	neg	saw
	bhí	ní	raibh
	was	neg	was

It might be claimed that whatever accounts for the appearance of the conjunct/dependent form with the particle in this small class of irregular Modern Irish verbs (a selectional relation between C° and Infl, for example) could also be responsible for the selection of the Old Irish conjunct forms. In fact, such a relation seems highly unlikely in Old Irish. The first problem we have with such an analysis comes from the fact that it draws unfounded conclusions about the parallels between the Old Irish and Modern Irish systems. Notice that the absolute/conjunct alternation is found in every simplex verb in Old Irish. In Modern Irish, the independent/dependent alternation is found in only eleven irregular (and highly suppletive) verbs. Six of these verbs show further irregularities in taking the present tense complementizer particles in the past tense. This alternation is clearly of a different and more limited form than the Old Irish situation, which is probably lexical and paradigmatic rather than syntactic. Second, we note that the Old Irish conjunct form is found without any complementizer at all (in Bergin's Law sentences). It would seem unusual to claim that a particular relation holds between a null C° and a non-initial verb (resulting in conjunct flexion), but that in an otherwise completely equivalent verb initial sentence, the same relation does not hold of the null C° and verb, thus resulting in absolute inflection. Finally, we have strong suspicions of an account that makes reference to a selectional restriction between complementizer particles and the verbal head. As will be seen below in section 3.3, not only is conjunct inflection found with conjunct particles, it is also found when the verb is compounded with a prepositional preverb and there is no overt complementizer particle present. If a selectional restriction between the C° and the verb is the trigger for the conjunct inflection, it is surprising that it should also be triggered by the presence of these pretonic prepositional preverbs. In modern Irish, there are no separable prepositional preverbs, and thus a selectional account of the dependent/independent alternation is available. Such an account does not extend to Old Irish, however. As will be seen below, the account presented here easily captures the complementary distribution of complementizers (and prepositional preverbs) and absolute verbal morphology in Old Irish.

15. See Zwart (1993a), where comparable morphological alternations are seen in Dutch verb second constructions.

16. This pattern is not unattested in Modern Irish; in some dialects, special relative forms of the verb can appear in relative clauses, as in (i) below.

(i)   an bhean a^L gheobhas   buaidh
      the woman that get.FUT.REL   victory
      "the woman who will conquer"

Again, this observation that there must be some relationship established between C° and the verb in Modern Irish is perfectly valid. However, the crucial difference between Old and Modern Irish here is that in Old Irish this agreement takes place (a) in absolute flexion and hence (b) only in the absence of an overt C°. In Modern Irish, by contrast, this form appears only when preceded by a relative complementizer (such as a^L). If we posited a null C° in a relationship with the verb giving the variation in absolute flexion, there is no principled reason why such variation should not appear in conjunct flexion as well.

17. In particular, the preverb *ro-* (PIE **pro* 'forward') performs this function, although *ad-* and *com-* are also sometimes found.

18. Except in the highly marked tmetic construction found in poetic works.

19. We use κ here instead of the more common C, in order to distinguish clitic groups from complementizers and conjunct particles.

20. Briefly, the changes are as follows: *as* is underlyingly /es/, 'out'. /e/ becomes /a/ (possibly schwa) in unstressed pretonic position, but remains /e/ when stressed as the first syllable of the compound verb. /s/ undergoes a morphophonological debuccalization process in this conditioning environment, becoming /h/ and then undergoing deletion, giving /ebur/, orthographically <epur>. See the references noted in the main text for a full account of these phenomena.

21. The gloss of the morpheme *rádi* is obscure from both primary and secondary materials; we believe this to be the correct translation, but this is speculation on our part.

22. However, there are some differences, as well, which keep us from embracing the account wholeheartedly. In Breton and other LHM languages, mechanisms exist for licensing Tense other than filling C° with a negative particle or non-finite participle. Rivero (1993) proposes that it can be licensed a C° heading a CP with a filled specifier, or by a C° which heads an L-marked CP. This last property accounts for the fact that LHM, being movement of a last-resort nature, is impossible in nearly all subordinate (hence L-marked) CPs in LHM languages. Since the facts for root and subordinate (relative) clauses in Old Irish are essentially identical, clearly L-marking cannot be relevant to the Old Irish case. Second, it is transparent that filling of the CP specifier is never possible in Old Irish, since no XP can ever precede the C°+Infl clitic group at the beginning of the clause, so it differs from the LHM languages in that fashion as well. A theoretical problem with the LHM approach lies in the fact that the structure of the dual movements depicted in the diagram in (34) above for Old Irish still involves a violation of the HMC even on the relativized minimality account. The movement of the particle to C° across Infl is legitimized because it is A-bar head movement, but the movement of the verb to Infl across the base position of the particle will still be blocked, because the

particle will be generated in an A-head position. (For a discussion of the reasons why the verb itself does not simply move up into C° see the discussion in section 4.3 below.) This problem is avoided in Breton where the paths of the movement are nested. One possible solution to this problem would be to suggest that the preverbs in Old Irish compound verbs head XP-shell projections below the verb root, which would itself then head the topmost VP. LHM would then take the lowest preverb and move it to C°, and other preverbs would left-adjoin to the verb root and incorporate with it into Infl, nested inside the LHM of the most embedded preverb.

23. So named in honor of Wackernagel's (1892) paper on second position clitics. See Duffield (1994), Anderson (1993), and the references therein for discussion of this kind of clitic.

24. We assume, following Thurneysen (1946), McCone (1987) and McCloskey (1978) here, that these elements are in fact real clitic pronouns rather than some kind of object agreement marker (see Eska 1996 for a different view). The distinction between an agreement analysis and an enclitic analysis makes no difference to the account we have presented here.

25. This form is replaced by *no-s•mbertaigedar*, with the "*do*-support"-like null preverb *no*, in later forms of Old Irish. However, the absolutive form continues to be used when there is no object pronoun. We will be concerned mainly with the period when object clitics adjoined after the main verb; it seems likely that the shift to insertion of a "dummy" preverb heralded the beginning of the shift to the Modern Irish system, in which the verb does not raise beyond expanded Infl.

26. It is possible that an account could be proposed according to which the enclitic looked for the first phonological word (ω) and affixed itself to the left (rather than the right). Such an approach would run into problems in the instances where no pretonic units appear in the verbal complex, (i.e., the absolutive verb forms). In these cases the enclitic adjoins to the right of the first phonological word, giving V-E order. Also, such an approach seems unnecessarily unusual; accounts of Wackernagelian cliticization tend to use suffixation to the first prosodic unit. Arguing for prefixation in the middle of the first prosodic unit seems particularly abstruse given that a clear syntactic constituent is available to the analysis at exactly the right place. See Eska (1996) for a diachronic perspective on the issue.

27. Old English clitics have been analyzed as marking the left edge of IP in a similar manner; see, e.g., Pintzuk (1991).

28. The account sketched here predicts, among other things, that cross-linguistically we might find more than one A-bar preverbal particle in front of verbs in VSO languages, depending upon whether they have A-bar head-movement or not. This seems to be the case, as in the Polynesian VSO languages where complementizers, question particles, negative markers, and sometimes mood each form their own particle to the left of V.

29. In this, we are following Schwartz and Vikner's claim that the word order is derived by moving the verb outside of the IP complex, unless the CP complex is filled by some other element.

30. This is similar to the approach suggested by Rivero (1993) and Borsley et al. (1996) where (long head) movement to C° occurs to license tense features.

31. In the face of a lack of evidence to the contrary, we are simply assuming that it is Platzack's [+F] feature which is driving the requirement of lexicalization. We note, however, that nothing crucial rests upon the choice of [+F] as the relevant feature for Old Irish. Given the fact that the initial "C°" element seems to bear [±wh] features, it might be the case that that is the relevant feature. We leave this open, and simply follow Platzack until evidence to the contrary emerges.

4

Tense and N-Features in Modern Irish

Eithne Guilfoyle

Within the Minimalist framework of Chomsky (1995), NPs check their N-features in the specifier of a functional category by LF at the latest. Several researchers have suggested that at spellout, Irish subjects check their N-features in the specifier of TP, while English subjects check their N-features in the specifier of AgrS, thus accounting for the VSO order of Irish as opposed to the SVO order of English (Bobaljik and Carnie 1996, Guilfoyle 1993, Noonan 1994). To this point, however, nobody has proposed an independent motivation for the cross-linguistic difference in the strength of the N-features of Tense and AgrS in the two languages.

In this chapter, I suggest that the strength of the N-features of Tense and Agr have consequences for the way in which event structure is mapped onto the syntax of the two languages. Specifically we suggest that Irish subjects check their N-features in the specifier of TP, and that there is a close relationship between the subject and the initiation point of the event. Tense is concerned with the timing of the event; therefore, it is appropriate that initiators (certain kinds of subject NPs) occupy the specifier of TP. This contrasts with English, where subjects check their N-features in the specifier AgrS. English subjects do not have to be initiators of the event (though they may be); rather, they are participants in the event (Van Voorst 1988). AgrS is concerned with referentiality—picking out an individual in the world; therefore, a wider range of argument types (e.g., instruments, experiencers) can appear in AgrsP at spellout than can appear in TP. Because of this cross-linguistic difference in the coding of the event structure, we find that the types of arguments that can function as subjects is much more restricted in Irish than in English. Specifically, Irish does not allow instruments, experiencers, or the single argument of unaccusative verbs to appear as a subject NP.

This chapter is organized as follows. In section 1, I present some background assumptions and examine and an account for Irish word order within the Minimalist framework. In sections 2 and 3, I present the proposal that Irish word order is related to the way argument structure is mapped into the syntax of Irish. In the final section, I show that this allows us to relate several seemingly disparate properties of Irish syntax, including the analysis of Irish non-finite clauses (Guilfoyle 1993), and the clause structure of early first language acquisition.

1. Word Order in Irish

1.1 Some Background Assumptions

Following Travis (1991) and Kratzer (1993), I assume that the VP is a bipartite structure, consisting of a lower VNP (verbal noun phrase) and an upper VP projection, each of which assigns a theta role within its own projection. The upper VP assigns the external argument, while the lower VP assigns the internal argument. In some languages, the lower VNP can appear without the upper VP. When this happens, there are restrictions on the realization of the external argument (see section 4.2 below). Modern Irish is an example of a language which places restrictions on the appearance of external arguments, and I will explore these restrictions in the following sections.

I also assume that the child builds structure, for which there is evidence in the data. This is expressed in the Principle of Minimal Projection (Grimshaw (1994:76):

(1)   THE PRINCIPLE OF MINIMAL PROJECTION
        Projections are legitimate only when they are motivated.

The Principle of Minimal Projection has the effect of prohibiting the generation of empty structure. In acquisition terms, this means that the child will posit only a projection that is motivated by the incoming data. This principle will be relevant to the discussion in section 4 below.

1.2 Irish VSO Order

The Irish non-finite form of the verb is known in traditional grammars as the "verbal noun" (VN). The categorial status of this form is controversial: It is either a noun with a verb-like argument structure, or a verb with a noun-like morphology. In Irish, V-movement correlates positively with Tense. Thus V-movement always takes place in finite clauses, but never in non-finite clauses. In the finite clauses in (2) and (3) below we see that V-movement has taken place, and the resulting word order is VSO:

(2)   D'fhan   Seán   sa   bhaile inniu.
        stay.PAST Seán   at   home today
        'Sean stayed at home today.'

(3)   Chuaigh Siobhán ar   scoil.
       go.PAST   Siobhan on   school
       'Siobhan went to school.'

In the non-finite clauses in (4) and (5), we see that there has been no V-movement, and the subject precedes the VN. Note that in (5) the non-finite clause in the answer is a root infinitival:

(4)   B'fhearr liom [tú   fanacht   sa bhaile inniu].
       COP'better with1S you   remain.INF home   today
       'I would rather you remain at home today.'

(5) Q: Caidé a   chuir sin i do   cheann?
       What COMP put   that in your head
       'What put that in your head?'

   A: Tú   a   bheith 'do   luí.
      You PRT be.VN lying down
      'The fact that you were lying down.' (lit. 'You to be lying there.')

Most recent treatments of Irish within generative grammar assume that the underlying word order is SVO, and that the surface VSO order found in the tensed clauses in (2) and (3) is derived by movement of the verb to clause initial position. Under this view, we expect that when the verb fails to move (for whatever reason), the non-finite verb-form appears following the subject. This prediction is borne out by the non-finite clauses shown in (4) and (5), where we can see that the non-finite verb-form appears following the subject. While there are many different analyses of the Irish VSO order, we will be concerned here with a recent account cast in the Minimalist framework.

2. Minimalist Approaches to Irish Word Order

Bobaljik and Carnie (1996) and Noonan (1994) have each proposed analyses of Irish clause structure within the Minimalist framework. Under these accounts, the verb again occupies the highest functional projection at spellout, while the subject occupies the specifier position of the second highest functional projection. Thus I have the tree given in (6), where V raises to AgrS, and the subject raises to the specifier of TP in finite clauses.

(6)

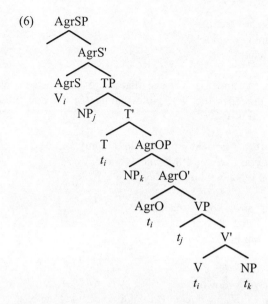

V-movement is driven by the requirement that the strong V- and N-features borne by Tense and Agreement heads are checked by spellout. Strong V-features are checked when the verb raises to the feature-bearing heads by spellout, while strong N-features are checked when an appropriate NP raises to the specifier of the feature bearing head by spellout. Thus, cross-linguistic variation in the position of the V and its argument NPs is due largely to variation in the feature specification of the functional heads which dominate VP. The features of Irish AgrSP and TP are given in (7):

(7) N- and V-features in Irish

AgrS	N	Weak
	V	Strong
Tense	N	Strong
	V	Weak

In tensed clauses, the strong V-features of AgrS force the verb to raise there. However, as the N-features of AgrS are weak, the subject does not have to occupy the specifier of AgrS. Tense has strong N-features and weak V-features, allowing the subject to check its features in the specifier of TP. The verb moves through Tense to AgrS. The object occupies the specifier of AgrOP, and we thus derive the VSO order of tensed clauses.

This proposal accounts well for the order in finite clauses, but we are still left with questions concerning the independent motivation for the features and the V-movement. First, we might ask what it means to say that a feature is strong or weak. Without independent motivation, the explanation is circular. V-movement takes place because of the strong feature in a functional head; but we know only that a feature is strong because the verb has raised. The strength or weakness of a feature does not correlate with any other property in the language. Any proposed analysis would be greatly improved if we could find any independent arguments for the features, or the movement. In what follows, I suggest that the surface VSO order of Modern Irish is related to the organization of event structure in the language.

3. The Status of the External Argument

3.1 The Specifier of TP and the External Argument

As we saw above, Minimalist accounts attempt to derive the contrast between the VSO order of Irish and the SVO order of English by appealing to differences in the N-features of AgrS and Tense in the two languages. In Irish the N-features of AgrS are weak, while Tense has strong N-features. In English, the reverse is true: Tense has weak N-features while AgrS has strong N-features. As a result, English requires the subject to occupy the specifier of AgrSP in tensed clauses. In Irish, the subject raises only as far as the specifier of TP. This kind of analysis provides an adequate description of the word order differences, but it could be argued that it is not really an explanation. In order for it to satisfy the criterion of explanatory adequacy we might expect to see further evidence that Irish subjects, unlike their English counterparts, occupy the specifier of TP. I explore this idea here and, drawing on proposals of Van Voorst (1988), I explore the relationship between event structure and word order in Irish.

3.2 The External Argument and Event Structure

Van Voorst (1988) argues that there are language-specific requirements on the realization of external arguments. He explores the cross-linguistic differences in these requirements using data from Dutch and English. His Event Structure Correspondence Rule is given in (8):

(8) EVENT STRUCTURE CORRESPONDENCE RULE   (Van Voorst 1988:10)

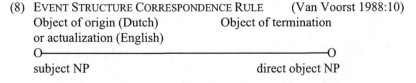

In (8), we see that while object NPs always coincide with the termination of events, subject NPs may coincide with the origin of the event, or they may coincide with an NP that actualizes the event. In Dutch, subjects are "objects of origin" and always play a role in initiating the event. English subjects, on the other hand, are crucial to the carrying out of the event—to its actualization—but are not necessarily involved in the initiation of the event. This is illustrated by the data in (9) and (10):

(9)   The key opened the door.

(10)   **Dutch**
       *De sleutel   opende   de deur.
       the key   open.PAST the door
       *'The key opened the door.'

In (9) *the key* is an instrument and clearly did not initiate the event; it is, however, crucial to the event's taking place, because it helped to actualize the event. Consequently *the key* is an acceptable subject NP in English. This is not so for the equivalent Dutch example in (10). This sentence is unacceptable. Dutch, unlike English, does not allow instruments to act as subjects because instruments never initiate the event described by the verb. If it is true that event structure can be encoded in different ways cross-linguistically, then we might expect that this encoding will have broader syntactic consequences. In particular, I consider what types of NPs can appear as subjects in Irish, and how this is encoded in the syntax.

First, I note that Irish, like Dutch, requires that the subject NP be an initiator of the event described by the verb. Irish instruments, like those of Dutch, cannot serve as an external argument. Therefore, (11) is ungrammatical:

(11)   *D'oscail an eochair an   doras.
        open.PAST the key   the door
       *'The key opened the door.'

This sentence is ungrammatical because the instrument *an eochair* 'the key' is not the initiator of the event, and cannot function as a subject. Note that when we replace *an eochair* with an animate subject the sentence becomes grammatical:

(12)   D'oscail   Seán an doras.
       open.PAST Seán the door
       'Sean opened the door.'

Likewise, it is acceptable to express the instrument in a PP:

(13)   D'oscail   Seán an doras leis an   eochair.
       open.PAST Seán the door with the key
       'Sean opened the door with the key.'

(14)   Diosclaíodh   an doras leis an   eochair.
       Open.PAST.IMP   the door with the key
       'The door was opened with the key.'

From these data we can see that instrumental subjects are not permitted in Irish, but rather must appear within a PP. This is so because an instrument can never be the initiator of the event. Further evidence for this claim is provided by the status of subjects more generally in Irish. Unless the subject is clearly an agent (an initiator of the event), there is a strong tendency for the "subject-like" element to appear as a PP internal to the VP rather than as an external argument. Thus, predicates expressing physical and psychological states typically appear as nominal predicates with PP experiencers. This is shown in the examples in (15):

(15) a. Tá eagla orm.
　　　 is fear on1S
　　　 'I am afraid.'

　　 b. Tá ocras orm.
　　　 is hunger on1S
　　　 'I am hungry.'

　　 c. Tá a fhios agam. . .
　　　 is its knowledge at1S
　　　 'I know. . .'

　　 d. Is maith liom é.
　　　 COP good with1S it
　　　 'I like it.'

All these predicates express states, and so their subject is not an agent; rather, it is an experiencer which cannot initiate the event in which they are participating. Consequently, the specifier of VP is not generated. It might be argued that the group of predicates is nominal rather than verbal, and, therefore, we cannot deduce anything about the structure of VP from such data. This, however, begs the question of why Irish lacks stative verbs with external arguments equivalent to English *like, fear,* and *know.*

　　Further evidence for our proposal is provided by the discussion of Irish unaccusative verbs by McCloskey (1996a). Under standard analyses, unaccusative verbs lack underlying subject. Their single argument is a complement of the verb, and the specifier of VP is not generated. In English, the single argument of the unaccusative verb raises to specifier of AgrS, with the result that the verb has an S-structure subject. McCloskey examines a group of verbs which he terms "salient unaccusatives." These verbs lack external arguments *both* underlyingly and on the surface, and they express their single internal argument as a prepositional phrase. Some examples of salient unaccusatives from McCloskey (1996a) are given in (16):

(16) a. D'eirigh   idir   na   fir.
   Rise.PAST between the   men
   'The men quarreled.'

   b. Théigh   fá dtaobh don   ghirseach.
   Warm.PAST about   the   girl
   'The girl became agitated.'

   c. Ghéaraigh   ar   a   choiscéim.
   Sharpen.PAST on   his   pace
   'His pace quickened.'

   d. Bhreisigh   ar   an   ghluaiseacht.
   Increase.PAST on   the movement
   'The movement increased.'

It is hard to characterize the thematic role borne by the single argument of these unaccusative verbs. Clearly, they are not agents, and they cannot be seen as the initiator of the event. In that case, they cannot be generated in the specifier of VP. The specifier of VP is unoccupied because there is no agent in the theta grid of the verb. The specifier of TP is also unoccupied because the event lacks an initiation point. I would go further and suggest that the lack of experiencer or theme subjects in salient unaccusatives, and in psychological predicates, reflects a deeper generalization: In Irish, the specifier of VP can be occupied only by the initiator of the event described by the predicate. Unaccusative verbs, and stative and psychological predicates, lack a point of initiation, regardless of whether they are tensed or non-tensed; thus, the VP in which they appear always lacks a specifier. Rather, the "subject" is generated as an experiencer or theme PP. I suggest then, that the specifier of VP in Irish is strongly associated with the beginning point of the event. Where an event lacks a clear point of initiation, the specifier of VP is not generated.

3.3 Two Language Types

In conclusion then, I have suggested that there are (at least) two language types:[1]

TYPE A: The external argument position is closely associated with the initiator of the event. If the event does not have an initiation point, an external argument is not assigned (e.g., Irish).

TYPE B: The external argument position is associated with a participant in the event. This argument does not necessarily have to be an initiator, although it often is (e.g., English).

In the next section, I briefly explore the consequences of this typology for three earlier analysis of issues in Irish syntax: Minimalist accounts of VSO order

(Bobaljik and Carnie 1996), the structure of Irish non-finite clauses (Guilfoyle 1997), and the acquisition of Irish (Guilfoyle, in press).

4. Some Consequences of the Proposal

4.1 Word Order: The Position of the Subject at Spellout

One obvious consequence of the typology given above is that type B languages allow a greater range of argument types in their subject position than do type A languages. A second consequence is that the subject in type A languages occupies a lower position in the tree at spellout, than does the subject in type B languages, and that has implications for the word order in the two language types.

In fact, the proposal that there are two types of languages provides independent support for the Minimalist analysis of the word order outlined in section 2 above. Recall that in Irish tensed clauses, the external argument raises to the specifier of TP. In English, however, the external argument of a tensed clause raises through TP to the specifier of AgrS. I would like to correlate this with differences between the two language types mentioned above. If a language chooses setting A, the strong N feature will be born in Tense, and the external argument will appear in the specifier of TP. This is because Tense places the event in time, and the external argument is associated with the beginning of the event in that language. If a language chooses setting B, then Agr bears the strong N feature, and the external argument will appear in the specifier of AgrS. This is so because the external argument is just a participant in the event, and Agr is concerned with identifying an individual in the event, rather than with the timing of the event. I am suggesting, then, that there is a direct relationship between the strength of the N-features of T or Agr and whether the language is type A or type B. Thus, it is no longer true to say that the "feature strength" account of VSO order is circular, because we now have an independent justification for the difference in the location of strong N-features in the two languages.

4.2 External Arguments in Irish Non-finite Clauses

As we saw in 1.2 above, Irish non-finite clauses are headed by a non-finite form of the verb known as the verbal noun (VN). This VN never appears to the right of the subject. In earlier work (Guilfoyle 1993, 1997), I argue that in Irish infinitivals the non-finite verb-form is in fact a nominal, and no true external argument is assigned. In fact, following the bipartite VP analysis of Travis (1991), VP lacks an upper projection. Thus, the intransitive non-finite clause in (17) has the representation shown in (19a), while the transitive non-finite clause in (18) has the representation shown in (19b):[2]

(17) B'fhearr   liom   [tú a   fanacht   sa bhaile   inniu].
     COP.better with1s   you PRT remain.VN   home   today
     'I would rather you remain at home today.'

(18) Ba mhaith liom   [PRO an   doras a   phéinteáil].
     COP good with1s   the door PRT paint.VN
     'I would like to paint the door.'

(19)   a.   b.

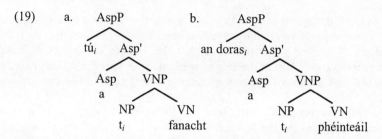

I refer the reader to my earlier work for further details of the proposals on the structure of Irish non-finite clause. For my purposes here, the crucial claim is that Irish non-finite clauses lack an external argument. It has been argued elsewhere that nouns lack a true subject (Grimshaw 1990). In the above-mentioned work, I relate this claim to the fact that they are headed by a nominal form. Note that whatever the merits of the claims for nominal status for the VN, the proposal that non-finite Irish clauses lack a true external argument is entirely consistent with proposals made here. Infinitival clauses in languages of type A cannot have a true subject because the clause lacks an initiation point. A language of type B, however, is entirely neutral as to whether a subject appears in non-finite clauses, because there is no direct link between initiation point and the subject in these languages.

4.3 Implications of the Proposal for the Acquisition of Irish

If the proposal made here is on the right track, we might ask a couple of questions from the perspective of language acquisition.

    a. If there are two language types, how would the child sort out which type of language was the language of the environment?
    b. Is there any evidence to suggest that children's first guess is that the language of the environment is of type A or type B?

In Guilfoyle (in press), I suggest that the child's first guess is that the language of the environment is type A. At a later stage the child will revise their analysis if the language of the environment provides evidence that a strict association between initiator and subject is too restrictive. This proposal can explain a number of characteristics of child grammars that have been widely reported in the literature. In particular, it can shed light on why children produce a high incidence of root infinitivals, and why their early structures appear to be truncated relative to the adult grammar.

For the last several years, there has been an ongoing debate over how many and what type of functional categories are available in early child grammars. To date, each side of the debate has been unable to answer fully the follow questions: If all functional categories are present and the child's grammar is constrained by UG, why does the child fail to use them in an adult-like way? On the other hand, if no functional categories are present, how can we explain the instances of V-movement in the early stages? There have been various attempts to address these problems. Both Haegeman (1995) and Rizzi (1993/4) suggest that root infinitivals in child grammars contain fewer functional categories than do tensed clauses. Children produce truncated structures which contain a VP but lack AgrS and Comp. However, these authors do not offer an explanation for this difference.

Wexler (1994) suggests that the functional categories are present from the earliest stages, but they are not used in the same way as in the adult grammar. Thus, while the functional head T is present in child grammars, it plays no role. As a result, children have the finite/non-finite distinction, but V-movement is "optional." This raises the question of why children would encode a distinction in their grammar that is essentially meaningless. It violates the Principle of Minimal Projection of Grimshaw (1994), because it would mean that the child is creating structure for which there is no motivation.

Our analysis can help resolve some of these issues. Roeper (1992) suggests that children know that the VP encodes events. If children acquiring any language assume that the external argument is associated with the initiation point of the event, we can explain why children produce truncated infinitivals, and why they correlate V-movement with Tense, rather than with an embedded/matrix distinction. They are, in effect, producing a grammar of type A. In this grammar, infinitivals lack external arguments because the event described by the verb has no initiation point. Finite clauses would project at least as far as TP so that the external argument could raise to its specifier. The child could revise this prediction, and move to a grammar of type B, where the language of the environment provides the evidence. Potential triggers that could cause the child to revise the hypothesis could include subjects in ECM contexts, or experiencer subjects.

(20)

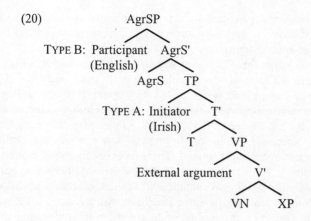

TYPE B: Participant AgrS' (English)

AgrS TP

TYPE A: Initiator T' (Irish)

T VP

External argument V'

VN XP

Note that the change from type A to type B language suggests that children's grammars may "grow" over time. However, this is a continuity rather than a maturational account. The change in the tree structure is driven by the incoming data rather than by a maturation of the grammar. Thus the "truncated" structure of early child grammars is just one of the options allowed within UG, and one that we expect to find in certain adult grammars. Note also that what can appear as an external argument in a type A language is a subset of what can appear as an external argument in a type B language. Initiators are participants in the event; however, participants are not necessarily initiators. If the child's first guess is that only event initiators can be external arguments, and they revise this hypothesis to event participants, they never have to retreat from the first grammar. They will simply loosen the restriction on the specifier of VP, and raise the external argument to the specifier of AgrS, rather than to TP.

5. Conclusion

In this chapter I have suggested that:

a. Languages differ with respect to the types of arguments that they permit to function as an external argument. Some language types require their subjects to be initiators of the event type A languages), while others allow a range of argument types to appear in the specifier of VP (type B).

b. Type A languages generate strong N-features in the head of TP. Type B languages generate strong N-features in the head of AgrSP.

c. This analysis is compatible with independent proposals on the structure of finite and non-finite clauses in Irish and children's early clause structure.

Notes

1. In fact, it appears that there may be a third language type, instantiated by German and Dutch. These languages place fewer restrictions on their subject position than does Irish, but more restrictions than English. As we saw in (14) above, these languages do not allow instrumental subjects, and they have a set of experiencer dative constructions similar to the psychological and physical predicates of Irish. Some examples from German are given below:

(i) a. Mir   ist   kalt.   b. Ihm   fehlt   die   Lösung.
        me.DAT is   cold   him.DAT lacks the solution
        'I am cold.'   'He hasn't the solution.'

However, there are also some psychological predicates which license experiencer subjects, such as:

(ii) a. Ich habe   Angst vor ihm.   b. Er   haßt   mich.
        I   have   fear   for him   he   hates   me
        'I am afraid of him.'   'He hates me.'

Thus, the typology given above is probably too restrictive, and a deeper investigation of the subject properties in languages like German may lead us to propose a three-way split, where German and Dutch are somehow 'intermediate' between type A and type B.

2. I have followed Travis (1991) and Guilfoyle (1993) and labeled the functional projection that dominates the VNP as AspP, but for our purposes it could just as easily bear the label AgrO. Crucially, however, it is not T, since there is no initiation point in these clauses.

5

VSO and Left-Conjunct Agreement
Biblical Hebrew vs. Modern Hebrew

Edit Doron

VSO word order may on principle be the reflection of very different clause structures. This chapter argues that for many languages where VSO order is attested (Semitic, Celtic, Romance, Greek), it reflects a particular clause structure, which I will call a "VSO clause," where the subject does not raise out of the c-command domain of the tense head of the clause:

A VSO clause is derived only if T has the following property:

(i)   T does not have the EPP feature.

VSO clauses exhibit the pattern of "left-conjunct agreement" observed in Irish by McCloskey (1986), and in Arabic by Aoun, Benmamoun, and Sportiche (1994), where the verb agrees with the leftmost conjunct of a postverbal conjoined subject, rather than with the full conjoined subject. Example (1) shows left-conjunct agreement in Biblical Hebrew[1]:

(1)   way-yiqqaḥ   šem   wa:-yɛpɛt   ʔɛt-haṣṣimla:
      and-took*3SM*   Shem   and-Japheth   ACC.the-garment
      'And Shem and Japheth took a garment.' (Genesis 9:23)[2]

This chapter shows that left-conjunct agreement follows from (i) above, and more precisely from the weaker (ii):

(ii)   T does not attract DP.

I assume (following Borer 1986 and Chomsky 1998) that what triggers the attraction of DP to T is the Agree relation between T and DP. Therefore, if T attracts DP, then they must be related by Agree. But if T has property (ii)—i.e., it does not attract DP—then T need not be related by Agree to DP. Rather, I propose that the Agree relation be defined to hold between T and the minimal D constituent closest to T which allows the derivation to converge. In a derivation which requires D to move, the minimal D that does not lead to a violation of the constraints on movement (such as the Coordinate Structure Condition) is the full subject DP. But in a derivation where D is not required to move, the minimal D constituent is a D head. In section 3, I show that in clauses with a conjoined subject, it is the head of the left conjunct that is the D head closest to T.

VSO clauses share property (ii) with another very different type of clause, those with an expletive subject. In this type of clause, T has the EPP feature—i.e., it does not have property (i). The EPP feature of T is satisfied by merging an expletive rather than by attracting the subject; that is, clauses with expletive subjects have property (ii). Yet both VSO clauses (which also have property (i)) and clauses with expletive subjects (which do not have property (i)) exhibit left-conjunct agreement, which shows that this kind of agreement follows from a property weaker than (i). It will be shown in section 3 that left-conjunct agreement follows from property (ii)—i.e., from the lack of DP-raising to T—either because T does not have the EPP feature (property (i)), or because the EPP feature is satisfied by merging an expletive.

Left-conjunct agreement is illustrated below for English, in a clause with an expletive subject, and for Modern Hebrew, in a clause with a null expletive:

(2)   a. In the school there **was** a library and a terminal room.
      b. ??In the school there **were** a library and a terminal room.

(3)   **Modern Hebrew**
      a. hayta   li   sipriya ve- ḥadar   maḥšeḇim
         was*3SF* DAT-me libraryF and roomM   computers
         'I had a library and a terminal room.'

      b. ??hayu   li   sipriya ve- ḥadar   maḥšeḇim
         were*3P* DAT-me libraryF and roomM computers
         'I had a library and a terminal room.'

In general, VSO clauses are not expletive constructions, since they do not show the definiteness effect found in (2) and (3). (1) above, for example, is a VSO clause which is clearly not an expletive construction, since its subject is definite. In addition, not every VSO sequence is a VSO clause. VSO word order is found in Modern Hebrew, but not VSO clauses. First, VSO word order occurs in Modern Hebrew in a null expletive structure such as (3) above. In addition, Modern Hebrew has VSO sequences following any preverbal constituent.[3] But there is no VSO sequence in Modern Hebrew which by itself constitutes a clause. Example (4) below shows that clause initial VSO is ungrammatical in non-expletive constructions, irrespective of the agreement features of the verb. (5) shows that VSO is possible only when some other constituent precedes the verb. The contrast between (5a) and (5b) indicates that left-conjunct agreement is disallowed. These constructions are therefore different is some crucial way from the expletive construction in (3), which allows left-conjunct agreement:

(4) **Modern Hebrew**

    a. *yiqaḥ   šem ve-yepet   ʔet-   hasimla
       will-take*3MS* Shem and Japheth ACC.the- garment
       *'Shem and Japheth will take the garment.'

    b. *yiqḥu   šem ve-yepet   ʔet-   hasimla
       will-take*3MP* Shem and Japheth ACC.the- garment
       *'Shem and Japheth will take the garment.'

(5) a. *maḥar   yiqaḥ   šem ve- yepet   ʔet-   hasimla
      tomorrow will-take*3MS* Shem and Japheth ACC.the- garment
      *'Shem and Japheth will take the garment tomorrow.'

    b. maḥar   yiqḥu   šem ve- yepet   ʔet-   hasimla
      tomorrow will-take*3MP* Shem and Japheth ACC.the- garment
      'Shem and Japheth will take the garment tomorrow.'

Left-conjunct agreement in non-expletive constructions seems to be attested in languages which, like Biblical Hebrew, have VSO clauses:

(6) a. **Standard Arabic**
      laʕibat   maryam wa- zayd   fi-l-bayt
      played*3FS* MariamF and ZaydM in-the-house
      'Mariam and Zayd played in the house.' (Rana Fahoum, p.c.)

    b. **Modern Irish**
      dá mbeinn   -se   agus tusa ann
      if beCOND1S EMPH and you there
      'if you and I were there' (McCloskey and Hale 1984: 31a)

    c. **Spanish**
      Estaba abierta la tienda y   el   mercado.
      was*3S* open3FS the shopF and the marketM
      'The shop and the market were open.' (Rodrigo Gutierrez, p.c.)

    d. **Greek**
      Irthe   o   Pavlos kai o   Giannis sto   parti.
      came3s PRT Paul   and PRT John to-the party
      'Paul and John came to the party.' (Anastasia Giannakidou, p.c.)

1.   Word Order in Biblical Hebrew and Modern Hebrew

The prevalent word order in Biblical Hebrew clauses is verb initial, as shown
again in (7) below. In Modern Hebrew, on the other hand, the prevalent word
order is SVO, as shown in (8a), whereas verb initial sentences are in general
ungrammatical, as shown again in (8b):

(7)   **Biblical Hebrew**
        V   S   O
        hirʔa-ni: yhwh ʔo:ṯka: mɛlɛk ʕal   ʔᵃra:m
        showed-me   God   ACC-you   king over   Syria
        'The Lord hath shewed me that thou shalt be king over Syria.'

                                                            (2 Kings 8:13)

(8)   **Modern Hebrew**
           S   V   O
        a. haseret   herʔa-li   ʔet-dani   menaceaḥ ba-taḥarut
           the.movie   showed-me   ACC-Dani   winning   in.the-race
           'The movie showed me Dani winning the race.'

           V   S   O
        b. *herʔa-li   haseret   ʔet-dani   menaceaḥ ba-taḥarut
           showed-me   the.movie   ACC-Dani   winning   in.the-race
           *'The movie showed me Dani winning the race.'

SVO is also often attested in Biblical Hebrew. Example (9), exactly as is, is a
perfectly grammatical sentence of both Modern and Biblical Hebrew:

(9)   **Biblical Hebrew**
           S   V   O
        u- mo:šɛ: ha:ya: roʕɛ: ʔɛt-co:n   yitro: ḥotno:
        and Moses   was3MS keepingMS ACC-sheep Jethro father-in-law.his
        'Now Moses kept the flock of Jethro his father-in-law.' (Exodus 3:1)

In Biblical Hebrew, the only sentences not introduced by an overt
complementizer are direct quotations, such as (7) above. Other main clauses are
always introduced by the complementizer *w-* 'and', also realized phonologically
as *u-* , as in (9) above, or as *way-* in (10):[4]

(10)   V   S   O
        way- yiqqaḥ   mo:šɛ ʔɛt-maṭṭe ha:ʔᵉlo:hi:m b- ya:do:
        and   took3MS Moses ACC-rod   the.God   in-hand.his
        'And Moses took the rod of God in his hand.' (Exodus 4:20)

In verb initial sentences such as (10), the complementizer 'and' cliticizes to the verb, yet it does not follow that the verb raises to C in Biblical Hebrew. Rather, the complementizer in both (9) and (10) lowers to cliticize to the left edge of the clause, similar to what is argued by Shlonsky (1988) for the Modern Hebrew complementizer *še* 'that' and by McCloskey (1996b) for Irish. Indeed, when sentences like (9) and (10) are preceded by adverbial clauses (themselves introduced by complementizers), then the main-clause complementizer *follows* the adverbial clause, as shown in (11a–b). Notice that it should not be inferred from the syntax of the corresponding King James translations that the clause following the adverbial clause is an embedded clause. In Biblical Hebrew, unlike English, a clause with an overt complementizer is possible as a main clause. In fact, the complementizer 'and' never introduces an embedded clause (cf. footnote 4):

(11) a. wa-yhi: l- šiḇʔaṭ hayya:mi:m **u-** me   hammabu:l
       and-was to-seven the.days   **and** waters the.flood

   ha:yu: ʕal   ha:ʔa:rɛc
   were upon the.earth
   'And it came to pass after seven days, that the waters of the flood were upon the earth.' (Genesis 7:10)

   b. wa-yhi: miq-qec ya:mi:m **way**-ya:ḇe   qayin mip-pri:
       and-was in-end days   **and**-brought Cain of-fruit

   ha:ʔᵃda:ma:
   the.ground
   'And in process of time it came to pass, that Cain brought of the fruit of the ground.' (Genesis 4:3)

2. Conjoined Subjects in Biblical Hebrew

As noted in the standard grammars of Biblical Hebrew (e.g., Gesenius 1910, Joüon 1923), the verb agrees fully with a conjoined subject in SV clauses, as in (12), but it agrees with the left conjunct in VS clauses, e.g., (13). I list here more examples of left-conjunct agreement simply because it is more exotic:

(12) u-mo:šɛ: ʔahᵃro:n w-ḥu:r   ʕa:lu: ro:š   haggiḇʕa:
     and-Moses Aaron   and-Hur climbed3MP head the.hill
     'And Moses, Aaron and Hur went up to the top of the hill.'
                                                    (Exodus 17:10)

(13) a. wat-tašar   dbo:ra: u:-ba:ra:q bɛn ʔ^abi:no:ʕam
and-sang3FS Deborah and-Barak son   Abinoam
'Then sang Deborah and Barak the son of Abinoam.' (Judges 5:1)

  b. way-ya:mot na:da:b wa-ʔ^abi:hu: lipne ʔ^abi:hɛm
and-died3MS Nadab   and-Abihu   before father.their
'But Nadab and Abihu died before their father.' (1 Chronicles 24:2)

  c. u-ba:ta: atta: w-ziqne yiṣra:ʔel ʔɛl mɛlɛk
and-will.come2MS you   and-elders Israel   to   king

micrayim wa-ʔ^amartɛm   ʔela:w
Egypt   and-will.say2MP to.him
'And thou shalt come, thou and the elders of Israel, unto the king
of Egypt, and ye shall say unto him...' (Exodus 3:18)

  d. way-yiqaḥ ʔabra:m w-na:ho:r   la:hɛm   na:ši:m
and-took3MS Abram   and-Nahor   DAT.themselves wives
'And Abram and Nahor took them wives.' (Genesis 11:29)

  e. wat-ta:qa:m ribqa: w-naʕ^aro:tɛyha: wat-tirkabna: ʕal
and-rose3FS Rebecca and-maids.her   and-rode3FP   on

hagg^əmalli:m
the.camels
'And Rebeka arose, and her damsels, and they rode upon the
camels.' (Genesis 24:61)

  f. wat-taʕan   ra:ḥel w-leʔa: wat-to:marna: lo:
and-answered3FS Rachel and-Leah and-said3FP   to.him

ha-ʕo:d la:nu: ḥelɛq w-naḥ^ala: b-bet   ʔa:bi:nu:
Q-yet   to.us portion and-inheritance in-house father.our
'And Rachel and Leah answered and said unto him, Is there yet
any portion or inheritance for us in our father's house?' (Genesis
31:14)

  g. way-yiṣṣa: da:wid w-ha:ʕa:m   ʔ^ašɛr ʔitto:
and-lifted3MS David and-the.people hat   with.him

ʔɛt-qo:la:m   way-yibku:
ACC-voice.their and-wept3MP
'Then David and the people that were with him lifted up their
voice and wept.' (1 Samuel 30:4)

In the examples in (13), the form of the verb is singular, yet the subject is clearly plural. It is implausible to analyze these examples as containing a singular subject combined with a comitative phrase, though this is the interpretation often offered by traditional interpreters of the Bible, such as Rashi (Rabbi Shlomo Yitshaki, 1040–1105), and traditional translations such as the King James Bible (see in particular the translation of 13c and 13e).[5] (13d), for example, involves the plural anaphor 'themselves' bound by the subject. (13g) involves the idiom 'X lifted up X's voice' which is obligatorily reflexive: There is no lifting up anybody's voice but one's own. But this entails, since X is marked as plural in the second part of the idiom, that the subject is plural as well. The examples in (13) are, therefore, examples with plural subjects.

The contrast between full agreement of the preverbal subject and partial agreement of the postverbal subject is also found in the other languages with left-conjunct agreement. Postverbal left-conjunct agreement, as in the (a) sentences below, alternates with full preverbal agreement, in the (b) sentences:

(14) **Standard Arabic**

    a. laʕibat   maryam   wa-zayd   fi-l-bayt

    played*3FS* MariamF   and-ZaydM   in-the-house

    'Mariam and Zayd played in the house.'

    b. maryam wa-zayd   laʕiba:/*laʕiba/*laʕibat   fi-l-bayt

    Mariam and-Zayd   played*3MDUAL/*3MS/*3FS*   in-the-house

    'Mariam and Zayd played in the house.'

(15) **Spanish**

    a. Estaba   abierta   la   tienda y   el   mercado.

    was3S   open*3FS* the   shopF and the   marketM

    'The shop and the market were open.'

    b. La tienda y   el   mercado estaban   abiertos/*estaba

    the shop and the   market   were3P   open*3MP/*was3S

    abierto/abierta.

    open**3MS/*3FS*

    'The shop and the market were open.'

(16) **Greek**

    a. Irthe   o   Pavlos   kai o   Giannis sto   parti.

    came*3S* the paul   and the John   to.the party

    'Paul and John came to the party.'

    b. O   Pavlos kai o   Giannis irthan/*irthe   sto   parti.

    the Paul   and the John   came*3P/*came3S* to-the party

    'Paul and John came to the party.'

3.   V-Raising and Left-Conjunct Agreement in VSO Clauses

First, we must establish that VSO word order in Hebrew indeed involves V-raising, similar to that in Irish (Chung and McCloskey 1987, McCloskey 1991, 1996a, 1996b, Koopman and Sportiche 1991, Duffield 1991, Guilfoyle 1993, Bobaljik and Carnie 1996) and Arabic (Mohammed 1990, Benmamoun 1992, and Fassi Fehri 1993), and unlike other types of VSO languages such as Chamorro (Chung 1990), where the subject lowers to VP rather than V-raising.

It has already been argued extensively that the verb in Modern Hebrew raises out of the VP.[6] First, there is evidence (Shlonsky 1987) that the verb can precede sentential adverbs, like *bevaday* 'certainly':

(17)   **Modern Hebrew**
    a. hamore   bevaday   yasbir   ʔet-hašiʕur
       the.teacher certainly   will.explain   ACC.the-lesson
       'The teacher will certainly explain the lesson.'

    b. hamore   yasbir   bevaday   ʔet-hašiʕur
       the.teacher will-explain   certainly   ACC.the-lesson
       'The teacher will certainly explain the lesson.'

Second, there is evidence (Shlonsky 1991) that quantifiers are floated from a postverbal position:

(18)   hayeladim   hebinu   kulam   ʔet-hašiʕur
       the.children   understood   all3MP   ACC.the-lesson
       'The children have all understood the lesson.'

Third, VP-ellipsis strands the verb (Doron 1990, 1999), which shows that the verb has raised out of the VP. The second reading available for (19) shows that VP-ellipsis has applied, stranding the verb in T:

(19)   ʔim mišehu   yedaber   ʕal   abodato,   gam dani   yedaber
       if   someone   will.speak   about work.his,   also Dani   will.speak
    a. 'If someone will speak about his work, Dani will speak too.'
    b. 'If someone will speak about his work, Dani will too.'

In Biblical Hebrew, it is possible to show that the verb may be found to the left of sentential adverbs, which indicates that it raises out of VP:

(20) **Biblical Hebrew**

we-lo: yiqqa:re: **ʃo:d** ʔɛt-šimḵa: ʔaḇra:m
and-NEG will.be.called **any more** ACC-name.yours Abram
'Neither shall thy name any more be called Abram.' (Genesis 17:5)

In addition, at least for the absolute form (ABS), the verb can be shown to raise out of VP, since ABS precedes not only T (i.e., the tensed form of the verb), but negation as well, as mentioned by Levin (1971)[7]:

(21) a. ra:ʔo: ra:ʔi:ti: ʔɛt- ʕ°ni: ʕammi: ʔˀˠšɛr b-micra:yim
seeABS saw1S ACC-affliction people.my that in-Egypt
'I have surely seen the affliction of my people which are in Egypt.'
(Exodus 3:7)

b. ba:ḵo: lo: tiḇkɛ:
cryABS NEG will.cry2MS
'Thou shalt weep no more.' (Isaiah 30:19)

The original position of ABS is within VP, as can be seen in untensed clauses. The order ABS-T observed in (21) is not found in imperative clauses, which are untensed. Rather, the order found in imperative clauses is T-ABS, as in (22):

(22) šimʕu: šamo:ʕa w-ʔal ta:bi:nu:
seeIMP seeABS and-NEG will.understand2MP

u-rʔu: ra:ʔo: w-ʔal teda:ʕu:
and-seeIMP seeABS and-NEG will.know2MP
'Hear ye indeed, but understand not; and see ye indeed, but perceive not.' (Isaiah 6:9)

I will therefore assume that V raises in tensed clauses in Biblical Hebrew, and I will attempt to answer the question posed as a consequence: How far does V raise in a VSO clause? The answer that Aoun, Benmamoun and Sportiche (1994) have given for Arabic is that V raises to functional head F *beyond* T. F is lower than C, since VSO order is possible in embedded clauses introduced by an overt C. The motivation for Aoun, Benmamoun, and Sportiche's answer is theory internal: Subject-verb agreement, according to them, is a relation which holds between T, the head of the clause, and its specifier, as shown in (23) and exemplified in (24). Therefore, the subject must be in the specifier of TP even when the verb precedes it. Accordingly, the verb must have raised to a functional head F higher than T in a VSO clause:

(23)

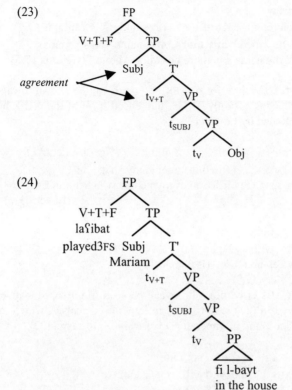

(24)

Yet if agreement is a relation which invariably holds between T and its specifier, then there is no structural difference between examples with left-conjunct agreement, such as (14a), and examples with full agreement, such as (14b). Indeed, Aoun, Benmamoun, and Sportiche deny the existence of left-conjunct agreement, and argue that such examples involve sentence conjunction where ellipsis of the verb and Right Node Raising have also taken place:

(25)

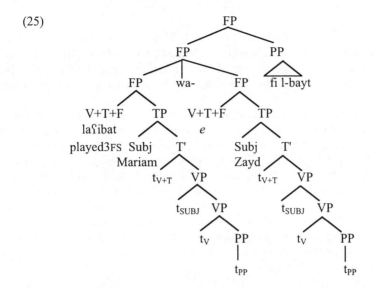

In (25), the second occurrence of the verb 'play' is ellided, whereas the PP 'in the house' is Right Node Raised (RNR). Yet this account is problematic even for Arabic. It predicts that the RNR constituent should show singular agreement, since this constituent supposedly originates from two singular clauses. This prediction cannot be tested with an RNR constituent such as 'in the house' in (25), which does not exhibit agreement. Yet in examples where the RNR constituent is a predicate with overt agreement, this prediction is systematically falsified. In (26), for example, the RNR constituent *yalʕaba:ni fi l-bayt* 'play3MD in the house' is obligatorily marked as dual (D), but if it were raised from two singular clauses, it should be marked as singular:

(26)   **Standard Arabic**
      ka:nat   maryam wa-zayd   yalʕaba:ni fi l-bayt
      was*3FS* Mariam and-Zayd   play3MD   in the.house
      'Mariam and Zayd used to play in the house.' (Rana Fahoum, p.c.)

Aoun and Benmamoun (1999) deny the existence of this problem by showing that it is not attested in either Lebanese or Moroccan Arabic. Yet this problem arises for Standard Arabic, as (26) shows, and moreover, it is also found in Irish and Biblical Hebrew. The relevant example from Irish is shown in (27), where the constituent which is Right Node Raised from two singular clauses (according to Aoun, Benmamoun, and Sportiche), *'nár suí*, is nevertheless plural:

(27)   **Irish**
      Bhínn féin   agus   an   seanduine   'nár suí.
      was*1S* EMPH and   the   old.fellow 1P   sitVN
      'The old fellow and I used to be sitting.' (McCloskey 1986:ex. 37)

In Biblical Hebrew as well, the putatively RNR constituents contain plural anaphors—e.g., *lahem* 'for themselves' in (13d), and *qolam* 'their voices' in (13g), which is an anaphoric part of the expression 'raise their voices'. The plurality of these anaphors would be completely unexpected if they originated from singular clauses.

Since the only argument in Aoun, Benmamoun, and Sportiche for raising V beyond T is to afford a unified account of agreement, and since this attempt is not successful, we are left with no reason to assume that V raises beyond T in VSO structures. Indeed, in McCloskey (1986, 1996a, 1996b), it is argued with respect to Irish that the verb does *not* raise beyond T. Rather, the verb is in T, while the subject is in a specifier of a head lower than T. For simplicity's sake, I assume that this lower head is V, though it is argued in Bobaljik and Carnie (1996) and McCloskey (1996b) that this head is actually a functional head below T and above temporal adverbs which follow the verb. Agreement in Irish holds between T and the lower subject, as shown in (28):

(28)

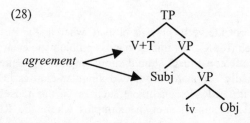

Something needs to be said about how the structure in (28) satisfies the EPP.[8] According to Chomsky (1995), the EPP is satisfied by covert raising of the features of the subject to T. Chomsky (1998) argues against covert feature movement, and moreover proposes to view the EPP as a feature not just of T but of functional heads in general. This feature is not necessarily a lexical property of functional heads, but can be added independently into the derivation. I propose that in a strictly VSO language such as Irish, T is not compatible with the EPP feature, neither as part of its lexical specification nor as an addition by the derivation. In Biblical Hebrew, Arabic, Romance, and Greek, on the other hand, an EPP feature may be added to T in some derivations, though it is not part of the lexical specification of T. Accordingly, in these languages, a VSO structure such as (28) is derived with a numeration which does not include the EPP feature. An SVO structure such as (29) is the outcome of a different derivation, one which includes an EPP feature but no expletive:

(29)

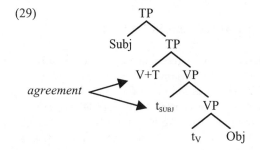

The two derivations in (28) and (29) have different agreement patterns, based on the same operation Agree:

The operation AGREE (adapted from Chomsky 1998)[9]

(a) The relation AGREE holds between the φ-features of T and the φ-features of D which is closest to T (in terms of c-command) in T's domain (all the nodes dominated by its sister).

(b) The values of φ-features are copied to T from the D related to it by AGREE.

(c) If T has an EPP feature, D is raised to T.

In (30), if T has an EPP feature not satisfied by the pure merging of an expletive, it enters into the AGREE relation with the highlighted DP, since this is the DP closest to T, and since this is the minimal constituent within the closest DP that may move without violating the constraints on movement:

(30)

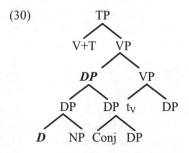

Yet, if T in (30) does not have an EPP feature (or if the EPP feature can be satisfied by a pure merging of an expletive), no movement is forced, and the AGREE relation holds with the closest D head, which is the boldfaced D in (30). Crucially, I assume the asymmetric structure of coordinate structures argued for by Larson (1990), where conjunctions head coordinate structures. I also assume that conjunctions lack any formal features, from which it follows that the category they project is that of the conjuncts themselves. Moreover, the number specification of a conjoined DP is not a morphosyntactic feature of the conjunction head, as argued by Farkaṣ and Zec (1995).

4. Subject-Verb Agreement in OVS Clauses

In section 3, I showed that left-conjunct agreement to postverbal subjects is a motivation for assuming VSO clause structure—i.e., a structure where the subject does not raise beyond T. The question now is whether such a structure is also motivated in clauses where V is not clause initial, e.g., OVS order. At first sight, it seems reasonable to continue assuming that in OVS clauses as well, the subject does not raise beyond T. OVS clauses are simply VSO clauses with subsequent fronting of the object. By this reasoning, the structure of (31a) should be (31b), which is derived from a structure like (28) by raising O to T:

(31)   **Biblical Hebrew**
   a. **O**   **V**   **S**
      we-ʔɛt-ʕ^ama:ṣa: ṣa:m   ʔabša:lom taḥat   yo:ʔa:b
      and-ACC-Amasa   appointed   Absalom   instead   Joab

   ʕal hacca:ba:
   on the.army
   'And Absalom made Amasa captain of the host instead of Joab.'

                                                           (2 Samuel 17:25)

   b.

OVS sentences like (31a) are also attested in Modern Hebrew. As mentioned in the introduction, Modern Hebrew allows postverbal subjects on condition that some other constituent—e.g., the object—precedes the verb. Indeed, (31b) is proposed by Borer (1995) as the structure of Modern Hebrew OVS sentences. Yet if this is the right structure for OVS sentences in Modern Hebrew, and if left-conjunct agreement is accounted for structurally, then the prediction is that (31b) should exhibit left-conjunct agreement in Modern Hebrew as well. But this is not the case, as already mentioned. In Modern Hebrew, only full agreement is attested:

(32)   **Modern Hebrew**
   a. *ʔet-haseper   sama   dvora   ve baraq   ʕal hamadap
      ACC.THE-.book put3FS   Deborah and Barak on   the.shelf
      *'Deborah and Barak put the book on the shelf.'

b. ʔet-haseper   samu   dvora   ve baraq ʕal hamadap
ACC.THE-.book put3*MP* Deborah and Barak on the.shelf
'Deborah and Barak put the book on the shelf.'

The lack of left-conjunct agreement in Modern Hebrew is puzzling in view of the fact that it exists in Biblical Hebrew. This leads us to suspect that the structure in (31b) cannot be the right structure for OVS sentences in Modern Hebrew. I claim that this is true for Biblical Hebrew as well.

Despite the grammar book generalization concerning Biblical Hebrew left-conjunct agreement, there *are* conjoined postverbal subjects in Biblical Hebrew where full agreement is attested:

(33) **Biblical Hebrew**
      w-hanno:teret   mimmɛnna: yo:klu:
      and-the.remainder   from.it   will.eat3*MP*

      ʔahᵃro:n u-ba:na:w
      Aaron   and-his.sons
      'And the remainder thereof shall Aaron and his sons eat.'
                                              (Leviticus 6:9/16)

(34) way-yhi: ʔahar haddᵊbari:m ha:ʔellɛ: ha:tʔu:
      and-was   after things   these   offended**3MP**

      mašqe   mɛlek micrayim w-ha:ʔo:pe: la-ʔᵃdo:nehɛm
      butler king Egypt   and-the.baker to-lord.their

      l-mɛlɛk   micra:yim
      to-king   Egypt
      'And it came to pass after these things, that the butler of the king of Egypt and his baker had offended their lord the king of Egypt.' (Genesis 40:1)

(35) w-ta:psu: bo: ʔa:bi:w   w-ʔimmo:
      and-will.hold3*MP* at.him father.his   and-mother.his
      'Then shall his father and his mother lay hold on him.'
                                              (Deuteronomy 21:19)

Full agreement is specially puzzling in examples such as (36a), since in the same chapter, three verses earlier, the same postverbal subject *does* trigger left-conjunct agreement, as shown in (36b):

(36) a. way-yer<u>d</u>u: Ɂela:w mɛlɛ<u>k</u>   yiṣra:Ɂel   w-i:ho:ša:pa:ṭ
      and-descended*3MP* to.him   king   Israel   and-Jehoshaphat

      u-mɛlɛ<u>k</u>   Ɂ^ε<u>d</u>o:m
      and-king   Edom
      'So the king of Israel and Jehoshaphat and the king of Edom
      went down to him.' (2 Kings 3:12)

    b. way-yelɛ<u>k</u>   mɛlɛ<u>k</u> yiṣra:Ɂel u-mɛlɛ<u>k</u>   yhu:<u>d</u>a: u-mɛlɛ<u>k</u> Ɂ^ε<u>d</u>o:m
      and-went*3MS* king   Israel   and-king   Judah   and-king Edom

      way-ya:so:bbu: dɛrɛ<u>k</u> šib̯ʕat ya:mi:m
      and-circled3MP   road   seven days
      'So the king of Israel went, and the king of Judah, and the
      king of Edom; and they fetched a compass of seven days'
      journey.' (2 Kings 3:9)

We must ask whether there is a structural difference between sentences with full agreement and sentences with left-conjunct agreement. The answer is provided by Moreshet (1967). In a comprehensive study of the complete prose of the Bible (excluding poetry), Moreshet found 235 sentences with a conjoined postverbal subject. In 210 of these sentences, agreement is with the left conjunct, whereas in 25 examples the verb fully agrees with the conjoined postverbal subject. Moreshet was able to discover a descriptive generalization which captures the distribution of full versus left-conjunct agreement. His generalization constitutes a necessary condition for full agreement:

THE MORESHET GENERALIZATION (adapted from Moreshet 1967)
The verb in Biblical Hebrew agrees with the leftmost conjunct of a
postverbal conjoined subject, unless either (I) or (II) hold:
    (I)   The verb is preceded in the clause by some constituent.
    (II) A clitic is attached to the verb.

Examples (33) and (34) above fall under clause (I) of this generalization, whereas (35) and (36a) fall under clause (II).[10] The problem is that the two clauses of the Moreshet Generalizaton do not seem to constitute a natural class of syntactic environments.
    Fortunately, the analysis proposed for clitics in Semitic by Doron (1996) and Doron and Heycock (1999) makes it possible to subsume condition (II) of the Moreshet Generalization under condition (I). According to this analysis, clitics may be viewed as anaphors bound by preverbal constituents, as in (37):

(37)   kol   habben hayyilo:<u>d</u> hayɁo:r-a: tašli:<u>k</u>u:-***hu:***.
        every son   born   the.riverALLAT you.will.throw-***him***
        'Every son that is born ye shall cast into the river.' (Exodus 1:22)

(37) is not an example of left-dislocation, as the constituent binding the clitic is the quantifier *kol habben hayyilo:d* 'every son that is born'. Quantifiers with 'every' do not undergo left-dislocation.

Crucially, the constituent binding the clitic is possibly empty, if previously mentioned in the discourse. This is clearly the case in (36a), for example, where the object clitic refers to the prophet Elisha, mentioned earlier in the text. The same is true for (35), where there is previous mention of a rebellious son, to which the clitic is anaphoric. These clitics may therefore be analyzed as bound by a preverbal constituents, just as in (37). The only difference is that the preverbal constituent is overt in (37), but it is null in (35) and (36a). Condition (II) therefore does not characterize any examples that do not already fall under (I). The two necessary conditions can be collapsed to a single one, which coincides with condition (I):

THE MORESHET GENERALIZATION (revised)
The verb in Biblical Hebrew agrees with the leftmost conjunct of a postverbal conjoined subject, unless the verb is preceded in the clause by some constituent.

The reformulation of the Moreshet Generalization is an improvement over the original formulation for yet another reason. It now accounts as well for cases where the anaphoric element which licenses full agreement is not a clitic attached to the verb, but some other anaphor. An example is shown in (38), where the anaphor is part of the conjoined subject itself (additional examples are Exodus 29:15, Leviticus 8:19,22, Numbers 20:10):

(38)   way-yo:ḵlu: way-yištu: hu: w-ha:ʔ°naːšiːm ʔ°šer ʕimmo:
       and-ate*3MP* and-drank*3MP* he and-the.men   that with.him
       'And they did eat and drink, he and the men that were with him.'
                                                            (Genesis 24:54)

The Moreshet Generalization in conjunction with our previous discussion provides a necessary condition for the raising of the verb beyond T. According to the conclusions of section 4, full agreement is the result of the subject raising to specifier of TP. Accordingly, if in a full-agreement structure the subject is found following the verb, then it must be that the verb has raised beyond T. The Moreshet Generalization states a condition on such a movement very similar to the condition on V-raising beyond T known from the discussion of Germanic languages (den Besten 1983, Platzak 1986a, and many others). This condition can be formulated as a V2 condition on V-raising beyond T:

THE V2 CONDITION
The verb in Biblical Hebrew does not raise beyond T unless preceded by some constituent.

In other words, the raising of V to a functional projection F beyond T is possible only if some constituent—e.g., the object—occupies specifier of TP:[11]

(39)

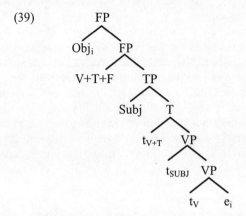

Descriptively, as we have seen, Modern Hebrew differs from Biblical Hebrew in two relevant respects:

(i)   The verb is always preceded by some constituent, not necessarily the subject.

(ii) There is no left-conjunct agreement when the subject follows the verb, other than in expletive constructions.

The difference may be reduced to a single factor if we simply assume that in Modern Hebrew, T has the EPP feature as a lexical property. This is why in Modern Hebrew, unlike Biblical Hebrew, there is always some constituent preceding the verb, and there is no left-conjunct agreement. Even where the object precedes the verb, the subject is in the specifier of TP and therefore triggers full agreement. Indeed, (39) is the structure proposed by Shlonsky and Doron (1992) for Modern Hebrew OVS sentences. In that chapter, independent evidence was presented in favor of (39) over (31b) as the structure for OVS sentences in Modern Hebrew. The distribution of left-conjunct agreement in Biblical Hebrew coupled with the lack of left-conjunct agreement in Modern Hebrew, is an additional argument to the same effect. The structure of Modern Hebrew SVO sentences, on the other hand, is argued by Shlonsky and Doron (1992) to be as in (29), the structure proposed here for Biblical Hebrew SVO sentences as well. A similar asymmetry between the position of a preverbal subject and a preverbal object is argued for in Germanic by Zwart (1993a).

Adopting the framework of Chomsky (1998) has made it possible to account for the different distribution of the EPP feature in the different languages. T in Modern Hebrew is assigned the EPP feature lexically (as in English). In Biblical Hebrew, it is not, but T may be enriched with an EPP feature as part of some derivations but not of others (the same is true of Arabic,

Greek, and Romance). In Irish, in contrast, T is incompatible with the EPP feature, which cannot be added to it either lexically or by the derivation.

Notes

1. All the Biblical Hebrew translations are from the King James Bible (1611), which is generally more literal than the other translations.
2. I am very grateful to Shraga Assif for the phonetic transcription of the Biblical Hebrew data.
3. The preverbal constituent may be null even when it is not expletive, as is generally assumed for "narrative inversion" and for "all-focus sentences," e.g.:

(i)   hitqašer   aba   šel<u>k</u>a

        called   father   yours

        'Your father called.'

4. The main clause complementizer 'and' has an important role for text cohesion (for recent discussion see de Caen 1995 and Hatav 1997). It is in complementary distribution with other complementizers—e.g., *ki:* 'for/that', *pen* 'lest', h^a 'Q' (a yes-no interrogative complementizer) —which only introduce embedded clauses:

(i)   ?al ti:r?i: ki: ša:maʕ   ?ᵉlo:hi:m ?ɛl   qo:l   hannaʕar

        NEG fear2FS   for   heard3MS God   to   voice   the.lad

        'fear not; for God hath heard the voice of the lad.'   (Genesis 21:17)

(ii)   ki: ?a:mru   pliˇti:m   pɛn yaʕᵃṣu: ha: ʕibri:m

        for   said   Philistines lest will.make3MP the   Hebrews

        _erɛ<u>b</u> ?o: _ᵃni:<u>t</u>

        sword or   spear

        'For the Philistines said, lest the Hebrews make them swords or spears.'

                                                    (1 Samuel 13:19)

(iii)   way-yo:mɛr   hᵃta_at   ?ᵉlohi:m ?a:no:<u>k</u>i:

        and-said3MS   Q instead God   I

        'and he said, Am I in God's stead.' (Genesis 30:2)

5. Genuine comitative phrases in Biblical Hebrew seem to be small clause adjuncts of the form [sc *and DP with him*], e.g.:

(i)   way-ya:<u>b</u>o: no:a_ [sc u-<u>b</u>a:na:w   w-?iˇto: u-nˇe

        and-came3MS Noah   and-sons.his   and-wife.his and-wives

        <u>b</u>a:na:w itto:]   ?ɛl hatte<u>b</u>a: mippne me   hammabbu:l

        sons.his with.him to   the.ark   because   waters the.flood

        'And Noah went in, and his sons and his wife and his sons' wives with him, into the ark, because of the waters of the flood.' (Genesis 7:7)

6. Borer (1995) presents arguments that V does not always raise in Modern Hebrew, but the validity of these arguments is disputed in Doron (to appear).

7. ABS is the absolute (i.e., non-construct) form of the verbal gerund used to reduplicate the verb for the purpose of strengthening the affirmative force of the utterance. It is usually translated as 'surely' or 'indeed'.

8. One approach to the question of how the structure in (28) satisfies the EPP is that of Alexiadou and Anagnostopoulou (1998). According to them, in *pro*-drop languages, V-raising to T itself satisfies the EPP, since V in these languages carries a clitic which has the feature [+D]. I will not discuss this proposal in the text, since it makes several wrong predictions. First, it predicts that every *pro*-drop language has VSO clauses, a prediction clearly falsified by Modern Hebrew. Second, by this approach, the subject cannot raise to the specifier of TP in *pro*-drop languages. Rather, any preverbal subject is purely merged to the specifier of TP, an A' position, and binds the thematic subject *pro* situated in the specifier of VP (or some other projection lower than T). Yet it can be shown that the subject does raise to the specifier of TP in *pro*-drop languages. Raised subjects differ in many of their syntactic and semantic properties from purely merged constituents, as amply shown for Standard Arabic, Modern Hebrew, and Japanese by Doron and Heycock (1999). For a very different view of the EPP in VSO languages, see Massam, this volume.

9. Chomsky's definition also includes an additional clause regarding the erasure of the non-interpretable φ-features of an agreeing T.

10. There exist a couple of apparent counterexamples to this generalization, yet it seems that even those can be explained away:

(i)   wa-ykah^a nu: ʔɛlʕa:za:r   w-ʔi:ṭa:ma:r

      and-served3MP   Eleazar   and-Ithamar

      'Eleazar and Ithamar executed the priest's office.' (1 Chronicles 24:2)

The verb in (i) shows full agreement to the postverbal subject, yet neither does it contain an object clitic, nor is it preceded by any constituent. But notice that (i) appears in the context of a detailed list of all the temple officials in King David's administration, at the point where the divisions of high priests, the descendents of Aaron, are listed:

(ii)   w-li-bne   ʔah^a ro:n   ma_lqo:ṭa:m bne ʔah^a ro:n na:da:b

      and-to-sons Aaron   divisions.their sons Aaron   Nadab

      wa-ʔ^a bi:hu: ʔɛlʕa:za:r   w-ʔi:ṭa:ma:r

      and-Abihu Eleazar   and-Ithamar

      way-ya:moṭ   na:da:b wa-ʔ^a bi:hu: lipne ʔ^a bi:hɛm u-ba:ni:m

      and-died3MS Nadab   and-Abihu before father.their and-sons

      lo: ha:yu: la:hɛm wa-ykah^a nu: ʔɛlʕa:za:r w-ʔi:ṭa:ma:r

      NEG were to.them and-served3MP   Eleazar   and-Ithamar

      'Now these are the divisions of the sons of Aaron. The sons of Aaron; Nadab and Abihu, Eleazar and Ithamar. But Nadab and Abihu died before their father, and had no children: therefore Eleazar and Ithamar executed the priest's office.' (1 Chronicles 24:1–2)

The passage in (ii) is an explanation for why there are only two divisions of high priests listed, not four, in spite of the fact that Aaron, the forefather of all high priests, had had four sons (about two centuries prior to David's time). The clause in (i), which is the last clause in (ii), is therefore probably not conjoined to the preceding clause, but rather contains it as an adverbial clause: 'Because Nadab and Abihu had died leaving no children while Aaron was still in office, only Eleazar and Ithamar succeeded him as high priests.' If this is so, then (i) does after all fall under the Moreshet Generalization.

11. In Arabic, Spanish, and Greek, left-conjunct agreement is optional, which may indicate that in those languages, T-raising to F is independent of the fronting of a constituent to the specifier of FP.

6

VSO and VOS
Aspects of Niuean Word Order

Diane Massam

This chapter explores the verb initial theme through an examination of predicate fronting in the Polynesian language Niuean. Beginning with the V-fronting analysis advanced by Emonds (1980) and Sproat (1983), among others, two questions are addressed: Where does the Niuean fronted element land? And what sort of constituent undergoes fronting? In answering the first question in section 1, it is shown that the Niuean verb does not front to C or T, since another head, namely NEG, can appear between the complementizer/tense morpheme and the verb. This necessitates positing an additional functional head between C and VP, which, following convention, I label Infl. Section 1 serves largely to describe Niuean fronting so as to place it in a typology of VSO languages. In sections 2 and 3, related issues are raised which have broader cross-linguistic and theoretical implications. In section 2, a brief examination of non-verbal predicate sentences, and of noun incorporation structures, leads to the conclusion that Niuean is not a verb-fronting language, but rather a predicate-fronting language. This is extended so that in all sentence types it is a maximal projection predicate that is fronted to specifier of IP. Thus, VSO order is in fact [Vt_o]SO order.[1] In concluding section 2, some empirical implications are examined regarding Niuean postverbal morphemes. In section 3, it is proposed that predicate fronting takes place, analogously to subject fronting in SVO languages (cf. Massam and Smallwood 1997), to check an Extended Projection Principle-related feature [PRED]. Thus, Niuean predicate fronting to IP, resulting in the so-called VSO order, is an externalization process, and is fundamentally different from the verb fronting to IP witnessed in SVO languages such as French (cf. Pollock 1989). Since it is claimed that predicates are syntactically externalized, it is necessary to define the notion of EPP predicate in a uniform fashion. An EPP predicate is defined as an X^o lexically determined predicate and its internal argument. The conclusion, section 4, reviews the findings of the chapter.

1.   Niuean Fronting is to IP, not CP

This section begins with a basic description of Niuean sentence structure, and an examination of word order.[2] First, arguments are provided against a flat structure; then arguments are provided that Niuean Tense is in C, and that VSO order derives from fronting to Infl and not to C (cf. McCloskey 1991, 1996b, for an overview of these two options).

Niuean exhibits a V-S-O-IO-Obl word order, as shown in (1) below.[3]

(1) a. Ne   tala aga   e   ia   e   tala   ke   he   tagata.
        PAST tell DIR3P ERG he ABS story to   PRT man
        'He told the story to the man.'

    b. Hifo   a   Lemani ki   tahi mo   e   vaka.
       go-down ABS   Lemani to   sea with ABS   canoe
       'Lemani went down to sea with a canoe.'

If we adopt the common assumption that the verb and its object originate within V', then all Niuean clauses with a verbal predicate involve some kind of movement. It could be taken simply as a theoretical assumption that the verb and object originate in V', but there is in fact some evidence for this, in that verbs form a closer D-structure bond with their objects than with their subjects. For instance, verbs can incorporate internal, but not external arguments, and verbs can form idioms in conjunction with their internal arguments (but not, it seems, with their external arguments).[4] Woolford's (1991) analysis of Niuean as having a flat VSO structure is thus not adopted.[5] The incorporation facts are shown below in (2), while (3) shows a verb-object idiom.

(2) a. Ne   inu   e   Sione   e   kofe.
        PAST drank ERG Sione   ABS coffee
        'Sione drank the coffee.'

    b. Ne   inu   kofe   a   Sione.
       PAST drink coffee ABS   Sione
       'Sione drank coffee.'

    c. Fā   totou he   tau faiaoga e   tau tohi.
       HAB   read ERG   PL teacher ABS   PL   book
       '(The) teachers often read books.'(S73)

    d. *Fā   totou faiaoga e   tau tohi.
        HAB read teacher ABS   PL   book
       *'Teachers often read books.'(S74)

(3) Loto a   au ke   oeli e   tau matahui, ti   koli.
     like ABS I SBJN oil ABS PL knee   then dance
     'I like to get a little drunk, then dance.'(S191)

Given a verb/object constituent at the level of thematic representation, I assume that the Niuean verb in sentences such as those above undergoes leftward movement to some c-commanding head position.[6] Following Chomsky (1995), it is assumed that the features of a functional head may contain a strong uninterpretable feature which requires checking prior to spellout, thus attracting some other element, which, as a result of Attract, immediately undergoes a Move operation. A central problem in the study of VSO languages is to determine to which functional head the verb is attracted. The debate usually focuses on C and Infl (or Tense) (cf. Hendrick, this volume, and Carnie, Harley, and Pyatt, this volume), so I begin the discussion with these categories.

In Niuean, the two categories of C and Tense are morphologically merged. The sentence begins with a particle which indicates the tense/aspect of the sentence.[7] These particles are given in (4). Note that the particles can be null, as in (1b) and (3).

(4) *Sentence-initial tense/aspect particles*

PAST	FUTURE	PROGRESSIVE	PERFECT	SUBJUNCTIVE
ne/na	to	hā ne	kua	kia

a. *Ne* tagi   a   ia.
   PAST cry   ABS   she
   'She cried.' (KeP)

b. *To* fano   a   ia.
   FUT go   ABS he
   'He will go.' (W12)

c. *Hā ne* nonofo a   mutolu i hinei.
   PROG stay   ABS   you   at this.place
   'Whilst you are staying here.' (M66)

e. *Kua* fano   tuai   a   ia.
   PERF go   PERF   ABS he
   'He has gone.'

The sentence initial particle expresses the tense or aspect of the sentence. These particles, however, also display complementizer-like properties, as discussed by Seiter (1980), in that the particles vary depending on the complementation status of the sentence, as follows. Matrix clauses begin with the particles listed above, as do sentential objects of some verbs—verbs of cognition, evaluation, observation, and speaking. These particles are in complementary distribution with other particles which do not have a tense function, such as the causal or factive particle *he*, seen in (5a). They are also in complementary distribution with the subjunctive particle *ke,* which introduces clauses embedded under modal verbs, and verbs of desire and intention as in (5b). Finally, we find a partially distinct series of tense/aspect markers in relative clauses and other operator-extraction contexts, as shown in (6):

(5) a. Gagao foki nī   a   au he hifo   a   Maka ki   tahi.
       sick also EMPH ABSI C   go-down   ABS   Maka to   sea
       'I'm also sick of Maka going down to the sea.' (S129)

    b. Ne   foa   e   lautolu e   vala vao ke   tā
       PAST clear ERG they   ABS bushland SBJN build

       aki   e   fale pola.
       INST ABS   house
       'They cleared the bushland to build a thatch house.'

(6)   *Sentence-initial tense/aspect particles in operator-extraction clauses*

PAST/PRESENT(NFUT)	FUTURE	PROGRESSIVE	PERFECT
ne	ka	ne fã e	(ne) kua

    a. Ne   inu   e   Sione e   kofe *ne*   taute e   au.
       PAST drink ERG Sione ABS coffee NFUT make ERG I
       'Sione is drinking the coffee that I made.'

    b. Ko e tau fale fã hanei *ka*   tā   he maaga.
       'Ko' PL house fourthese FUT   build in village
       'These are the four houses that are going to be built in the village.'
       (Sp135)

    c. e   tagata *ne fã e* onoono hake ke he mahina
       ABS man   PROG   look   up   to PRT moon
       'the man who's looking up at the moon' (S93)

    d. Ko Fao hanā *ne kua* iloa ko ia ne   tā   mai
       'Ko' Fao this PERF   know 'ko' he NFUT bring from

       a   Avatele mo Kavatele mai i   Fonuagalo.
       ABS   Avatele and Kavatele from LOC   Fonuagalo
       'It was this Fao who is known for bringing Avatele and Kavatele
       from Fonuagalo.' (NAH4)

Sentence initial particles thus express information both as to the tense/aspect of the sentence, and to the grammatical status of the clause (matrix, subject clause, object clause, relativizing clause, etc.). In the case of object clauses, they also express information as to the selectional properties of the governing verb—i.e., whether it selects a subjunctive or a fully tensed clause. Given these facts, the initial particle is posited to be a portmanteau Complementizer/Tense element, CTP (i.e., Comp/Tense Phrase).[8]

We can now question whether the verb-fronting operation in Niuean involves fronting to CTP. In fact, this appears not to be the case. This can be seen by an examination of the Niuean verbal complex, beginning with the preverbal elements, as shown below.

(7)   *Sentence-initial elements*

C/Tense	Negative	Auxiliaries	Verb

    To nākai liu   feleveia   foki   a   taua.
    FUT not   again meet   also   ABS   we
    'We will never again meet.' (S16)

Note that the negative morpheme and auxiliary verb(s) intervene between the verb and the sentence initial CT particle. This means that if the verb is considered always to move to CT position, there must at some point in the derivation be an X^0 of the form: [T-NEG-AUX-Verb]. It might be the case that the entire complex is a constituent at D-structure, in which case the entire complex moves to CT. Or, one or both of the AUX and NEG elements could appear in a head position, with the verb complex moving first to AUX, then to NEG, and so on.

These views are problematic, because NEG appears to be an independent stem, itself able to host verbal clitics. There is a postverbal perfect marker *tuai* which often co-occurs with the CT perfect marker *kua*. It appears above in (4e). In a negative sentence, instead of appearing after the verb, *tuai* appears after the negative element.

(8)   Kua   nākai tuai   fano   a   ia.
    PERF not   PERF   go   ABS   he
    'He has not gone.' (Mxviii)

As well as the perfect particle, there is another verbal clitic which shifts to the post-negative position in a negative sentence. This is an emphatic marker, *lā,* seen in (9). (Note the negative element *nākai* alternates with a different form *ai* which appears in (9)). *Lā* often co-occurs with another emphatic marker, *ia*. In a negative sentence *lā* appears on the NEG, while *ia* occurs on the verb.[9]

(9) a. Ai lā   kitia   e   au   e   pusi.
      not EMPH   see   ERG   I   ABS   cat
      'I have not yet seen the cat.' (Sp169)

   b. ... ko e   mena kito   taute lā ia   he   tau
      ... 'ko'   thing recent make   just   LOC   PL

    magahala fakamui nai.
    period-of-time-after-this
    ' a thing just recently done.' (NAH2)

c. Nākai lā   nofo ia   a   au he ha   motu tufa a   Niue.
   not EMPH live EMPH ABS I   on NSP island like ABS Niue
   'I've never before lived on an island like Niue.' (S16)

A constituent question marker can also appear after the negative element:

(10) Ai kia kitia e   koe   e   laa kua   tokoluga?
     not Q see   ERG you ABS sun PERF high
     'Didn't you see the sun high up?' (S26)

It has been argued (Chung 1970) that in other Polynesian languages the negative element is in fact a verb, since, for example, it houses verbal affixes and it takes as its complement a phrase which begins with an embedded CT element (cf. also Bauer 1997, Hohepa 1969, Pearce 1997, and Waite 1987). In Niuean, the negative element does not seem to be a full-fledged verb, since it does not appear with the complete range of verbal clitics (outlined below), and it does not take a CTP complement. However, its behavior is that of a syntactic head, rather than a lexical affix or clitic.

Since none of the material surrounding NEG is phrasal, it might still be possible to maintain the claim that [NEG-*lā*-*tuai*-AUX-Verb-. . .] is a single X° at some level. (See below for discussion of postverbal clitics.) But this necessitates a varying templatic morphology since the order of morphemes within the complex head would differ depending on whether or not it contained a negative morpheme. (In an affirmative sentence we find [AUX-Verb-. . . -*lā*-Y-*tuai*-. . .].) It is hard to explain this variation in morpheme order under a V-to-CTP view, whereas if we assume that NEG intervenes between CT and the fronted verb, we can explain why *tuai* and *lā* appear on the NEG element simply by observing that they are always on the head of the phrase that is a sister to CT (i.e., in the second head position, or "governed" by CTP). It is reasonable that a perfect morpheme need be governed by perfect tense, and that a temporal emphatic such as *lā*, meaning 'just/yet', need be governed by tense. There is no comparable reason why their relative order within a single head should matter.

Finally, as well as being an independent morphological head, NEG has sentential scope rather than scope over the verb alone. It is preferable, then, to consider NEG as an independent item in the syntax. I thus rule out the movement of V to CTP.

The argument presented above for not considering V-movement to be to CTP is based on negative sentences. In sentences where there is no NEG, it might appear that V to CT movement is a possibility (and note that NEG to CT movement remains a possibility). However, this would be true only if the so-called V-fronting is actually head movement. Below I argue that what is fronted is in fact a maximal projection (VP, PP, AP). If this is the case, it is clear that the projection could not move to the Spec of CTP and appear, as it does, to the right of the head of CTP. Note that if the claim of this chapter is granted (i.e., that VSO in Niuean involves maximal or remnant predicate fronting), the ordering of C before the predicate is an argument against movement to CTP in both affirmative and negative sentences.

For the sake of completeness, let us briefly examine auxiliaries. Auxiliaries in Niuean, unlike NEG, are morpho-syntactically inert, in that they never vary in their position with respect to other particles or phrases. They include desideratives, habituals, and elements meaning 'look like', 'nearly', 'begin', among others (see Seiter 1980). An example (*fia* 'want') appears below:

(11)   Ne fia   evaeva a   ia ka e   nākai talia
        Pst want walk   ABS he but   not   let

        he matua ke   taute pihia.
        Erg parent SBJN do so
        'She wanted to go for a walk, but her parent wouldn't let her do so.'
        (Sp75)

Auxiliaries appear between NEG and V. They do not show evidence of independence from the verb, since their position is fixed and no material may intervene between the auxiliary and the verb.[10] While, as seen above, in a sentence with NEG, the perfect element *tuai* and the emphatic *lā* appear on NEG rather than on the verb, in a sentence with no NEG, but with an auxiliary, *tuai* and *lā* appear on the verb, not on the auxiliary. Thus, auxiliaries, unlike NEG and V, do not display the head-like property of taking particles. As stated above, *tuai* and *lā* appear on the first head after CTP. They never appear on auxiliaries; hence auxiliaries are not heads. Instead, I consider that the auxiliaries are verbal prefixes, or perhaps more correctly, that they form compounds with verbs. Under the entry for *fia* Sperlich (1998) states that ". . . some speakers may want to consider such constructions either as compounds or as verbs with a prefix. . ." This view is supported by the fact that the auxiliaries appear to be completely inert syntactically. It is further (weakly) supported by Seiter's observation that one auxiliary is orthographically represented as a prefix on a verb (*fiakai* 'hungry, lit. 'want-eat', *fiamohe* 'sleepy', lit. 'want-sleep'). Similar support is found in the fact that several auxiliaries are redundant expressions of portions of meaning of the verb with which they appear, e.g., *fā* 'habitual' with *mahani* 'typical', or *fia* 'desiderative' with *loto* 'want' or with *manako* 'desire'.

Given the discussion above, we can adopt the structure in (12) for the Niuean clause, where there is a C/Tense phrase, then a Negative phrase, then the position to which the verb fronts. This position is followed by the VP. Following a convention commonly adopted for other languages, I call the position to which the verb fronts Infl. Since the tense morphology does not actually appear in this slot, and since I claim that what does appear here is a predicate EPP feature, this position might also be termed Pred (cf. Bowers 1993), but here I maintain the more familiar term. I leave aside here detailed discussion of exactly where the subject and object should be positioned at spellout, but see (18), (21), and (25) below, and Massam (1998b).

(12)   [$_{CTP}$ CT [$_{NEGP}$ NEG [$_{IP}$ Infl [$_{VP}$ Subject V Object]]]]

Niuean VSO order is thus preliminarily considered to arise from movement of V to Infl, with the understanding that Infl does not contain tense features. (This will be revised in section 2 to accommodate predicate fronting of maximal projections.) Note, however, that the attracting feature in Infl is yet to be fully discussed.

2.   Maximal Projection Predicate Fronting (VSO is [V$_{to}$]SO)

2.1. Non-Verbal Predicate Fronting (PredSO not VSO)

A central fact of word order in Niuean is that in many instances it is not a verbal element (as it is in 13a) which appears in the V-slot, but that instead it can be an apparent nominal element, as seen in (13b–e), or a prepositional element, as in (14). In these examples, the predicate and its following particles are shown in brackets. This observation has been made for a variety of VSO languages (e.g., for Tahitian by Lazard and Peltzer 1991). The theoretical significance of this fact, however, is not always appreciated (but cf. Carnie 1993, 1995, for Irish, and Lee, this volume, for Zapotec). Predicate nominals are marked with *ko* (proper) and *ko e* (common), which I gloss here simply as 'ko', reserving further discussion of its category and meaning until section 3.2 below.

(13) a. [Ne   inu]   e   Sione e   kofe.
        PAST drink ERG   Sione ABS   coffee
        'Sione drank the coffee.'

     b. [Ko   Mele]   e   faiaoga.
        'Ko' Mele   ABS   teacher
        'The teacher is Mele.'

     c. Ai [ko e faiaoga] a   Mele.
        not 'ko'   teacher ABS   Mele
        'Mele's not the teacher.'

     d. [Ko e tipolo agaia   nī]   ne   inu   ai   a   lautolu.
        'Ko'   lime still   EMPH NFUT drink PRON ABS   they
        'It's still only lime juice that they are drinking.' (S100)

     e. [Ko e fale   ke   lima   aki]   e   fale   i   kō.
        'Ko' house SBJN five   INST ABS house LOC   there
        'That house over there is the fifth house.' (S53)

Seiter (1980) provides evidence that the fronted *ko (e)* nominal is in the same slot as the fronted verb, since it follows the NEG (13c) and precedes the usual postverbal adverbs (13d).[11] In (13e), we see a clear example of a fronted maximal projection, namely a nominal with a modifying relative clause (literally translated as 'the house that (one) fives with'.) Other examples with clearly phrasal predicates are given in (16) and (23) below.

There are two immediate theoretical consequences of the observation that the verbal slot may be filled with a maximal projection. First, Niuean VSO order results at least some of the time from non-verbal predicate-fronting rather than from V-fronting. In Minimalist terms, this means that the strong attracting feature in Infl that provokes the predicate initial word order must be [PRED] rather than the purely categorial feature [V] (cf. Bowers 1993). Second, it appears to be the case that the fronted predicate is at times an X°, as in the case of V-fronting as in (13a), and at times an XP, as in the case of predicate nominal (13b–e) or prepositional fronting as in (14).

(14)   Hā   he fale a   ia.
       PRED in house ABS she
       'She is in the house.' (M66)

Maintaining a conservative view of X-bar theory (vs., for example, Carnie 1995 or Chung 1990), wherein only non-phrasal X° elements can appear in or adjoined to head positions, it must be the case that phrasal predicates (e.g., 13e) are fronting to the specifier position of IP, rather than to the head position of IP.[12] If, as assumed, in all instances the moved element is fronting to check a [PRED] feature, this raises questions regarding Pied Piping. (15) would appear to hold:

(15)   *Bifurcated description* [PRED] *checking* (to be resolved below)
       a. If the predicate is verbal, it alone moves to check [PRED], none of its arguments may move with it.
       b. If the predicate is nominal or prepositional, it moves along with a subset of its phrasal arguments/modifiers (obligatorily).

There are two problems with this situation. We must ask what particular separate paths of movement the two predicate types take (head to head vs. specifier to specifier), and whether these might not be expected to correlate with other word order differences (cf. Rackowski and Travis, this volume). I leave this issue aside for now. In addition, there is a philosophical difficulty, namely that there is no apparent reason why predicate types should behave differently in this way. Instead of trying to formulate a justification for this bifurcation in predicate behavior, let us explore the possibility that all [PRED] checking (even purely verbal [PRED] checking) involves the fronting of a maximal projection. In the case of verbal predicates, this will involve so-called remnant VP-fronting (cf. Lee, this volume). To support this position, I first show that there are sentences where verbal [PRED] checking clearly does involve the fronting of a maximal projection.

2.2.   *VP Predicate-Fronting: Noun Incorporation (VSO vs. VOS)*

In this section, I show that "V-fronting" can, at least in some cases, involve VP-fronting. In order to show this, we first corroborate and extend Seiter's (1980) observation that so-called Noun Incorporation (NI) in Niuean can incorporate non-head material, as seen below. In (16a), for example, the nominal *sipi mo e ika mitaki* 'good fish and chips', which would not be considered an X°, is claimed by Seiter to have incorporated onto the verb. In each example below, the "incorporated" nominal is bracketed. (See Massam 1998b, for a more detailed discussion of Niuean NI and of the analysis presented briefly here.)

(16) a. Ne   kai [sipi   mo   e   ika   mitaki]   a   Sione.
        PAST eat chip COM ABS fish good   ABS Sione
        'Sione ate good fish and chips.'

b. Ne   holoholo   [kapiniu kiva] fakaeneena   a   Sione.
   PAST wash   dish   dirty   slowly   ABS Sione
   'Sione is washing dirty dishes slowly.'

c. Kua   leva   lahi   e   amaama aki   ke
   PERF longtime very ABS awaiting INST   SBJN

   fai [pepa pehē   nai] kua   tohia   ke   fakamau aki   e
   be   book like   this PERF written SBJN retain   INST ABS

   tau puhala gahua lima he   motu ha   toutolu ko   Niue...
   PL ways   work hand of   island of ours   'ko'   Niue
   'There has been a long time of waiting for there to be a book like this, which was written to retain the ways of handiwork of our island. . .' (TKL:Introduction)

Although Niuean sentences such as these have traditionally been labeled as NI sentences, they cannot be accounted for by analyses of NI, since the putative incorporated nominal is not an X°. We can instead account for sentences such as (16) in Niuean as does Massam (1998b). In that article, I argued that the "incorporated" nominal (bracketed in 16) originates as an NP direct object, rather than a DP direct object, such as found in non-NI transitive clauses. This claim is supported by the fact that incorporated nominals may not be preceded by any of the case number and determiner particles (e.g., *tau* 'PL', as in 2c), which usually appear at the beginning of a DP constituent. An NP object cannot check the absolutive Case, so it does not move out of VP to a checking position, but instead remains *in situ* within the VP, and gets fronted along with the verb by predicate-fronting.

In (17), we see a structure with so-called noun incorporation. Here, the external DP argument is generated in specifier of AbsP, and an NP is base-generated in object position. This NP cannot check the absolutive Case feature, since an NP (as opposed to a DP) has no Case feature Hence, this NP could not move out of complement position to establish a checking relation with the [+ABS] feature. As a result, when VP fronting occurs, it will involve the movement of the VP in bold to the specifier of IP. In other words, the NP object will front along with the verb.

(17)   *"noun incorporation"*

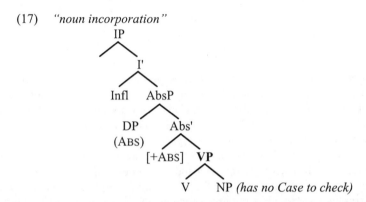

This analysis, which accounts for all of the basic "NI" facts in Niuean, shows us that non-head material can also be fronted in cases where the predicate is a verb, as well as when the predicate is a DP or a PP. The apparent norm then becomes the exception; that is, the cases where a simple V appears to be fronted are unusual (albeit more common), since most cases of predicate fronting appear to involve XPs rather than X°s. We can gather the one exception into the generalization by considering that in non-"NI" verbal VSO sentences too, the VP is the constituent that moves (in fact, it is the VP remnant, since all that remains in the VP is the verb). This is shown below. (18a) illustrates a transitive clause, where the DP object moves to AbsP to check the absolutive Case feature. (18b) shows the same situation in an intransitive clause. In these two cases, when the VP fronts to check the [PRED] feature in Infl, the trace of the moved DP fronts also. (Following Legate 1997; I assume obligatory predicate reconstruction at LF, thus allowing the moved DP to c-command its VP-internal trace at LF.)

(18)   a. *transitive*   b. *intransitive*

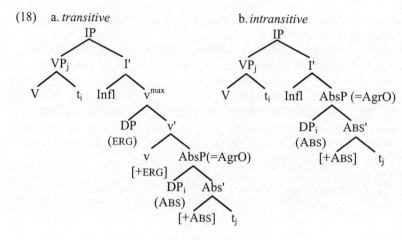

Thus, in non-incorporating verbal predicate sentences, no argument is fronted with the verb, because if the arguments are DPs, PPs or CPs, they will be in Spec of AbsP, rather than included in VP; hence, they are not moved along with VP (see also Lee, this volume).[13] This position (which receives independent support from the ordering of adverbs, as argued in Rackowski and Travis, this volume) raises questions about the nature of the elements that can check [PRED]. In particular, we must account for why indirect objects and obliques do not undergo predicate-fronting along with the verb, whereas equivalent elements do undergo fronting along with a nominal predicate. This question will be further discussed below.

2.3 Postverbal Particles and Indirect Objects/Obliques

As noted, the analysis proposed has implications for Niuean postverbal particles—which are shown in (19), with examples following in (20)—and for oblique arguments. In particular, they cannot be analyzed as verbal affixes. This section presents a structural analysis for these particles and obliques which is compatible with the claim that Niuean clauses involve the fronting of a maximal projection to specifier of Infl. (19) shows the ordering and nature of the postverbal particles that are exemplified in (20). For each particle in (19) I indicate which example(s) in (20) it appears in.

(19)   *Postverbal particles*

Advs	*aki* 'with'	*oti* 'all'	*ai* 'PRON'	ASP-ADV	EMPH	PERF	Q
a,b,c,g,i	e	f	g	h	c,h,i	e,f,i,j	j

Adverbs (directional and manner particles): mai 'towards 1PL', *atu* 'towards 2p', *age* 'towards 3p', *hake* 'upwards', *hifo* 'downwards', *lahi* 'very', *fakamitaki* 'well', *fakaeneene* 'carefully'

Aspectual adverbs: *t ūmau* 'always', *hololoa* 'frequently', *agaia* 'still', *agataha* 'immediately'

Emphatic particles noa 'only', *nī* 'indeed', *foki* 'also', *lā* 'just' *(ia), koa* 'indeed'

(20) a. Kua   hoge *lahi*   e   motu.
       PERF starve greatly ABS   island
       'The island is greatly starving.' (Sp172)

   b. Ne   ō   *mai*   a   lautolu ki   hinei.
       PAST goPL *DIR1* ABS   they   to   this.place
       'They came here.' (M180)

   c. Mumui   *mai*   *nī*   a   lautolu he motakā ha   lautolu.
       followPL *DIR1* *EMPH* ABS they   in   car   of   them
       'They'll just follow (us) in their car now.' (S18)

   d. Kua   hele *tuai*   e   Sione e   falaoa aki   e   titipi haana.
       PERF cut *PERF* ERG Sione ABS bread with   ABS knife his
       'Sione has cut the bread with his knife.' (S243)

   e. Kua   hele *aki* *tuai*   e   Sione e   titipi haana e   falaoa.
       PERF cut *with* *PERF* ERG Sione ABS knife his   ABS bread
       'Sione has cut the bread with his knife.' (S244)

   f. Kua   iloa   *oti* *tuai* e   lautolu a   au.
       PERF know *all* *PERF* ERG   they   ABS me
       'They all know me.' (L)

   g. ti   laga   aki   *hake* *ai*   e   Ataraga a   Maui ki luga . . .
       Then cause move *up*   *then* ERG Ataraga ABS Maui to top. . .
       'Then Ataranga raised up Maui ...' (C98)

   h. Kata *tumau nī*   a   ia.
       laugh *always just* ABS he
       'He's just always laughing.' (S24)

   i. Kua   uku *hifo* *foki tuai* a   au   ke he toka.
       PERF dive *down* *also PERF* ABS I   to PRT bottom
       'I have dove down to the bottom before.' (S24)

   j. Ita   *tuai* *nakai*   a   patu nā?
       angry *PERF* Q   ABS guy   that?
       'Is that guy angry?' (S25)

The first four particle types in (19) all involve relations between the verb and other elements below IP (e.g., directional specification, instrumental Case/theta assignment, completion, and signaling a missing oblique). Accordingly, I consider them to be generated below IP. Further, these particles all move with the VP, so they must also be below AbsP. As shown in (21), I consider these particles to be adjoined to VP. These elements do not seem to occur with nominal or prepositional predicates, and hence they adjoin only to VP. The aspectual adverbs, the emphatics, the perfect, and the question marker (*nakai*), on the other hand, have sentential scope and can appear with verbal, nominal, or prepositional predicates. I therefore propose, that they appear either as a clitic complex in Infl, or as a string of heads projected outside VP, above AbsP and V^{max}.[14] This is shown in (21). Evidence from predicate nominals and incorporated structures together argues against any of the particles in (19) being simply base-generated directly on the verb, since each of them may also appear after a maximal projection predicate, whether [V NP] or [DP]/[PP].[15]

Niuean verbal clauses thus contain a VP, consisting of a verb, its object or the trace of its object, and optionally a sequence of clitics (i.e., directional/manner particles, *aki*, *oti*, and *ai*). This VP raises to specifier of IP, where it appears at PF, followed (in Infl) by aspectual adverbs, emphatics, the perfect marker (in non-negated sentences), and the sentential question marker. This is displayed in tree form below (for an intransitive verb). In a negative sentence, some of the particles in Infl would instead appear in NEG, as discussed above.

(21)

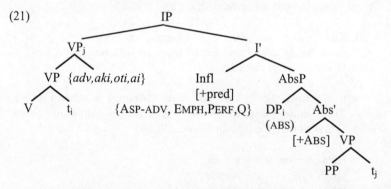

Note that obliques, which never front with the predicate, must appear above the VP, but below the positions in which the subject and the object appear in regular (non-incorporating) clauses, since the word order is VSO-Obliques. I therefore propose that they are adjoined to VP, and that predicate-fronting moves only the minimal VP. (Below I discuss why the counterparts of these oblique phrases in nominal predicates do front along with the nominal predicate.)

3. Predicate-Fronting as an EPP Reflex

3.1. Why does the Predicate Move?

What is the nature of the Niuean predicate-fronting? I claim that it is an EPP (Extended Projection Principle) reflex, as argued in Massam and Smallwood (1997). Niuean predicate-fronting obviously differs from V-raising to Infl in languages such as French and English, where maximal and non-verbal predicates never substitute for V. Another difference between Niuean and most European languages is that the latter require a grammatical subject, due to the EPP requirement instantiated by the [D] feature in Infl (Chomsky 1995). However, Niuean, a strict VSO language, provides no evidence for [D] in Infl. (This is also argued to be the case for Irish by McCloskey 1996b; see also Doron, this volume). Subjects c-command objects, as evidenced by binding facts (according to Seiter 1980), but are otherwise not much structurally distinguished (by extraction, including raising, quantifier float, etc.). Further, Niuean has no expletives. This is in contrast to English, where a strong nominal [D] in Infl forces a subject-predicate structure for all clauses, resulting in some cases in the presence of an expletive subject as in (22) (cf. Chomsky 1995, and Smallwood 1996, who extends this requirement to small clauses).

(22)   There are students in the classroom.

Niuean (but not English) predicates can check features in Infl, and English (but not Niuean), requires a grammatical subject. Massam and Smallwood (1997) relate these two properties by claiming that the Niuean head of IP has no [D] feature; thus, the specifier need not be filled by an element checking [D], but instead can be filled by the predicate checking the [PRED] feature (which they actually refer to as a Tense feature) on the head of Infl. In this way they account for predicate nominals in Niuean. In this chapter I extend this claim to encompass all clause types in Niuean. Thus, regular verbal predicate clauses and NI clauses, as well as predicate nominals and PPs, involve the fronting of a maximal projection to the specifier position of Infl. It is thus impossible for a language with a true predicate- (as opposed to V-) fronting requirement to instantiate initial subjects, since the specifier of Infl is filled by the predicate. Thus, as in Massam and Smallwood (1997), the Niuean [PRED] feature parallels the English [D] feature, in that the strict EPP nature of English is mirrored by the strict VSO nature of Niuean. [D] and [PRED] are thus in complementary distribution and can be seen as two reflections of a single EPP predication feature. This might explain the noted correlation between VSO and the absence of copular verbs, since maximal non-verbal predicates can undergo predicate-fronting and there is no need for a V in Infl.

3.2 What is a Predicate? (X + YP)

It is claimed that the notion of predicate is central to the grammatical structure of Niuean in that each clause must externalize its predicate following the EPP. It is thus important to be clear as to what constitutes a Niuean predicate. It was noted above that when the predicate is nominal, it appears to front with its arguments, whereas when it is verbal, it seems that only the verb itself fronts. It was argued that it is preferable and possible to regard predicate-fronting as uniformly moving a maximal projection. But, in a sense, this has merely shifted the question sideways. While we now consider predicate-fronting always to move a maximal predicate, we must ask why, when the predicate is a nominal, it can front along with an apparent external argument (a possessor) and an internal argument, but when the predicate is a verbal or prepositional phrase, only the internal argument may front (overtly in case of NI, and as a trace in non-NI clauses). That a nominal predicate can include external and internal arguments is seen in (23).[16]

(23) [Ko e poka-aga   he   tama   e   maka]
      'Ko' push-ING   GEN   child ABS rock

      [ati   matakutaku ai   e   kulī].
      [reason$_i$ fear   PRON$_i$ ABS dog]
      'The reason the dog was afraid was the child's pushing the rock.' (L)

Of course, the apparent main difference between the nominal and verbal predicate sentences is that in an example like (23) it appears to be the entire DP (including the external argument *he tama* 'the child') which is acting as the predicate. This predicate then has an additional external argument (namely, *ati matakutaku ai e kulī* 'the reason the dog was afraid'). In verbal predicate examples, the verbal predicate can have no subject independent of one of its own thematic arguments (either the external agent in a transitive, or the moved object in an intransitive).

We can eliminate this last remaining asymmetry, however, by paying attention to the fact that predicate nominals in Niuean always appear with the pre-nominal marker *ko (e)*, as we observed above. In (13b–e) and (23), for example, the nominal phrase is marked by the preposition *ko (e)*, (Likewise, a predicate PP requires an extra preposition, *hā*, to render it a predicate.) Seiter considers this to be a prenominal predicate marker. In Massam (1996), however, it is argued that *ko (e)* is best considered a preposition (following Clark 1976). This preposition marks a nominal phrase as being a non-argument.[17] In this view, predicate nominals in fact reduce to predicate PPs.

Given the identification of predicate nominal and predicate prepositional phrases, we can now unify the notion "predicate" across Niuean clause types, and explain why nominal arguments other than direct objects can front with a nominal predicate but not with a verbal predicate. Quite simply, the predicate in (13b–e), just as the predicates in (3) and (14) consists of a [–N] element (either *ko (e)*, or another preposition, or a verb) and its complement. The external arguments of all the prepositional predicates, as well as any modifying obliques, are not considered as part of the predicate, just as in the case of verbal predicates.

The notion "predicate" can thus be uniformly defined in Niuean as in (24), which is the revised form of (15). The clitics mentioned in the definition are the first four in (19)—those which appear adjoined to VP, namely the directional and manner particles—and *aki*, *oti*, and *ai*. Remaining unclear is exactly why EPP predicates should be so defined, and the exact role of the clitics in Niuean syntax.

(24)   *Unified description of what checks [Pred]*   (Revision of 15)
       [[X YP]+clitics], where X is a lexical predicate, YP its internal
       argument.[18]

Thus, while a verbal predicate sentence has the structure in (18) (with or without "NI"), or in (21), which shows the clitics, a nominal or prepositional predicate sentence will have the structure in (25).

(25)

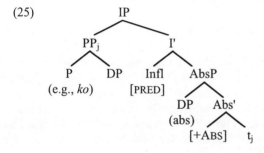

The DP argument of the preposition, unlike that of a verb, will always undergo movement as part of the predicate because it receives inherent Case from the preposition, and thus never undergoes movement to AbsP to check Case. All predicate types can thus receive a unified treatment, if we allow that the head predicate in a predicate nominal sentence is not the head of the nominal phrase, but instead is the prepositional element *ko (e)*.

4.   Conclusion

This chapter has analyzed the nature of Niuean VSO, arguing that this order is derived, and that it is derived not by movement to C, nor to Tense, but rather to a lower functional head, labeled Infl (or Pred), which houses an uninterpretable EPP feature [PRED]. Next, it was shown that verb-fronting is to be more properly considered as predicate fronting in this language, since maximal phrases which are demonstrably non-verbal also front to the same slot. This raises the question of why there should be a bifurcation in the language between X° verbal predicates and XP non-verbal predicates. Evidence from so-called Noun Incorporation in Niuean allows us to see that at least in some cases in verbal sentences it is VP rather than V° which is fronted. From this, I posited that in all cases predicate-fronting involves XPs, but in case of an object DP, the object will have moved out of VP prior to movement of VP, so that what fronts is a VP remnant consisting of the verb and the trace of the object. Implications of the analysis regarding postverbal elements were discussed. The claim was made (following Massam and Smallwood 1997) that predicate fronting in Niuean is in complementary distribution to subject externalization in SVO languages, and that in both cases the movements are a reflection of an Extended Projection Principle feature: [D] in SVO and [PRED] in VSO. A reanalysis of predicate nominals as predicate prepositional phrases allowed for the notion "Predicate" to be uniformly defined in Niuean as a lexically defined predicative head plus its internal argument and clitics.

This work puts forward the notion that at least in some cases, VSO languages belong to a parametrically different class than SVO languages, in that the former can involve a [PRED] feature rather than a [D] feature as the EPP feature. This chapter can thus be placed within a growing body of work which argues that VSO order is in some cases to be viewed as a variant on VOS order.

Acknowledgments

Many people have contributed to the ideas expressed in this chapter. In particular, I would like to thank (in New Zealand) Chris Lane, Elizabeth Pearce, Lagi and Moka Sipeli, Lingi Igasia, Harry Manamana, and Wolfgang Sperlich, and (in Canada) Andrew Carnie, Elizabeth Cowper, Jila Ghomeshi, Alana Johns, and Yves Roberge. I am also grateful to the anonymous reviewers for their valuable comments. I especially thank Carolyn Smallwood as portions of this chapter grew out of joint work with her.

Notes

1. See Rackowski and Travis (this volume) for support of this position from Niuean adverbial ordering. They also discuss the relationship between VSO and VOS order. Cf. Freeze and Georgopoulos (this volume), who take a base-generated view of verb initial order. Lee (this volume) also proposes a VP-fronting analysis to accommodate non-verbal predication in Zapotec.

2. Data in this chapter come from a variety of sources. Data elicited during my own consultations are unmarked for source, but all other sources are indicated after the relevant sentences. The source abbreviations used are: C=Chapin (1974); L=Lane (1978); M=McEwen (1970); S=Seiter (1980); Sp=Sperlich (1998); W=Whittaker (1982); KeP = *Ko e Pusi* by Angeline Hamiora; NAH = *Niue: a history of the island*, published jointly by the Institute of Pacific Studies of the University of the South Pacific and The Government of Niue; and TKL = *Tau koloa fakamotu ha Niue: tau koloa laufa (Cultural crafts of Niue: Pandanus weaving)* by Shari Cole and Vitolia Kulatea. Rex et al.

(undated) and Kaulima and Beaumont (1994) were also of use. Glosses for some sentences are my own and orthography has been changed in places for consistency. Abbreviations used are ABS: absolutive, C: complementizer, COM: comitative, DIR1/3: towards 1st/3rd person, EMPH: emphatic, ERG: ergative, GEN: genitive, HAB: habitual, INST: instrumental, LOC: locative, (N)FUT: (non)future, NOM: nominalizer, NSP: nonspecific, PERF: perfect, PERS: person marker, PL: plural, PRON: pronoun, POSS: possessive Case, PROG: progressive, PAST: past, Q: question, SBJN: subjunctive. *Ko (e)* is not glossed, but is a preposition which precedes a non-argument nominal.

3. Niuean has an ergative case marking system. The case particles encode a common/proper distinction not indicated in the glosses. This explains why the absolutive is *e* on the common object in (1a), but is *a* on the proper subject in (1b). Ergative is realized either as *he* (common) or as *e* (proper or pronoun).

4. I do not have evidence that verb-subject idioms do not exist in Niuean, but I have not encountered any. In Seiter (1980) we find (i), but it arguably involves an unaccusative verb:

> (i) Kua   teitei   pouli tei   a   fafo.
>   PERF nearly   dark   PERF ABS outside
>   'It's nearly dark.' (S190)

5. There are also arguments from binding (Seiter 1980) that the subject c-commands the object, which also argues against a flat VSO structure (though not necessarily for a V' constituent). In addition, there are strong reasons for assuming that at least absolutive arguments appear at PF in a non-thematic position, since they can be in positions to which they have been raised. This also argues against a flat structure.

6. I adopt here, without discussion, a verb-fronting approach to VSO. Others (e.g., Chung 1990) have presented different analyses, such as subject-lowering, as discussed in the Introduction to this volume.

7. The semantics of the tense/aspect system is not discussed here, and I will consider the two categories to be one, labeled Tense, for the purposes of this chapter. Krupa (1982) considers that each particle denotes either tense or aspect, but not both. The analyses of these particles in Clark (1976), Krupa (1982), McEwen (1970), Seiter (1980), and Whittaker (1982) differ in detail. For example, Whittaker states that *kua* is present tense, while McEwen considers *kua* to indicate present, past, or future. Seiter states that it is perfect, whether past, present, or future. In addition, it appears that in the absence of an initial particle, the sentence might be past, present, or future. I essentially follow Seiter's (1980) analysis here.

8. It might also be the case that there is a separate CP and TP, where T raises to C. If the two were adjacent in the tree, there would be no empirical difference between the two analyses. If, on the other hand, Tense were to be generated in Infl, thus non-adjacently to CP, below NEG, then this would result in a violation of the head-movement constraint, since Tense would have to move across NegP to reach the head of CP. Alternatively, we could consider Tense to move first to NEG, then to C. But we would then need special rules to account for the ordering of morphemes, since Tense appears merged with C, and not with NEG. See Jelinek (this volume) and Carnie, Harley, and Pyatt (this volume) for discussion of similar issues in other verb initial languages.

9. There are several emphatic elements. The first of these (*lā*) appears after NEG if it is present, but the others always appear after V.

10. One auxiliary, *liga* 'likely', does show evidence of being an independent item, since it is followed by a tense marker and can appear in front of NEG. I leave this auxiliary aside here.

11. When examined more closely, this supports the division of the postverbal particles into two groups as discussed below in 2.3, namely those base-generated in VP and those base-generated outside of VP, since the former do not seem to appear after *ko (e)* NP, although they do appear on maximal predicates in NI structures.

12. I thank Jila Ghomeshi for illuminating discussion on this point.

13. As discussed in Levin and Massam (1984, 1986), Niuean verbs that take sentential internal arguments divide into two classes: those with ergative subjects (a small group) and those with absolutive subjects. The CP in the latter group is an indirect object, hence would not be inside the fronting predicate at any level. The CP in the former class is base generated inside VP, and it then moves to check Case, just as a DP object does. Although in many object movement analyses CPs are held not to move (perhaps because they do not check Case), the Niuean CP objects that co-occur with ergative subjects must receive absolutive Case, since ergative Case appears only if there is an absolutive argument in the clause. Hence, it seems correct to state that these CPs move to Spec of AbsP to receive Case. I thank Andrew Carnie for pointing out to me the importance of CP objects in a VP remnant movement analysis.

14. In a negative sentence, of course, as discussed above, *lā* and *tuai* would be generated on NEG (or, if they are heads, then between NegP and IP).

15. An alternative is that each clitic appears as the head of a phrase, and movement takes place through or along with the clitic heads. See Rackowski and Travis (this volume) for an analysis of Niuean along these lines. I am taking a cautious approach here, since there is much not yet known about these clitics. The analysis presented here is similar in spirit, though not in detail, to that of Steuart (1996). Steuart argues for movement to what she calls Mood Phrase, which houses the emphatics and the question marker. The examination of NEG, *lā* and *tuai*, as outlined in this chapter has led me to modify her analysis.

16. The internal structure of Niuean DPs remains unexplored, and I make only reasonably uncontroversial statements about it here. For analysis of DP structure in the related language Māori, see Waite (1994) and Pearce (to appear).

17. The decision to consider *ko (e)* to be a prepositional element rather than a verbal copular or a predicate-making element is based on the fact that it appears in a variety of contexts where it does not act as a predicate in any active sense. For example, *ko (e)* precedes nouns in clefts, *wh*-questions, topics, appositions, titles, conjunctions, and in isolation. An apposition example is seen in (16c). Similarly, this argues against treating *ko (e)* as a complementizer, as Carnie (1995) treats Irish *is*.

18. Massam (1998) argues that unaccusatives and unergatives in Niuean are intransitives (contra Hale and Keyser, 1991 who consider that unergatives are underlying transitives). Thus, all clauses in Niuean will have an internal argument (a YP in 24).

7

V-Initial Languages
X or XP Movement and Adverbial Placement

Andrea Rackowski and Lisa Travis

Kayne (1994) proposes a restrictive view of phrase structure which derives many aspects of X'-theory and also derives a universal underlying order of SVO. Cinque (1999) proposes an account of adverb ordering which includes a universal hierarchy of functional categories which introduce adverbial expressions into the syntax. In this chapter we investigate two verb initial languages within the context of Kayne's view of phrase structure and Cinque's view of adverbs. Given the restrictiveness of both these systems, we are forced to posit what would otherwise be very controversial structures to account for the word order of these languages (see, for example, the discussion in Freeze and Georgopoulos, this volume). However, we believe that these controversial structures lead us to questions that would not have otherwise been asked and to generalizations that would not have otherwise been observed.

According to Kayne's (1994) theory of phrase structure, the word order of verb initial languages must be derived from a base-generated SVO structure. There are two obvious possibilities: the verb initial order may come about either by V-movement or by VP-movement. *A priori*, it seems that the difference between these two derivations would be immediately clear, with V-movement resulting in VSO languages and VP-movement resulting in VOS languages. Recent work, however, has shown that determining what type of movement has occurred is not so simple. There are languages such as Chamorro (e.g., Chung 1990) and Niuean (e.g., Massam and Smallwood 1997) which show VSO order when the clause contains a verbal predicate—as in (1a) and (2a)—but show XP order when the predicate is an NP or PP as in (1b, c) and (2b, c)).[1]

(1) **Chamorro** (Chung 1990:565, 571)
    a. Ha-bisita   si Dolores si Juan.   VSO
       INFL.3SG-visit   D.   J.
       'Dolores visited Juan.'

b. I   rigalu   ginin   as   nana-hu   esti na   aniyu.   NP S
the present from OBL mother-AGR.1SG this L   ring
'This ring is a present from my mother.'

c. Ginin ichi'lu-hu   esti na   katta.   PP S
from the.sibling-AGR.1s   this L   letter
'This letter is from my sister.'

(2)   **Niuean**   (Massam and Smallwood 1997)
a. Ne tala aga   e   ia   e   tala   ke   he   tagato.   V S O
PST tell.DIR.3P ERG he   ABS story   to   LOC man
'He told the story to the man.'

b. Ko   e   tau   kamuta   fakamua   a   lautolu.   NP S
ko ABS   PL   carpenters before   ABS they
'They were carpenters before this.'

c. Haa   he   fale   gagao   a   ia.   PP S
haa   in   house sick   ABS she
'She is in the hospital.'

Carnie (1995) argues, using data from another VSO language (Irish), that this apparent difference in movement to pre-subject position (X in the case of V and XP in the case of N and P) is, in fact, not a problem for syntactic theory. He claims that the distinction between the X level of a category and the XP level is a more flexible distinction than previously assumed. Apparent XPs may move to X positions in a system where the level of a category may be underspecified. Massam (1998b, this volume), on the other hand, argues that in Niuean, all predicate movement is XP movement. The VSO order in (2a) is accounted for by object and PP movement out of the VP (see also Lee, this volume).

In this chapter, we reexamine the nature of predicate movement by investigating a different part of the syntax, the order of adverbs. Cinque (1999) argues that the order of adverb placement is universal and that adverbs are placed in the specifier positions of functional heads which contain a meaning similar to the meaning of the adverb.[2] Cinque argues that adverbs in Italian are placed in specifier positions, based on evidence from participle placement. In (3), the participle *rimesso* 'put in order' can appear in a variety of positions (marked with an X) with respect to the adverbs.

(3) *Participle placement in Italian* (Cinque 1999)
   a.... non hanno   **rimesso** di solito.
      ... NEG have   **put**   normally not

   X   mica X più   X   sempre X completamente X
       any   longer   always   completely

   tutto bene in   ordine.
   all   well in   order
   'Since then, they haven't usually not any longer always put
   everything well in order.'

In this chapter, we look at two languages—Malagasy and Niuean—where adverbial elements appear in the exact opposite order from that described by Cinque. Our goal is to determine whether anything can be revealed about the phrase structure of the language from this unexpected adverbial placement. Despite the fact that these two languages share a reversed adverbial order, there are significant differences in other aspects of word order between the two languages. We attempt to address questions of the similarities and differences between the word order facts of the two languages. Following work by Massam (1998b) and Pearson (1998), we develop a typology of languages according to which some languages front predicates, and others front arguments. Verb initial languages like Malagasy and Niuean, obviously, fall in the first type; languages like English into the second. From this we will derive the adverbial ordering facts as well as several surprising differences between the two types in the behavior of arguments. Within the predicate fronting type, the differences between Malagasy (a primarily VOS language) and Niuean (primarily VSO) follow from the different extent to which these predicate initial languages utilize object movement. Finally, our system predicts the relative rarity of OVS languages and gives this typological observation a theoretical explanation.

1. Opposite Orders and VP Movement: Malagasy

Malagasy[3] is a VOS language in which adverbials occupy a position either directly before the verb phrase, as in (4) or after the verb phrase, as in (5). Postverbal adverbials optionally occur between the verb and a definite complement, as shown in (5).

(4)   Efa   nanasa   lamba   Rakoto.
       already PST.AT.wash   clothes Rakoto
       'Rakoto has already washed clothes.'

(5) a. Manasa   lamba   tsara   Rakoto.
       PRES.AT-wash   clothes well   Rakoto

   b. Manasa   tsara   ny   lamba   Rakoto.
      PRES.AT.wash   well   DET   clothes   Rakoto
      'Rakoto washes clothes well.'

While the order of preverbal adverbial elements in Malagasy conforms to Cinque's universal adverbial hierarchy, postverbal adverbials are in the mirror order. This is exemplified in (6)–(9) and schematized in (10)–(11). (6) shows that indefinite objects precede the adverbial while definite objects may follow the adverbial; (7) gives a sample of some of the preverbal adverbials, and (8) and (9) some postverbal adverbials (see Rackowski 1998 for additional relevant data).

(6) a. Tsy   manasa   **lamba**   *mihitsy*   ve   Rakoto?
       NEG PRES.AT.wash   clothes   at-all   Q   Rakoto

   b. *Tsy manasa *mihitsy* **lamba** ve Rakoto?

   c. Tsy   manasa   *mihitsy*   **ny lamba** ve   Rakoto?
      NEG PRES.AT.wash   at-all   DET clothes Q   Rakoto
      'Does Rakoto not wash clothes at all?'

(7)   *Efa*   *mbola tsy*   mahay   lesona
      already still   NEG   PRES.AT.know   lesson

      Rakoto no   mbola   mitabataba.
      Rakoto FOC   still   talkative
      'Not only does Rakoto not know his lessons, but he is talkative also.'

(8) a. Manasa   lamba   *tsara foana*   Rakoto.
       PRES.AT.wash   clothes well   always   Rakoto
       'Rakoto always washes clothes well.'

   b. *Manasa lamba   *foana tsara* Rakoto.

(9) a. Tsy manasa   lamba   *tanteraka   intsony* Rakoto.
       NEG PRES.AT.wash   clothes completely anymore Rakoto
       'Rakoto does not completely wash clothes anymore.'

   b. *Tsy manasa lamba *intsony tanteraka* Rakoto.

(10)   *Cinque's hierarchy:*

      1   2   3   4   5   6

   (speech act) > Generally > Neg > Already > Still > (at-all) >

      7   8   9   10

   Anymore > Always > Completely > Well

(11)   *Malagasy order:*

               2   3   4   5   (3)

   Na(dia > Matetika > Tsy > Efa > Mbol > Tsy > VERB >

   'Even' > generally > Neg > Already > Still > Neg VERB >

   10   9   8   7   6   1

   Tsara > Tanteraka > Foana > Intsony > Mihitsy > Aza > Ve

   Well>Completely>Always>Anymore >At-all > though> Speech Act

1.1 Intraposition Movement

This order cannot be accounted for by cyclic head movement and adjunction of adverbials to the verb, since adverbs appear after the object (i.e., at the right edge of the VP).[4] We claim that postverbal adverbials are in head positions, allowing iterative VP movement through their specifiers, which creates an onion-skin-type "intraposition" structure as in (13).[5] Because of the positions of the "framing adverbs" (Keenan, in press), which occur with one member at the beginning of VP and one at the end (such as *tsy...mihitsy* in (6) above), Rackowski (1998) posits the structure in (12), which allows members of the framing pair to select one another.[6]

(12)

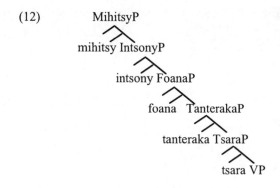

              MihitsyP

        mihitsy IntsonyP

          intsony FoanaP

            foana TanterakaP

              tanteraka TsaraP

                  tsara VP

(13)

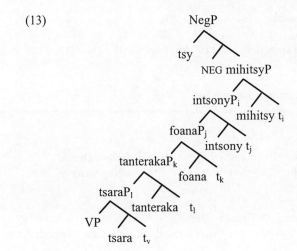

Since preverbal adverbials remain in their merged positions in the specifiers of functional projections, center-embedding of adverbials must stop at the last available specifier of an adverbial phrase being blocked by *tsy* in specifier of NegP from raising any further. The postverbal reversal of Cinque's order in Malagasy thus results from intraposition movement, which is made possible by the presence of empty specifiers in the postverbal adverbials.

1.2 Predicate-Fronting

Speech-act adverbials are predicted by Cinque to be very high in the hierarchy and functional structure. In Malagasy, however, they appear last before the clause final subject. This order can be explained by positing movement of TP around the Speech Act Phrase (veP) and into the next-highest specifier, as shown in (14).[7,8]

(14)

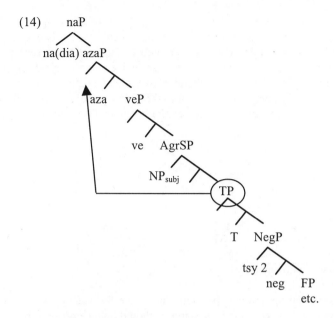

Movement of TP correctly predicts the position of the subject last in the Malagasy clause. Everything below AgrSP (which contains the subject) has raised above it, explaining why the verb and object never follow the subject. PPs, which sometimes follow the subject, can optionally merge between TP and AgrSP, remaining, as expected, unmoved when TP raises to azaP.

Evidence for the movement of TP comes from the behavior of the framing pair *na(dia) ... aza*, which translates roughly as 'even ... though'. The first half of the pair, *na(dia)*, always occurs first in the clause, while the second half, *aza*, is always after the other adverbials but before the speech act particles and subject.

(15) (Faly ve Rakoto) *na dia* tsy   manasa lamba   intsony
      happy Q Rakoto   'even'   NEG   wash   clothes anymore

      mihitsy *aza*   izy?
      at-all   'though' 3P
      'Is Rakoto happy even though she doesn't wash clothes at all
      anymore?'

(16) *Na dia* tsy   manasa lamba   intsony   *aza*
      'even'   NEG   wash   clothes anymore   'though'

      ny mpiasa rehetra ...
      DEF worker all
      'Even though all the workers don't wash clothes anymore ...'

The structure that we propose here has the advantage of allowing one half of this framing pair to select the other half, creating a local relation between the two. The VP and adverbials intervene between the two partners in the sentence, however, indicating that this material must have arrived in this position via movement to the specifier of the lower member of the pair (azaP), as shown in (17) below. The process of predicate fronting to the specifier of azaP thus allows the framing pair to maintain a tight, local relation even as TP intervenes in the linear order.[9]

(17)

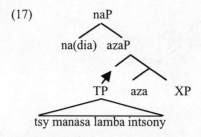

The predicate-fronting analysis predicts that, since the subject is the only argument not contained in some kind of island, it should behave differently from the other arguments. It is therefore unsurprising that only the subject may be *wh*-extracted in this language. As noted in Pensalfini (1995), TP movement of the clause around the subject leaves the subject as the only DP that is not in a restricted position, accounting for the well-known Austronesian *wh*-extraction facts.[10] *Wh*-extraction of any non-subject argument results in ungrammaticality. If an object or oblique is questioned, this element must first be promoted to the subject position through morphological marking on the verb. The structure in (14) straightforwardly explains the restriction by having the subject free from islands, while the rest of the arguments in a clause are inextricable. Examples are given in (18)–(20) (Pensalfini 1995).[11]

(18) a. *Iza   no   mividy   ny   vary ny   lehilahy?
      who FOC PRES.AT.buy DET rice   DET man

    b. *Iza   no   vidin'   ny   lehilahy ny   vary?
      who FOC TT.buy   DET man   DET rice

    c. Iza   no   ividianan' ny lehilahy ny vary?
      who FOC CT.buy   DET man   DET rice
      'Who was bought rice (for) by the man?'

(19) a. *Inona no   mividy   ho an' ny ankizy   ny lehilahy?
      what   FOC PRES.AT.buy for ACC DET children DET man

    b. Inona no vidin'   ny lehilahy ho an' ny ankizy?
        what FOC TT.buy   DET man   for ACC DET children
        'What did the man buy for the children?'

    c. *Inona   no   ividianan' ny lehilahy ny ankizy?
       what   FOC   CT.buy   DET man   DET children

(20) a. Iza no mividy   ny vary ho an' ny ankizy?
        who FOC PRES.AT.buy DET rice   for ACC DET children
        'Who bought the rice for the children?'

    b. *Iza   no   vidina   ho an' ny ankizy ny vary?
       who FOC TT.buy   for ACC DET children DET rice

    c. *Iza   no   ividianana ny vary ny ankizy?
       who   FOC CT.buy   DET rice   DET children

In (18), since the benefactive is the target of extraction, only the Circumstantial Topic (CT) construction is possible because this is the verb form which signals that an oblique has become the subject (see the discussion of this in section 4.2 below). In (19), where the theme is being questioned, the verb must be in the Theme Topic (TT) form, indicating that the theme is in subject position; and in (20) where the agent is being questioned, the verb must be in the Actor Topic (AT) form.[12]

1.3 Object Shift

Definite objects in Malagasy optionally appear among or after postverbal adverbials. The position to which they raise appears to have no fixed location, since they may occur either before or after the same adverbial.

(21) a. Tsy manasa   foana   **ny lamba** *mihitsy* Rakoto.
        NEG PRES.AT.wash always   DET clothes at all   Rakoto
        'Rakoto does not always wash the clothes at all.'

    b. Tsy manasa   intsony   *mihitsy* **ny lamba** Rakoto.
       NEG PRES.AT.wash no longer at all   DET clothes Rakoto
       'Rakoto does not wash the clothes at all anymore.'

As in some Germanic languages (e.g., Swedish; Holmberg, p.c.), when the object is definite, it optionally raises out of the VP to AgrP, and when it is indefinite, it remains in the VP (Diesing 1992, Diesing 1996, Diesing 1997).[13] In many languages, object shift "depends on information structure, in particular something like the contrast between specific and non-specific ... AgrOP has to

do with the mapping from syntax to semantics, and nothing to do with case"
(Bobaljik and Thráinsson 1998).

Material within the VP in many languages receives default focus (see
Jelinek, this volume, for more on focus in predicate initial languages). As
Diesing (1997) explains (also Diesing and Jelinek 1995), definite objects must
escape existential closure in the VP (Diesing 1992) in order to avoid being
focused and interpreted as new information. Anders Holmberg (p.c.) also points
out cases of movement out of VP for reasons of defocusing objects (which then
show up as definites) in Finnish and Danish. The same interpretation
requirements are evident in Malagasy, where the position closest to the verb is
obligatorily focused. Definite objects thus escape the existential closure and
default focus of the VP by overtly shifting out to a higher position.

Since objects move for configurational and interpretational reasons rather
than for Case-checking or other featural motivations, it is unclear to what
position they are raising; we call the position AgrOP. There is a general
necessity in Kayne's (1994) framework for either a number of empty phrases to
be available as landing sites for movement, or for a mechanism by which empty
phrases can be inserted into the syntax in certain positions or ranges of positions.
One way of explaining the position of objects in Malagasy is to allow the
insertion of AgrOP anywhere between the lowest NegP to VP (rather than
consistently occupying one set position); this causes the appearance of the object
between any of the postverbal adverbials, which, as heads of AdvPs, are
constant in their positions.[14] Object movement and AgrOP insertion are
demonstrated in (22).

(22)

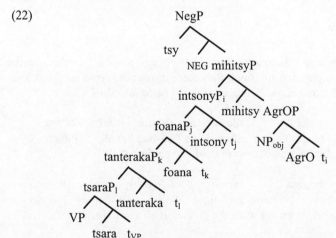

'Tsy manasa tsara tanteraka foana intsony mihitsy **ny lamba** Rakoto.'

Once AgrOP has been inserted into the tree and the object has raised to it, it
must become invisible to movement in order to force the phrase below it to
raise. If, instead of forcing the next AdvP to raise, the AgrP were itself to raise

to the next-highest specifier, an impossible order would result, with the object before the verb.

(23)   *   NegP

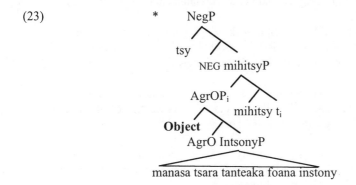

manasa tsara tanteaka foana instony

*'Tsy **ny lamba** manasa tsara tanteraka foana intsony mihitsy Rakoto.'

To avoid this ungrammatical derivation, there must be a restriction in the grammar such that non-contentful phrases like AgrP are invisible to movement and cannot themselves move. In contrast to this, contentful phrases like AdvPs can and, in this case must, move. This is one alternative to Chomsky's (1995) theory that AgrPs do not exist because they do not project a label. Here, lack of a label would instead mean "structurally present but invisible for syntactic processes." While we make some speculations concerning such categories in section 4.4 of the chapter, we leave the details of it here as a departure point for future research.[15]

2. The Case of Niuean

Niuean is a VSO language, as shown in (2) above. There is debate, however, as to whether there is XP or X predicate movement. In this section, we show that the ordering of pre- and postverbal adverbial particles suggests that there is XP predicate movement in Niuean. The order of particles is given in (24) below (taken from Massam 1998b).

(24) Tns/C Neg Modal VERB Dir Man *aki oti ai* Asp-Adv Emph Perf Q

There again seems to be a correlation between preverbal elements which appear in their hierarchical order and postverbal elements which are in the reverse order. For instance, preverbally, tense appears above the modals, as predicted by Cinque. Postverbally, manner adverbs occur before adverbs like *always*. As we can see in the Italian example in (3) and the schema in (10), the opposite order occurs in Italian.

Massam (1998b, this volume) argues that Niuean has VP movement—the object may appear adjacent to the verb and within the verbal complex, as in (25) and (26) (see also Lee, this volume, for a related analysis of Zapotec).

(25) Ne holoholo kapiniu kiva fakaeneene a   Sione
      PST wash   dish   dirty slowly   ABS John
      'John is washing dirty dishes slowly.'

(26) Kua kai ika mo   e   talo a   mautolu   he mogonei.
      PERF eat fish with ABS taro ABS we.PL.EX   at now
      'We are eating fish and taro right now.'

The reason why Niuean is generally VSO, however, is that definite objects move out of the VP before the VP moves. In Niuean, in contrast to Malagasy, object shift of the definite object is obligatory.[16]

As shown already for Malagasy, the only way to have the tense particles preverbally and the Q morpheme postverbally is by assuming long-distance VP-movement.[17]

(27) a. [CP [QP [AgrP [AgrP [TP [ModalP [Asp-AdvP [aiP [ManP [DirP [VP · · ·

b.

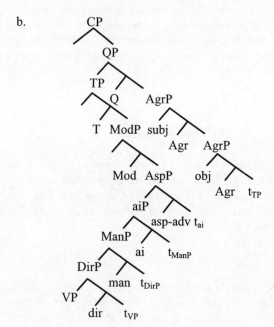

This tree accurately captures the word order in (28), as desired.

(28)   Tns/C Neg Modal VERB Dir Man *aki oti ai* Asp-Adv Emph Perf Q

The structure in (27) is very similar to the one proposed for Malagasy in the previous section. Adverbs are in their universal order, as predicted by Cinque, and the linear ordering occurs through iterative movement of VP through the lower specifiers. The high Speech Act particle becomes ordered last in the sentence through TP movement to a position above it, which positions the VP and adverbs before it and the subject. Final position for definite objects is the result of obligatory object shift to an unmovable AgrOP, which is always located above TP (see Massam, this volume, for more examples).

The difference between Malagasy and Niuean basic order, then, comes from the requirements on and position of object shift in the two languages. A moved object in Niuean will still be outside any island—and thus extractable—since it is in the AgrOP above the TP which raises (which is exactly what Massam and Smallwood (1997) describe, although they give no examples to show it).[18] This is in contrast to Malagasy, where even shifted objects are always within the TP that raises and are thus within islands. These differences in object movement requirements result in the Malagasy "basic" order of VOS and the Niuean order of VSO.[19]

3.   Predicate vs. Argument Movement

Before turning to some arguments for why using a restrictive view of phrase structure and a looser view of movement offers some empirical gains, we discuss a possible typological distinction between languages like Malagasy and Niuean and languages like English. Massam (this volume), following ideas presented in Massam and Smallwood (1997), claims that Niuean differs from English in terms of what element satisfies the EPP. In English (and other SVO languages), it is the subject that raises to the specifier of IP to check the D feature in Infl. In Niuean, however, it is the predicate that raises to the specifier of IP. Massam argues that this is due to a [PRED] feature in Infl in Niuean. Her proposal, then, is that there is [PRED]-fronting to the specifier of IP. The two types of languages would be as shown below.[20]

(29)

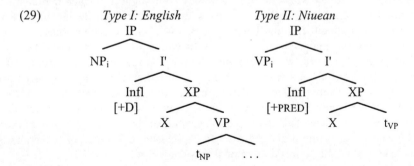

Pearson (1998), looking at word order variations within the VP in a variety of languages, proposes a similar parameter which affects a different portion of the tree. He claims that there are two types of VO languages. While we simplify his analysis considerably here, one can say that Type I languages (English, French, Indonesian, Italian, Dutch, Turkish, Japanese, German) move XPs that do not contain the V, and Type II languages (Malagasy, Tzotzil, Palauan, SLQ Zapotec) move XPs that still contain the V within the VP. Given Massam's claim about what happens above VP, and Pearson's claim about what happens within VP, we would like to suggest that there are more generally argument fronting languages and predicate-fronting languages—where a predicate is seen simply as the extended projection of a verbal category. VP-first languages like Malagasy and Niuean would be predicate-fronting languages, while subject first languages would be argument-fronting languages. It is interesting that in Pearson's typology, Type II VO languages are either VSO or VOS but never SVO. All the SVO languages are Type I. This suggests that his two types and Massam's two types are co-extensive.

If it is true that there are predicate-fronting languages and argument fronting languages, we would expect that there would not only be differences in word orders (predicate first vs. argument first) but also in the status of the arguments. This is suggested by Massam and we offer further support for this below.

4. The Status of Arguments in a Predicate-Fronting Language

While we have shown that the ordering of adverbials in Malagasy and particles in Niuean can be accounted for within a restrictive view of phrase structure set up by Kayne and Cinque, we have not shown that it *must* be done this way. Further, given the complications of intraposition, one might claim, as Ernst (1998) does, that intraposition is an unnecessary process which flies in the face of the general notions of economy and minimalism. In this section, we show that it is not only possible, but also preferable, to have an account of word order which includes the process of intraposition. One advantage is that by being forced to posit intraposition in the case of Niuean to explain Q-particle placement, we find an easier explanation for the indefinite object placement facts discussed by Massam (this volume). We suggest further that there is generally a distinction between objects in predicate-fronting languages and objects in argument-fronting languages. Below we discuss four areas in which this distinction may appear. While confirmation of this distinction requires further detailed work, we believe that the preliminary findings are suggestive. The distinction in the status of arguments in predicate-fronting languages, we claim, stems from the fact that they move for reasons other than checking features. We have seen above that the projection to which they move is invisible to further movement. This is needed to account for the word order facts of these languages, but it might also be used to explain the difference of behaviors of these elements. It is to this discussion that we now turn.

4.1 Binding in ECM Constructions

Travis (in press) discusses binding facts in Malagasy and compares them to binding facts in Balinese as presented by Wechsler and Arka (1998).[21] Like Malagasy, Balinese has a verbal system that allows a variety of arguments of the verb to appear in subject position, depending on the verbal morphology. In the examples below, we see an Actor Topic (AT) form of the verb with an agent subject and a Theme Topic (TT) form of the verb with a theme subject.[22]

(30) Tiang numbas bawi-ne punika.   (W&A: ex. 3)
      1SG AT.buy pig-DEF that
      'I bought the pig.'

(31) Bawi-ne   punika   tumbas tiang.[23]   (W&A: ex. 2)
      pig-DEF   that   TT.buy 1SG
      'I bought the pig.'

Both languages differ from English in that movement to subject position in many cases does not affect binding. In other words, an element in the VP may bind an element outside the VP. Relevant examples for both languages are given below.

(32) **Balinese**
      Awakne tingalin-a.   (W&A: ex. 41)
      self   TT.see-3SG
      '(S)he saw himself/herself.'

(33) *Wayan tingalin-a   teken awakne.   (W&A: ex. 42)
      Wayan TT.see-3SG PREP self
      *'Wayan was seen by himself.'

(34) Ia ningalin awakne.   (W&A: ex. 43)
      1SG AT.see   self
      '(S)he saw herself/himself.'

(35) **Malagasy**
      Novonoiny   ny   tenany.
      PST.TT.kill.3P DET   body.3P
      'S/he killed himself/herself.'

(36) *Novonoin'ny   tenany   izy.
      PST.TT.kill'DET body.3P 3P
      *'S/he killed himself/herself.'

(37)   Namono   ny tenany   izy.
       PST.AT.kill   DET body.3P   3P
       'He killed himself.'

(38)   *Namono   azy   ny tenany.
       PST.AT.kill   him   DET body.3P
       *'Himself killed him.'

In (32) and (35), the agent within the VP binds the theme in the subject position. In (33) and (36), we see that a theme subject may not bind an agent within the VP. In other words, in both languages, binding appears to be determined more by theta-role than by surface syntactic position. The agent may bind the theme no matter what the syntactic configuration, while the theme can never bind the agent no matter what the configuration. We leave aside the issue of why these languages differ in binding from languages like English and refer the reader instead to Travis (in press) and Wechsler and Arka (1998). There is, however, a distinction between these two languages in their binding systems that we tentatively suggest might be due to the difference in their word orders (VOS vs. SVO). The phenomenon involves binding in ECM constructions. Both languages have ECM:

(39)   **Balinese** ECM
       Tiang nawang   Nyoman Santosa mulih.   (W&A: ex. 22b)
       1SG   AT.know   Nyoman Santosa go.home
       'I knew that Nyoman Santosa went home.'

(40)   **Malagasy** ECM
       Mihevitra   an'iBakoly   ho   hajain'iSoa   Rakoto.
       PRES.AT.think   ACC'Bakoly   PRT PRES.TT.respect'Soa   Rakoto
       lit: 'Rakoto thinks Bakoly to be respected by Soa.'

Both languages also allow the subject of the embedded verb to be bound by an antecedent in the matrix clause as shown in (41)–(44) below. The distinction is that Malagasy (44) but not Balinese (42) further allows a pronoun to appear in this position co-indexed with the same antecedent.

(41)   **Balinese**
       Ia$_i$ nawang   awakne$_i$ lakar tangkep   polisi.   (W&A: ex.110a)
       3SG AT.know   self   FUT   TT.arrest police
       'He$_i$ knew that the police would arrest self$_i$.'
       lit: 'He$_i$ knew himself$_i$ to have been arrested by the police.'

(42)   *Ia$_i$ nawang   ia$_i$ laka   tangkep   polisi.   (W&A: ex.110c)
       3SG AT.know   3SG FUT   TT.arrest police
       lit: 'He$_i$ knew him$_i$ to have been arrested by the police.'

(43)   **Malagasy**
Mihevitra   ny tenany$_i$ ho hajain'iSoa   Rakoto$_i$.
PRES.AT.think   DET body.3P PRT TT.respect'Soa Rakoto
lit: 'Rakoto$_i$ thinks himself$_i$ to be respected by Soa.'

(44)   Mihevitra   azy$_i$ ho hajain'iSoa   Rakoto$_i$
PRES.AT.think   3P PRT TT.respect'Soa Rakoto
lit: 'Rakoto$_i$ thinks him$_i$ to be respected by Soa.'

This variability of binding occurs in Malagasy only in the case of ECM constructions. In other words, objects that receive a theta-role directly from the matrix verb may not be co-indexed with the subject of that verb, as shown below.[24]

(45)   *Manaja   azy$_i$ Soa$_i$.
PRES.AT.respect   3P   Soa
'Soa$_i$ respects him$_i$.'

At the very least, the ECM objects in Balinese and Malagasy are behaving quite differently, and the ECM object in Balinese (an SVO language) is behaving in the same way that an ECM object in English (another SVO language) behaves. This is true despite the fact that Balinese binding appears to work very differently from English binding in other respects. Malagasy binding, which in these very respects works the same as Balinese, differs when it comes to derived (raised) objects. While not conclusive, we believe that this is due to the fact that arguments in predicate-fronting (VP-initial) languages have a different status from arguments in argument-fronting (SVO,SOV) languages. In a language like English, the ECM object must have moved to a position that may be assigned Case by the matrix verb. This position is restricted and fixed. In Malagasy, without knowing the details of which position the object moves to, we do know that this position is much more variable (as shown by the adverbial facts in section 1 above). We speculate that it is this variability that allows variability in the binding facts.[25]

4.2 Derived Objects in General

We have just seen ECM objects in Malagasy acting differently from ECM objects in English. In fact, many constructions that arguably have derived objects work differently in Malagasy (and other verb initial languages) than they do in SVO languages. Consider the case of applicatives and possessor raising.

Malagasy, like many other Austronesian languages, can promote a variety of NPs to subject position by adjusting the morphology on the verb. Below we have a case where Actor Topic (AT) morphology promotes the agent to the subject position, Theme Topic (TT) morphology promotes the theme to the subject position, and Circumstantial Topic (CT) morphology promotes some oblique NP (in this case a benefactive.)

(46) Manasa   lamba ho an'ny   ankizy ny lehilahy.
      PRES.AT.wash clothes for ACC'DET children DET man
      'The man washes clothes for the children.'

(47) Sasan'   ny   lehilahy ho an'ny   ankizy ny lamba.
      TT.wash'   DET   man   for ACC'DET children DET clothes
      'The clothes are washed by the man for the children.'

(48) Anasan'   ny lehilahy ny lamba   ny ankizy.
      CT.wash'   DET man   DET clothes DET children
      'The children are washed clothes for by the man.'

In the Malagasy CT construction, the oblique preposition is incorporated into the verb, and the oblique argument surfaces as the subject. In SVO languages, the effect of applicative constructions is the incorporation of oblique prepositions and the promotion of the oblique to the *object* of the verb. The following Indonesian example illustrates this fact (taken from Baker, 1988:234, due to Chung 1976).

(49) **Indonesian**
      a. Saja mem-bawa   surat itu kepada Ali.
         I   TRANS-bring letter DET to   Ali
         'I brought the letter to Ali.'

      b. Saja mem-bawa-kan   Ali surat itu.
         I   TRANS-bring-to Ali letter DET
         'I brought Ali the letter.'

In (49a) *Ali* appears as an oblique, but in (49b), where there is an applicative morpheme *kan* on the verb signaling P-incorporation, the oblique NP now behaves like the object of the verb. The difference, then, between Malagasy and Indonesian is that in Malagasy (a VOS language) P-incorporation has the effect of promoting an oblique to subject position, while in Indonesian (an SVO language) P-incorporation has the effect of promoting an oblique to object position.[26] Possessor raising shows similar effects. In Chichewa, an SVO language, a non-object can become the object of a verb as in (50). In Malagasy, while there is possessor raising, it occurs only with adjectives, unaccusatives, and passives as shown in (51).

(50) **Chichewa**   (Baker 1988:11)
      a. Fisi a-na-dy-a   nsomba za kalulu.
         hyena SP-PST-eat-ASP fish   of hare
         'The hyena ate the hare's fish.'

b. fisi   a-na-dy-er-a   kalulu   nsomba.
hyena SP-PST-eat-APPL-ASP hare   fish
'The hyena ate the hare's fish.'

(51) **Malagasy**   (Hung 1988)
a. Marary   ny   zanako.
PRES.sick DET   child-1SG
'My child is sick.'

b. Marary   zanaka aho.
PRES.sick child   1SG

c. Nianjera   ny tranon-dRabe.
PST.AT.collapse DET house-Rabe
'Rabe's house collapsed.'

d. Nianjera   trano Rabe.
PST.AT.collapse house Rabe

The possessor never raises to object position, only to the subject position. Some languages have processes by which a non-object can become an object (promotion to object), as in ECM, applicatives, and possessor raising; Malagasy has similar processes, but the elements never become objects. In ECM, the raised NP appears to stay in a lower binding domain (much like specifier of DP in English). In applicatives and possessor raising constructions, the elements are promoted directly to subjects.[27] We take this as a further indication that the object position in Malagasy is unlike object positions in other languages. More to the point, the object position of Malagasy, a VOS language, is unlike the object position of English, an SVO language. We claim that this is not accidental.

4.3 Coordination

In this section, we look at two types of coordination facts that support the intraposition account for the phrase structure of Malagasy. Guilfoyle, Hung, and Travis (1992) (henceforth GHT) propose a structure for languages such as Malagasy that, in a very simple manner, accounts for the facts of Malagasy word order. The structure is given in (52) below.

(52)

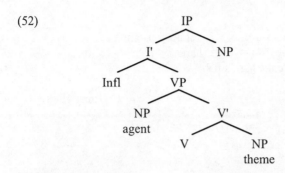

The main purpose of this structure is to account for the fact that the non-subject agent can intervene between the verb and its object, as in the following Malagasy sentence.

(53)   Nividian'ny   renin-dRakoto   lamba   aho.
       PST.AT-buy'DET   mother-Rakoto   clothes   1SG
       'I was bought clothes by Rakoto's mother.'

Note that the object is indefinite in this case. As we have seen above (6b), generally indefinite objects have to appear adjacent to the verb so, for example, an adverbial cannot intervene. It might seem surprising, then, that a complex NP, when it is the agent, can intervene between a verb and its indefinite object. The GHT account explains this difference through phrase structure. When the V moves to Infl in the tree given in (52) above, the object remains *in situ* as an indefinite object should. Then the only material that may appear between the moved V and the indefinite subject will be the agent which also remains *in situ*.

As nicely as the GHT structure captures this observation, Keenan (in press) has shown that it runs into problems elsewhere. In the GHT structure, the V and the agent never form a constituent which excludes the object. If this is true, then we would not expect to be able to conjoin the V and agent with another constituent. Keenan, however, gives the following examples where this is possible. The sentences in (54a) and (54b) show that each individual sentence related to the conjoined structure is possible, and (54c) gives a case where a Circumstantial Topic verb-form and the corresponding agent can conjoin with an AT form of the verb. Keenan's conclusion is that the structure in GHT cannot be accurate since at no point do the V and agent form a constituent which excludes the object.

(54)   **Malagasy**   (Keenan, in press: ex. 43)
       a. Nividianako   ilay boky ianao.
          PST.CT.buy-1SG   that book 2SG
          'You were bought that book by me.'

b. Namaky   ilay boky ianao
   PRES.AT.read   that book 2SG
   'You read that book.'

c. Nividianako sy   namaky   ilay boky ianao.
   PST-buy-1SG and PRES.AT-read   that book 2SG
   'You [were bought+for by me and read] that book.'

Keenan claims that the appropriate tree for Malagasy first combines the V with the agent and only then combines that constituent with the theme. His proposed tree for (55a) is given in (55b) below. Here we have a theme topic sentence, but it is clear that the agent is combined with the verb form before any other material from the VP is.

(55) a. Novidin-dRabe   ho   an-dRasoa   ilay satroka.
     PST.TT.buy-Rabe   for ACC-Rasoa   that hat
     'That hat was bought for Rasoa by Rabe.'

b.

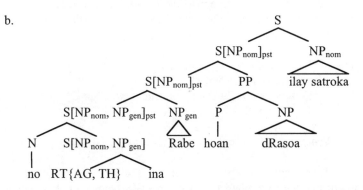

An intraposition account, however, can explain all Keenan's data. It can also explain an additional piece of data which is problematic for him. First, consider how our tree can capture the coordination facts given above. Once the object has moved out of the VP, the remnant of the projection just above the VP contains the V followed by the agent—precisely the constituent we needed for coordination.

(56)

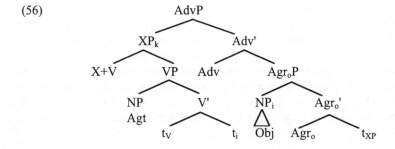

Recall that in Keenan's example, the object is definite. For us, this means that movement out of the VP is possible, allowing for the coordination of the V+agent. In fact, we predict that if the object is indefinite, such coordination should not be possible. Keenan's structure makes no such prediction. We can now empirically test the two accounts. Note first that an indefinite object may appear in a V+agent construction:

> (57)   Nividianako   boky ianao.
>   PST.CT.buy-1SG   book 2SG
>   'You were bought a book by me.'

Both accounts are able to produce such a sentence. In the intraposition account, this is done by simply leaving the object *in situ* and moving the V over the agent, as in (52) above. In this situation the V+agent constituent includes the object. In Keenan's structure, the data in (57) can be represented by simply combining the indefinite NP with the V+agent constituent. In this case, however, the V+agent still forms a constituent. As we can see below, only the intraposition account makes the right prediction. Coordination is possible only with a definite object.

> (58)   *Nividianako   sy namaky   boky ianao.
>   PST.CT.buy.1SG   and PRES.AT.read book 2SG
>   'You [were bought+for by me and read] a book.'

4.4 OSV Languages

As a final, very speculative consequence of the language typology we propose, we might be able to explain the rarity of OVS languages. If languages in fact divide into predicate-fronting languages and argument-fronting languages, we would not expect to find a language that fronts both arguments and predicates in the course of deriving its basic word order.[28] Languages like Malagasy and Niuean place the V in front of the subject because they are *predicate*-fronting languages. The explanation has been that in order to check relevant features, they move predicate projections to specifier positions. When arguments do move in these languages, since they are not moving to check features, they create constituents which cannot be targeted for further movement (though, of course, a larger constituent that contains them may move). On the other hand, we are hypothesizing that SOV languages move the object in front of the verb because they are *argument*-fronting languages. In other words, for a language to be OV, it would have to be an argument-fronting language. The O would be moved to a position before the verb to check features. If this VP were to front so that the O and the V would appear before the S, it would have to be a predicate-fronting language, something we have excluded by hypothesis. This last claim is clearly the most speculative of all and requires a careful investigation of OVS languages such as Hixkaryana.

5. Conclusion

In this chapter, we have shown that the order of adverbial elements in both Malagasy and Niuean indicates that it is XP, rather than X movement, that creates the word order in basic clauses. In Malagasy, as a VOS language, it is relatively unsurprising that VOS order results from movement of the VP. By comparing the order of adverbials in Malagasy and Niuean, we have shown that Niuean word order also results from VP movement, supporting arguments made by Massam (this volume) on the basis of other evidence. Assuming the theory of Cinque (1999), we have demonstrated that the only way to derive the actual order of adverbials in these languages is through intraposition movement of the VP and AdvPs and predicate-fronting of TP.

We have also shown that, although the Kayne and Cinque theories require a much richer array of functional categories than has often been assumed, the structures that they create account far better for word order and other phenomena in these verb initial languages than do other analyses. Theories which allow right-adjunction and headedness variation are certainly no simpler than our analysis, and, in fact, they fail to account for many of properties of the languages.

Acknowledgments

The authors would like to thank the following people and groups for valuable input. Thanks to Andrew Carnie, David Pesetsky, and Noam Chomsky for comments on an earlier draft, and Mark Baker, Jonathan Bobaljik, Nigel Duffield, Anders Holmberg, Diane Massam, Susi Wurmbrand, and the Syntax Project at McGill University for discussion of the ideas. The first author thanks funding from an NSF graduate fellowship and the second author thanks FCAR (97ER0578) and SSHRCC (410-98-0452) for crucial support of this research. Many thanks also to Saholy Hanitrinianina for native speaker judgments and data. Errors are our own.

Notes

1. The following are abbreviations used in glosses: ABS: absolutive, AGR: agreement, ACC: accusative, APPL: Applicative, ASP:Aspect, AT: Actor Topic, CT: Circumstantial Topic, DET: Determiner, ERG: Ergative, EX: Exclusive, FOC: Focus, FUT: Future, L: Linker, LOC: Locative, NEG: Negative, OBL: Oblique, P: Person, PRT: Particle, PERF: Perfective, PL: Plural, PREP: Preposition, PROP: Proper, PRES: Present, PST: Past, Q: Question, SG: singular, SP: subject agreement, TRANS: Transitive, TT: Theme Topic.

2. We will use the label "adverbial" so as not to prejudge whether the element appears in the head position or the specifier position.

3. The analysis of Malagasy presented in this section is largely a summary of the account given in Rackowski (1998).

4. This is clearly not a case of object incorporation (where V+O would raise and head-adjoin to adverbials) because of the existence of coordinated and complex objects in this position, which is generally not possible with incorporation. See Massam, this volume, for a related discussion of Niuean.

5. Placing these adverbials in head positions may appear controversial. In Cinque's framework, adverbs in specifier position have a related head position, and we believe that in Malagasy, some adverbials appear either in or adjoined to this head position (see Travis (1988) for an head-adjunction analysis of adverbs). By having adverbials in head positions, we can have intraposition without creating additional semantically empty projections for predicate-fronting.

6. See Nilsen (1998), Pearson (1998), and Ernst (1998) for similar movement processes and discussion.

7. *na*P and *aza*P, because of their complementizer-like semantics, may be parts of an iterated CP phrase or series of CP phrases, as in the theory of Rizzi (1997), although we leave the question of their exact status open here.

8. Duffield (1995) makes similar claims about Irish looking not only at the order of adverbials but also at object pronoun placement.

9. An alternative would be to have the first C left-branching and the second C right-branching, but this allows for a completely unrestricted and anti-Kaynean phrase structure.

10. Pensalfini (1995) eventually rejects the predicate-fronting explanation for Malagasy word order because his version considered only TP raising to the specifier of CP, leaving no intervening positions between CP and AgrSP for adverbials or PPs. With the structure in (14), however, these problems are solved, and the explanatory power of the movement for adverbial order, subject position, and extraction restrictions remains.

11. The glosses have been changed to correlate with the ones used in this chapter. Also, translations are given only for the grammatical questions. The ungrammatical questions would have the same translation.

12. An obvious prediction here is that the same restrictions on *wh*-movement will not appear in VOS languages and SVO/VSO languages. An interesting further study would explore the differences in the restrictions on *wh*-movement in SVO languages like Indonesian, a VSO language like Chamorro, a VOS language like Malagasy, and Tagalog where the word order is fairly variable between VSO and VOS.

13. The position is unlikely to be vP (the object shift position in Chomsky 1995) because that should not have the variable placement options exhibited here, being part of verbal phrase shells. Also, if it were vP, there should be no adverbs allowed between it and VP, since this would interfere with theta considerations (see Chomsky 1995 for details).

14. Alternatively, there could be many empty functional projections in the structure—perhaps one between every phrase that there is evidence for—and movement to any of them would satisfy the configurational requirements of definite objects. Here we adopt the other hypothesis, for the reason that variable insertion seems more restrictive than allowing so many contentless functional projections in the structure, but both are possible in principle.

15. Because of lack of space, we will not go into the obvious alternative analysis of right-adjoining the adverbs as in Ernst (1998). We feel, however, that being forced into the intraposition account leads to interesting questions with interesting results as discussed in section 4.

16. This is similar to the obligatory object shift in Danish for definite pronominal objects (Anders Holmberg, p.c.).

17. Massam (this volume) and Massam and Smallwood (1997) also argue for predicate-fronting to explain verb initial order. In those analyses, XP movement to Infl is driven by the need to check off an EPP feature—a feature which is satisfied in SVO languages by DP movement, and in verb initial languages by predicate movement.

18. We predict there should be an extraction asymmetry between indefinite and definite objects, but since *wh*-movement imparts its own sort of focus on a moved DP, this may be an untestable hypothesis.

19. Object shifting for Irish, a VSO language, has been proposed by Bobaljik and Carnie (1996) and Duffield (1995).

20. XP in this tree should be taken to represent any number of categories that might appear between the highest functional projection (here IP) and VP.

21. Wechsler and Arka (1998) have a different analysis of Balinese and therefore use different terminology. We refer the reader to their article for an interesting discussion of the ergativity of Balinese.

22. See Aissen (this volume) for a discussion of related binding facts in Jakaltek.

23. This example, from Wechsler and Arka (1998), is from Balinese high register, while the other examples are from low register. The difference that is relevant here is in the form of the pronoun.

24. There are verbs that do allow a pronoun to be bound by the subject (see Zribi-Hertz and Mbolatianavalona 1999), but these are lexically determined and vary from speaker to speaker.

25. Obviously much more work is needed here to sort out the facts and the details of the analysis. For example, objects in Malagasy are required to be assigned Case, but one could argue that Case assignment is not restricted to one designated position. While this variability in the binding facts is reminiscent of the cases of logophoricity in Reinhart and Reuland (1993), we don't believe that the reflexive is logophoric. It must have a local antecedent which c-commands it, and it does not appear to carry any focus.

26. There are verb initial languages that appear to have promotion to object position e.g. Kimaragang Dusun (Kroeger 1990). We take Indonesian and Malagasy as a minimal pair since they both use suffixes to designate the preposition incorporation. Kimaragang Dusun uses prefixes, which may point to a different sort of process.

27. There is interesting evidence from the interpretation of bound pronouns which suggests that when an oblique becomes a subject, it has to, in some sense, pass through the object position in the course of the derivation. See Travis (in press) for details.

28. Obviously there will be predicate-fronting of a sort in argument-fronting languages. For example, there is VP-fronting in English constructions such as 'Eat the cake, they will'. Further, SOV languages will be able to front the OV constituent in such topicalization structures. Here, however, we are discussing movements that are needed to derive the basic word order of the relevant language.

8

VP Remnant Movement
and VSO in Quiaviní Zapotec

Felicia Lee

A common theme in the literature on VSO languages is the claim that clause initial predicates are verbal heads (Emonds 1980, McCloskey 1991, Koopman and Sportiche 1991, among others). This claim, however, poses problems for a number of VSO languages: Irish, for instance, allows complex nominal predicates to occupy the same position as verbal heads (as noted by Carnie 1995); and Quiaviní Zapotec[1], the language examined in this chapter, also allows verbs and phrasal expressions to appear interchangeably in certain syntactic contexts. This work will propose an alternate analysis for the derivation of VSO word order that accounts for the non-head-like behavior of predicates in VSO languages: VP remnants, rather than verbal heads, raise to pre-subject position. Subjects and objects base-generated within VP raise into their respective agreement projections, while the VP, which itself contains traces of these arguments, raises to clause initial position. (The non-head-like behavior and morphological patterning of predicates in other VSO languages have recently prompted other researchers to reach similar conclusions independently; see Massam, this volume, and Rackowski and Travis, this volume).

I introduce this proposal with an examination of three syntactic constructions in Quiaviní Zapotec (QZ), a VSO Otomanguean language spoken in Oaxaca, Mexico. In the constructions that I discuss, verbs either appear interchangeably with XPs such as nominals and prepositional phrases, or show other movement and distributional properties that cannot be accounted for by head movement, but can be accounted for if verbs are taken to be VP remnants that undergo XP movement through specifier, rather than head, positions. I then outline the VP-raising proposal and show that it correctly predicts the grammatical distribution of QZ verbs. In the appendix, I show, following arguments made by Lee (to appear), that QZ verbal morphology cannot be accounted for by verbal head movement, but can be easily explained, in a manner consistent with Baker's (1985) Mirror Principle and Kayne's (1994) principles of Antisymmetry, if inflected verbs in QZ are assumed to be VP remnants.

1. QZ Verbs as XPs: Some Evidence

In a number of syntactic contexts, QZ verbs share the same movement and distributional constraints as bona fide XP constituents (such as proper names and prepositional phrases). This section discusses two of the most striking cases: attraction to adverbial clitics and constituent negation. I also present another verbal construction, which involves the stranding of pronominal subject agreement clitics, and show that while this can be easily accounted for if QZ V-movement is taken to be VP movement, it is unexpected under the standard assumption that V-movement is always head movement.

1.1. The Placement of Adverbial Clitics

One piece of evidence against the head status of inflected QZ verbs comes from the distribution of adverbial suffixes that modify both DPs and inflected verbs. In the following examples, the modal clitic *-zhya'* 'might' and adverbial clitic *-ga'* 'instead/ for the time being' attach to DPs, PPs, and verbs:[2]

(1) N-u'uh-*zhya'*-rëng   Lohs Aa'nngl.
    NEUT-exist-MIGHT-3P Los   Angeles
    'They might be in Los Angeles.'
    [i.e., it might the case that they are in Los Angeles]

(2) Lohs Aa'nngl-*zhya'*   n-u'u-rëng.
    Los   Angeles-MIGHT   NEUT-exist-3P
    'They might be in Los Angeles.'
    [i.e., it might be Los Angeles where they are]

(3) La:a'ny yu'uh-*zhya'*   n-u'uh   liebr.
    in   house-MIGHT   NEUT-exist book
    'The book might be in the house.'
    [i.e., it might be in the house where the book is]

(4) Lia Oliieb-*ga'*   b-gya:a'ah.
    Ms. Olivia-INSTEAD   PERF-dance
    '*Olivia* danced instead (of someone else).'

(5) B-gya:a'ah-*ga'*   Lia Oliieb.
    PERF-dance-INSTEAD Ms. Olivia
    'Olivia *danced* instead (of doing something else).'

These examples show that the scope of the adverb (and thus the interpretation of the sentence) varies according the constituent to which it is affixed. In (1), where the modal suffix *-zhya'* appears affixed to the verb 'be', the modality scopes over the entire event denoted by the VP (their being in Los Angeles is a possible state of affairs). When *-zhya'* 'might' is attached to 'Los Angeles' in (2), the modality takes scope only over 'Los Angeles' (i.e., 'It might be Los Angeles where they are'). The differing placement of *-ga'* 'instead/for the time being' in (4) and (5) results in similar contrasts. In (4), for example, *-ga'* 'instead' takes scope over the nominal 'Ms. Olivia', indicating that Olivia was the participant selected to dance instead of some other person previously introduced in the discourse. In (5), *-ga'* takes scope over the verb 'dance', with the meaning that Olivia chose dancing instead of some originally intended activity. In other words, *-ga'* serves to distinguish the constituent to which it is suffixed as an object or activity selected as an alternative to some other option.

These examples also show that the relation between adverbial suffixes and the constituents they modify is syntactic as well as semantic: nominals modified by *-ga'* 'instead/for the time being', for instance, must appear preverbally, rather than in their canonical postverbal argument positions:

(6) Lia Oliieb-*ga'*   b-gya:a'ah.
     Ms. Olivia-INSTEAD   PERF-dance
     '*Olivia* danced instead (of someone else).'

(7) *B-gya:a'ah Lia Oliieb-*ga'*.
     PERF-dance Ms. Olivia-INSTEAD
     '*Olivia* danced instead (of someone else).'

The same constraint holds for nominals modified by *-zhya'* 'might':

(8) *N-u'u-rëng   Lohs Aa'nngl-*zhya'*.
     NEUT-exist-3P Los   Angeles-MIGHT
     'They might be in Los Angeles.'

This suggests that adverbial suffixes force movement of the constituents they modify. I assume that these adverbial suffixes are generated in specific functional projections (following Cinque 1999), and that constituents modified by these adverbials adjoin to them, thus appearing on their left. This movement licenses the scopal relationship between the adverbial and the affected constituent.

Because the presence of these adverbials blocks the movement to normally available preverbal positions, I claim that *-zhya'* 'might' or *-ga'* 'instead' are generated above TP (which I assume to be the position in which verbs ordinarily surface). An example of how the fronted subject in (4) might raise to adjoin to an adverbial is seen in (9); irrelevant projections are omitted from the tree below (the verb is placed in the head of TP for expositional simplicity, although it will soon be made clear why this is wrong):[3]

(9) a. Lia Oliieb-*ga'*   b-gya:a'ah.
     Ms. Olivia-INSTEAD   PERF-dance
     '*Olivia* danced instead (of someone else).'

b.

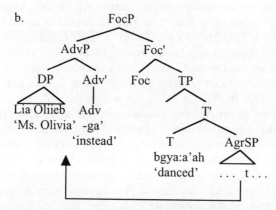

Consider the following evidence that constituents adjoined to adverbials undergo additional movement after adjoining to the adverbial. This movement is clearly visible in constituents modified by the modal clitic -*zhya'*. The fact that such movement is required of both XPs (such as nominals and prepositional phrases seen in (2–4)) and verbs modified by -*zhya'*, as in (1) and (5), supports the argument that QZ verbs are XPs.

A partial derivation for a sentence with a nominal modified by -*zhya'* such as (10), repeated from above, is as follows:

(10)   Lohs Aa'nngl-*zhya'*   n-u'u-rëng.
       Los   Angeles-MIGHT   NEUT-exist-3P
       'They might be in Los Angeles.'
       [i.e., it might be Los Angeles where they are]

Because -*zhya'* expresses modality, I assume it is generated in MoodP:

(11)

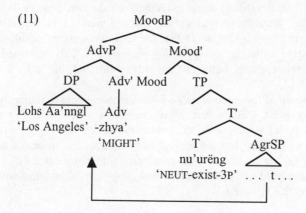

1.1.1   A Digression on Functional Categories

Let us digress slightly to discuss the relative placement of FocP and MoodP. Because *-zhya'* is generated in MoodP, the ordering of these projections will be crucial for the following analysis of *-zhya'*. The placement of MoodP above TP is due to the fact that the modal interpretation of verbs with certain aspect markers is changed under negation (Lee 1996). Verbs with the irrealis marker, for example, have simple future readings when used as matrix clause predicates (12), but receive indirect imperative readings when they appear in standard clausal negation structures (13):

(12)   *G*-wu:all-rëng liebr.
       IRR-read-3P   books
       'They will read the books.'

(13)   R-eihpy Lia Pamm la:a'rëng   cëi'ty *g*-wu:all-dya-rëng   liebr.
       HAB-tell Ms. Pamm 3P   NEG IRR-read-NEG-3P   book
       'Pam told them not to read the books.'
       ≠ 'Pam told them they will not read the books.'

Negation in QZ is clause-initial. The fact that modal interpretations can be triggered by movement of verbs into NegP suggests that negated verbs must raise through MoodP in order to reach clause initial NegP, and in cases where modal features are active, the verb will receive a modal rather than non-modal interpretation. The placement of the modal projection above TP is also consistent with Barbiers's (1995) proposal that Dutch modals with non-epistemic readings take IP (=TP) complements. See also Hendrick (this volume) for more discussion of MoodP.

The placement of MoodP below FocP is motivated by the fact that sentences with modal verbs still allow focus-fronted arguments:

(14)   Gyeeihlly ch-ille'eh   y-se:e:i'dy   ra   mni'ny.
       Mike   IRR-be.allowed IRR-teach   PLUR   children
       '*Mike* will be allowed to teach the children.'

MoodP, where *-zhya'* is presumed to be generated, appears above the normal landing position for verbs (TP) but below the preverbal focus projection FocP. We can use this ordering as a diagnostic for structure in the next section.

1.1.2   Co-occurrence Restrictions with Focus and -zhya'

At first glance, then, the structure in (11) predicts that focused constituents should be able to precede constituents modified by *-zhya'*, since constituents modified by *-zhya'* apparently adjoin to *-zhya'* in MoodP, and focus projection above MoodP is unfilled. This, however, is not the case:

(15)   *Gyeeihlly   Lohs   Aa'nngl-zhya'   n-u'uh.
        Mike   Los   Angeles-MIGHT NEUT-exist
       *'*Mike* might be in Los Angeles.'

Access to the focus position appears to be blocked. This suggests that 'Los Angeles' itself must occupy the specifier of the focus projection, rather than the Mood projection.

One possible explanation for this is that adverbial suffixes such as *-zhya'* are heads of matrix clause projections, rather than specifiers, as in (9) and (10). First, the constituent to be modified by *-zhya'* would raise into the empty specifier of MoodP, for scope reasons:

(16)

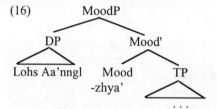

Subsequent movement of *Los Angeles* into FocP is motivated by an Antisymmetry-driven constraint: Koopman's (1996) Generalized Double-Filled Comp Filter (GDCF). This constraint states that no projection may have overt lexical material in both its head and specifier simultaneously; thus, in a syntactic structure such as (16), either the head or the specifier of MoodP must undergo further movement. Koopman suggests that the many cases cross-linguistically in which both heads and specifiers of CP appear to be filled actually involve the head and specifier of two separate projections: The head occupies the lower projection, and the constituent that appears to occupy the specifier of this projection actually occupies the specifier of a higher projection with an empty head. The motivation behind the GDCF is a desire to preserve the general principles of Kayne's (1994) Antisymmetry proposal, while allowing segments, as well as categories, to participate in c-command (and thus, linear ordering) relations.

A few clear patterns emerge from the discussion above: Adverbial clitics such as *-zhya'* and *-ga'* are generated in positions above TP, and nominals modified by these suffixes raise into specifiers of the projections they occupy. The GDCF forces further movement of modified nominals to higher projections. This movement is clearly XP movement. In the next section, I will show that QZ verbs are subject to the same movement constraints as other constituents modified by *-zhya'* and *-ga'*.

1.1.3   Verbs Modified by -zhya' and -ga'

In this section, I show that these parallel constraints indicate that verbal heads and nominal phrases undergo identical movement processes.

Like suffixed nominals, verbs modified by adverbial clitics must also surface in positions above the normal landing position for verbs. While QZ subjects and objects may appear fairly freely in preverbal position when given contrastive focus readings, verbs cliticized by *-ga'* or *-zhya'* disallow preverbal arguments. This is seen in the contrast between (17) on one hand, and (18) and (19) on the other:

(17)   Gyeeihlly b-da'uhw   bxaady.
         Mike   PERF-eat   grasshopper
         '*Mike* ate grasshoppers (not someone else).'

(18)   B-da'uhw-al-ru-zhya'   Gyeeihlly bxaady
         PERF-eat-ALREADY-MORE-MIGHT Mike   grasshopper
         'Mike might have already eaten more grasshoppers.'

(19)   *Gyeeihlly   b-da'uhw-al-ru-zhya'   bxaady.
         Mike   PERF-eat-ALREADY-MORE-MIGHT grasshopper
         *'*Mike* might have already eaten more grasshoppers.'

The fact that preverbal subjects may not precede verbs suffixed with *-zhya'* suggests that verbs suffixed with *-zhya'*, like modified nominals, must move past TP into the preverbal subject position.

The striking similarities in distribution and structural constraints on nominals and verbs modified by adverbial clitics suggest a parallel derivation for both types of structures. Both modified nouns and verbs necessarily raise past TP. This points toward an analysis in which verbs modified by *-zhya'*, like nominals, raise past TP and MoodP into FocP, thus rendering the focus projection unavailable for other constituents. By Occam's Razor, the same factors should motivate movement of both NPs and verbs past MoodP into FocP. If this is the case, then verbs, like nominals, must be XPs: Like nominals modified by *-zhya'* they raise to spec, MoodP to check their modal features. Also like nominals modified by *-zhya'*, they are also forced by well-formedness conditions to raise out of MoodP into FocP. If *-zhya'* is a head and is generated in the head of MoodP, then constituents in spec, MoodP are forced to raise out by the GDCF:

(20) a. N-u'uh-*zhya'*   Gyeeihlly Lohs Aa'nngl.
         NEUT-exist-MIGHT Mike   Los Angeles
         'Mike might be in Los Angeles.'

b.[$_{FocP}$[$_{VP}$t$_i$ nu'uh t$_j$]$_k$FOC[$_{MP}$ t$_k$-*zhya* '[$_{TP}$ t$_k$ T[$_{AgrSP}$ Gyeeihlly$_i$ Los Aa'nngl$_j$ t$_k$]]]]

Here, the arguments of the verb ('Mike' and 'Los Angeles'), base-generated within VP, have moved out of VP into their respective agreement projections for case-marking purposes. The VP-remnant itself then raises into specifier of TP to license its own tense features. From this point, its movement is exactly parallel to that of a modified nominal: It raises into the specifier of MoodP (whose head contains -*zhya*') for feature checking, then into the specifier of FocP to avoid violation of the GDCF.

To sum up, either DPs or verbs may be targeted for this movement. The identical constraints on both nominals and verbs modified by modal or adverbial clitics suggest that the syntactic processes they must undergo must also be identical. Inflected verbs in QZ undergo the same type of movement as XPs, which suggests they should be treated as XPs themselves.

1.2. The Distribution of Verbs and XPs under Negation

Further evidence against the head status of inflected verbs comes from their distribution and behavior under negation. In this section, I show that verbs may appear interchangeably with unambiguously phrasal constituents (DPs and PPs) in QZ's constituent negation construction.

QZ negation is most commonly expressed by two discontinuous negative morphemes; negated constituents appear between these two morphemes. Standard clausal negation in QZ, for example, consists of a clause-initial negative morpheme *cëi'ty* followed by the negated verb and the morpheme -*dya'*, then the subject or pronominal subject clitic:

(21)   *Cëi'ty*   gw-a:a'z-*dya'* Gyeeihlly Lieeb.
        NEG   PERF-beat-NEG Mike   Felipe
        'Mike didn't hit Felipe.'

Assuming that such two-part negation constructions require specifier-head agreement of the two negative morphemes in NegP (as has been shown for French *ne . . . pas* constructions by Moritz and Valois 1994, among others), negated verbs should appear in the head of NegP under standard assumptions about V-movement. Such a structure, shown below, was proposed in Lee (1996) (irrelevant projections omitted):

(22)

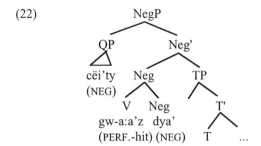

A head-movement account of verb placement between the two negative morphemes in clausal negation, however, fails to account for other common negation structures in QZ. Contrastively focused verbs, for instance, may be negated with the constituent negation marker *a'ti* instead of the clausal negation marker *cëi'ty:*

(23) *A'ti* gw-a:a'z-*dya'* Gyeeihlly Lieeb, b-cuuni'-ëng Lieeb.
      NEG perf-hit-neg Mike Felipe PERF-hit-3S Felipe
      'Mike didn't *hit* Felipe, he kicked Felipe.'

At first glance, it appears that the only difference between (21), the negated sentence with *cëi'ty,* and (23), the sentence with negated contrastive focus (with *a'ti)* is that *a'ti* appears preverbally instead of *cëi'ty.* The verb raises by head movement to the head of NegP in both constructions. This, however, poses problems for other typical negative constructions with *a'ti:*

(24) *A'ti* San Luuc-*dya'* gw-e:eh Pamm.
      NEG San Lucas-NEG PERF-go Pam
      'Pam didn't go to *San Lucas* (but rather somewhere else).'

(25) *A'ti* cuann tenedoor-*dya'* b-da'uhw Gyeeihlly gueht.
      NEG with fork-NEG PERF-eat Mike tortilla
      'Mike didn't eat tortillas with a fork.'

Since proper names (assumedly DPs) and PPs may appear between the negative markers *a'ti* and -*dya',* the idea that negated constituents raise into NegP by head movement is problematic. Equally problematic is the possibility of allowing either heads or XPs to be selected by negation, and positing different movement strategies to derive nearly identical structures. The fact that inflected verbs pattern with clear non-head constituents under focus negation indicates that they should be treated as XPs, rather than as heads.

In Lee (1996), I claimed that the first of the two discontinuous negative elements in clausal negation construction was base-generated in the specifier of NegP, and negated verbs, along with the negative morpheme -*dya',* raised into the head of NegP. This is clearly unworkable for the focus negation cases such as (24) and (25), in which the negated constituent is clearly an XP. Rather, an alternative analysis all negated constituents—including verbs—are headed by a quantifier like *cëi'ty*, and this QP moves into the specifier of NegP:[4]

(26)

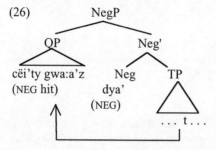

Movement of the negative phrase headed by *cëi'ty* into the specifier of NegP is motivated by the need for the negative phrase to have its features checked against those of the head of NegP.[5]

2. Stranding of Subject Agreement Clitics

More evidence against a head movement analysis of verbs in QZ is the possibility of stranding pronominal subject clitics. Pronominal subjects in QZ are expressed with post verbal subject clitics that are prosodically bound to the verb. This makes QZ verbs appear "head-like": The cliticization of person/number morphemes onto the verb appears, at first glance, to be the result of incorporation of the verb into an agreement morpheme. I show, however, that pronominal subject markers are not syntactically bound to the verb. Evidence for this is seen in the following examples, in which the verb *bda'uhw* 'ate' may raise to the left of the adverb *al* 'already', leaving the pronominal subject clitic *-rëng* behind:

(27) *Al*   b-da'uhw-*rëng* bxaady.
      ALREADY PERF-eat-3P   grasshopper
      'They already ate grasshoppers.'

(28) B-da'uhw-*al-rëng*   bxaady.
      PERF-eat-ALREADY-3P   grasshopper
      'They already ate grasshoppers.'

The possibility of such movement is unexpected under the standard assumption that postverbal subject clitics are heads of inflectional projections (such as AgrSP) into which verbal heads have incorporated.

   It might be argued that *al* 'already' can be base-generated either preverbally or postverbally, and no V-movement is involved in these sentences. There is evidence, however, that this is not the case. While *al* generally may either immediately precede or follow the verb, it may only appear to the left of the verb in the presence of preverbal topicalized subjects:

(29) A   Gyeeihlly *al*   b-i:i'lldy   liebr.
      TOP Mike   ALREADY   PERF-read   book
      'Mike already read the book.'

(30) *A   Gyeeihlly b-i:i'lldy-*al*   liebr.
      TOP Mike   PERF-read-ALREADY   book
      *'Mike already read the book.'

This asymmetry can only be explained by moving the verb: The ungrammaticality of (30) suggests that movement of the VP-remnant past *al* is blocked by the presence of the preverbal subject. On the other hand, the acceptability of (29) and ungrammaticality of (30) are unexplainable under the assumption that preverbal *al* is base-generated above postverbal *al*.

Another context in which postverbal *al* is disallowed is in the presence of preverbal independent pronouns. QZ generally expresses pronominal subjects with postverbal subject agreement clitics, such as those seen in (27) and (28). However, separate, prosodically independent pronominal forms may also be used for emphasis: These "independent" pronouns, when used as subjects, can only appear preverbally (i.e., they cannot appear in the canonical postverbal subject position), and must co-occur with postverbal subject agreement clitics (32):

(31) B-to'o-ng   ca'rr.
      PERF-sell-3S car
      'He/she sold the car.'

(32) *Laang* b-to'o-ng   ca'rr.
      3S   PERF-sell-3S car
      'It was he/she that sold the car.'

When independent subject pronouns appear, *al* shows the same distributional restrictions that hold with preverbal topics, in that it may only appear preverbally:

(33) Laang *al*   n-ac-ëng   me's.
      3S   ALREADY   NEUT-be-3S   teacher
      'He/she is already a teacher.'

(34) *Laang n-ac-*al*-ëng   me's.
      3S   NEUT-be-ALREADY 3S   teacher
      *'He/she is already a teacher.'

In these cases, as in the preverbal topic cases, postverbal *al* is disallowed in the presence of preverbal constituents. This again suggests that the preverbal constituent blocks movement of the verb past *al*.

While the distribution of independent subject pronouns pronominal subject clitics in QZ appears reminiscent of pronominal argument behavior in number of other indigenous American languages (see for example, Jelinek, this volume), the fact that pronominal subject clitics may be separated from the verb by raising of the verb past *al* indicates that these clitics occupy projections distinct from the verb, and should not be considered to be incorporated agreement heads. Indeed, while QZ pronominal subject clitics are prosodically bound to verbs, I will argue that they occupy the same position as postverbal lexical subjects.

Evidence for this comes from the ordering of subjects with certain other adverbs. The adverb *nsehe's* 'quickly', for example, generally appears clause-initially or clause-finally, but may appear (less preferably) between verbs and lexical subjects:

> (35) ?Al   b-iːi'lldy   *nsehe's*   Gyeeihlly liebr.
>   ALREADY PERF-read QUICKLY Mike   book
>   ?'Mike already read the book quickly.'

It may not, however, appear between the subject and object:

> (36) *Al   b-iːi'lldy Gyeeihlly *nsehe's*   liebr.
>   ALREADY PERF-read Mike   QUICKLY book
>   *'Mike already read the book quickly.'

These constraints also hold for pronominal subjects. While not fully acceptable, adverbs such as 'quickly' may (marginally) appear between the verb and pronominal subject clitic:

> (37) ??Al   b-iːi'lldy   *nsehe's*-rëng liebr.
>   ALREADY PERF-read QUICKLY-3P book
>   ??'They already read the book quickly.'

Such adverbs are completely disallowed, however, between the subject agreement clitic and object:

> (38) *Al   b-iːi'lldy-rëng *nsehe's*   liebr.
>   ALREADY PERF-read-3P QUICKLY book
>   *'They already read the book quickly.'

These data support the idea that subject agreement clitics are syntactically distinct from the verbs they cliticize to, and that they occupy the same position as lexical subjects.

2.1 Further Consequences of Pronominal Clitic Stranding

The possibility of stranding pronominal subject clitics—and the fact that they behave syntactically like lexical subjects—also supports the idea that arguments necessarily raise out of VP before VP itself raises to TP or a higher position. Assuming the generally accepted theory that arguments are base-generated within VP (Koopman and Sportiche 1991, among others), the fact that verbs can move independently of their arguments, as seen in the preceding examples, indicates that arguments surface in positions outside of VP. I assume that the need for arguments to raise out of VP is motivated by Case requirements: These requirements can only be met by movement of arguments into (or through) their respective agreement projections.

One could argue, alternately, that arguments remain within VP and the verbal head itself raises to clause initial position in VSO languages, as proposed by Koopman and Sportiche (1991). There is strong evidence against this in QZ. First, as shown in section 1 above, verbs undergo the same movement processes and are subject to the same syntactic constraints as XPs. This is unexplainable if verbs are taken to be heads. Second, if subjects and objects remained in VP, one would expect subjects and objects to be able to behave together as a single constituent (as argued for Irish subjects and objects by McCloskey 1991). For example, if we assume for the moment that QZ verbs undergo head movement, and VP remnants left behind after verb raising contain the base-generated arguments, then it would be potentially possible for the VP remnant itself to raise to FocP, fronting and focusing both the subject and object:

(39)

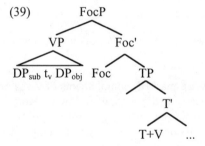

This prediction, however, is not borne out. Such constructions are ungrammatical:

(40) *Gyeeilly ca'rr b-to'oh.
       Mike   car   PERF-sell
     *'*Mike* sold *the car.*'

QZ allows only one non-coordinated constituent per sentence to appear in focus position. The fact that subjects and objects together cannot raise to Focus seems to indicate that they do not form a single constituent, and thus cannot be posited to be stranded in VP (however, cf. a discussion of a similar set of facts from Irish in McCloskey 1991).

To sum up this section, the distribution of pronominal and lexical subjects, and particularly their behavior in the presence of adverbs such as *al* 'already' and *nsehe's* 'quickly', demonstrate that arguments necessarily raise out of VP to their own licensing positions. Despite the prosodic dependency between pronominal subject clitics and verbs, they are syntactically independent entities rather than incorporated heads. This is consistent with the arguments made earlier in this chapter that QZ verbs are VP remnants rather than heads.

3. VP-Raising and Clausal Arguments

A potential problem for the VP remnant proposal is the status of clausal complements: If embedded sentences are generated as complements of V, and the entire VP necessarily raises to TP, then this model predicts that clausal complements raise along with VP. This would result in clausal complements being ordered before matrix clause subjects and objects, as in the following template:

(41)   *[V CP] S O

This pattern, however, is completely unattested in QZ. Rather, clausal complements in QZ necessarily follow all matrix clause arguments:

(42)   V S O CP

To explain this, I claim (following Stowell 1981) that clausal complements, like nominal arguments, necessarily raise out of VP into the matrix clause before VP itself raises to TP.

I assume that clausal (that is, non-Case-marked) complements of verbs raise into a functional projection LP (for Licensing Projection, following Koopman and Szabolcsi 1997). Since embedded clauses in QZ generally appear after matrix clause subjects and arguments, I assume that these clausal complements, like nominal arguments, raise out of the matrix VP into a licensing position in the matrix clause before the matrix VP itself raises to clause-initial position. Because complement clauses appear after matrix clause objects, I assume that LP is below AgrOP:

(43)   B-quilly   Lieeb Gyeeihlly [y-to'oh Gyeeihlly ca'rr].
       PERF-persuade Felipe Mike   IRR-sell Mike   car
       'Felipe persuaded Mike to sell the car.'

(44)

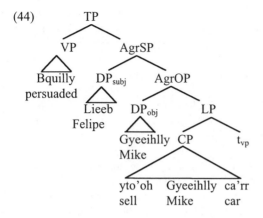

While this may appear to be an ad hoc mechanism to save the VP-raising theory, it has independent theoretical motivation in earlier work on Case and theta-role assignment of complement clauses (Emonds 1978, Stowell 1981, among others). More recently, the raising of complement clauses to higher projections has been posited as a means of handling apparent cases of right-adjunction in a manner consistent with the principles of Antisymmetry (Kayne 1998, Koopman and Szabolcsi 1997).

Stowell (1981) presents a number of arguments that clausal complements in English surface in positions other than their base-generated complement positions. He notes that gerund clauses may appear as objects of prepositions and subjects of complements of exceptional Case-marking verbs, while tensed clauses may not:

(45) a. He blamed it [on [Bill's being too strict]].
    b. *He blamed it [on [that Bill was too strict]].
    c. I consider[[John's having come home] to be fortunate].
    d. *I consider [[that John came home] to be fortunate].

(Stowell 1981: 148–149)

Furthermore, tensed-clause complements may not appear directly after tensed verbs:

(46) a. Paul knew from experience [that the law was unfair].
    b. ?*Paul knew [that the law was unfair] from experience.

Stowell postulates that the ungrammaticality of (45b, d), and (46b) can be attributed to the clashing requirements of Case and theta-role assignment in these structures. He assumes the following requirement for theta-role assignment (proposed in Chomsky 1981):

(47)   Theta-roles can only be assigned to A-chains that are headed by a position occupied by PRO or Case. (Chomsky 1981, as cited in Stowell 1981:111)

Case assignment, however, is subject to the following constraint:

(48)   THE CASE RESISTANCE PRINCIPLE (CRP):
Case may not be assigned to a category bearing a Case-assigning feature. (Stowell 1981: 141)

Since Case-assigning property is linked to tense, tensed clauses are subject to the CRP, and are thus blocked from appearing in Case-marked positions. Stowell notes, however, that there are many cases in which tensed clauses appear as subjects or complements of tensed verbs in apparent violation of the CRP:

(49) a. [That Brian dyed his hair] proves nothing.
  b. Paul already knows [that Jim lives with his sister].
(Stowell 1981:152, 159)

In the case of tensed-clause subjects, he suggests—adopting earlier ideas by Emonds (1976) and Koster (1978)—that the tensed clause raises to a higher topic position. This is supported by the fact that tensed-clause subjects only appear in constructions in which topics can also appear, and are blocked in environments in which topics may not appear (such as relative clauses):

(50)   *John's belief [[that you took the course] helped you] is unfounded.
(Stowell 1981:153)

Stowell also proposes that tensed-clause complements of tensed verbs, such as that in (49b), are also extraposed from their base (Case-marked) position. He suggests (following Emonds 1976) that these extraposed clauses move rightward to a postverbal position to fulfill the CRP. This accounts for the clause final position of the tensed-clause complements in (49b).

The idea that clausal complements must move to positions distinct from their base-generated positions is not new or theoretically unmotivated. Stowell's proposals can be easily updated to be consistent with Minimalist assumptions: Most obviously, it must be assumed that tensed complement clauses raise leftward, not rightward, to fulfill the CRP. Also, the CRP itself can be restated in terms of feature licensing conditions: since Case assignment is now assumed to be licensed by specifier-head agreement within Agr rather than by head government by the verb stem, I assume that tensed-clause complements must appear in positions distinct from nominal complements because they cannot receive the Case features assigned by Agr. In other words, clausal complements of tensed verbs raise to a licensing projection analogous to Agr, but that differs from the nominal agreement licensing projections in that it does not assign Case.

4. Conclusion

In this chapter, I have shown that VSO word order in QZ can best be accounted for by positing movement of a VP-remnant, rather than a verbal head, to clause initial position. This movement strategy provides a unified account for both the ordering of morphemes within verbal expressions, and the distribution of verbal expressions in different syntactic constructions. Notably, this approach provides a principled account for the fact that phrasal expressions and verbs participate interchangeably in a number of syntactic constructions, such as negation and adverbial modification.

Appendix: QZ Verbal Morphology

In this appendix, I provide a brief overview of the somewhat complex verbal morphology of QZ, and show that the verbal morpheme order of QZ cannot be derived by head movement. This, in turn, provides further evidence for the VP status of QZ verbs. I will also show that while the ordering of verbal morphemes in QZ cannot be accounted for under a head movement account, it can be derived in a straightforward way under the VP-remnant raising account proposed above.

QZ verbs may be marked with affixes on both their left and right edges. All QZ verbs obligatorily appear with one of seven aspect markers, which also encode tense and sometimes mood. These markers appear on the leftmost edge of the verb:

(51)   *Ca*-taːaʼaz Lieeb Gyeeihlly.
       PROG-beat Felipe Mike
       'Felipe is beating Mike.'

QZ shows no person or number agreement marking on verbs with lexical subjects. Pronominal subjects and third-person singular pronominal objects are expressed as clitics on the right edge of the verb:

(52)   Ca-taːaʼaz-*ëng*   Gyeeihlly.
       PROG-beat-3S.PROX   Mike
       'He/she is beating Mike.'

(53)   B-toʼo-*ng-niːi.*
       PERF-sell-3S.PROX-3S.DIST
       'He/she sold it.'

Directional markers (reduced forms of the verbs *ried* 'come' and *rihah* 'go')[6] and causative markers may also appear on the left edge of the verb after the aspect marker:

(54)   R-*id*-ta'uhw   Gyeeihlly.
       HAB-COME-eat Mike
       'Mike comes to eat.'

(55)   B-*z*-ya'a'ah   Lieeb   Gyeeihlly.
       PERF-CAUSE-dance Felipe   Mike
       'Felipe made Mike dance.'

A number of affixes, such as the comitative suffix *-ne:e*, may appear on the right edge of the verb theme:

(56)   Cay-a'uw-*ne:e*   Gyeeihlly Lieeb.
       PROG-eat-WITH   Mike   Felipe
       'Mike is eating with Felipe.'

Adverbial markers may also appear on the right edge of the verb, before subjects or subject and object agreement markers. Multiple adverbials may appear:

(57)   Z-auw-*daan-zhya'*   Gyeeihlly.
       DEF-eat-MUCH-MIGHT   Mike
       'Mike will probably eat a lot.'

Thus, an abbreviated template for possible inflected verb forms in QZ is as follows:

(58)   Asp(dir)(caus)Verb(applic)(adv)(adv)(adv)(Subj)(Obj)

This template poses serious problems for the standard assumption that verbal inflection is derived by head-movement. If we adopt the standard assumption that verbs are inflected through head-movement, morphemes are affixed in the order in which they occur in the syntax (following Baker's (1985) Mirror Principle), and only left-adjunction is possible (Kayne 1994), the order of morphemes would have AgrO over AgrS, and the VP over T. This kind of order is clearly undesirable. First, placement of AgrO above AgrS is virtually unattested in linguistic theory, as is the idea that aspect/tense inflection is generated below the verb.

   A possible option for deriving the morpheme ordering in (8) from a more conventional underlying structure is to assume that heads may adjoin to either the left or right edge of the verbal head as it raises up through the structure. Thus, the Aspect and Causative heads adjoin to the left edge of the verb, and the others adjoin to the right edge. This approach is problematic for several reasons. First, it clearly violates the Mirror Principle. Second, it violates Kayne's (1994) Linear Correspondence Axiom by forming structures that branch in more than one direction.[7] Although it has been suggested (Potter 1995) that languages may select the directionality in which adjoined heads surface at PF (some languages spell out adjoined heads at the left edges of phonological structures at PF, others to the right), it is not possible under Potter's theory for a language to spell out material in both directions simultaneously.

The simplest option would be to adopt a non-ordered feature-checking approach, consistent with Chomsky 1995 (contra Baker, Kayne, etc.): Features checked by movement may be checked in any order, and feature-checking is not constrained by the physical ordering of morphemes. This would be the best option to adopt if it were the case that inflected verbs in QZ behaved consistently like heads in all contexts. As shown in the previous sections of this paper, however, this is not the case. Thus, even under the loosest possible correspondence between morphological ordering and underlying syntactic structure, it is impossible to derive the verbal structure of QZ from head movement. However, VP-remnant movement might allow both the morphological ordering of QZ verbs and their syntactic behavior to be accounted for in a unified way.

Acknowledgments

Support for this work was provided by the NSF project *San Lucas Quiaviní Zapotec: Dictionary, Grammar, and Texts* (Pamela Munro, principal investigator), at the UCLA Linguistics Department, and by a grant from the UCLA Institute of American Cultures/Chicano Studies Research Center. Thanks are due to Pamela Munro, Hilda Koopman, Jamal Ouhalla, Tim Stowell, and the audiences at the UCLA Syntax and Semantics Seminar and the UCLA American Indian Seminar for their questions and suggestions. I am also grateful to Andrew Carnie, Richard Kayne, and an anonymous reviewer for their comments and suggestions on an earlier draft of this chapter. QZ data were provided by Rodrigo Garcia, except where noted. Any errors are my own.

Notes

1. This language has also been called San Lucas Quiaviní Zapotec (SLQZ) in previous literature (Munro and Lopez 1997, Lee 1996), following the Mexican convention of assigning indigenous villages Catholic saints' names along with names in indigenous languages. In the interest of brevity, I use only the indigenous community name here (QZ).

2. QZ vowels may have one of four phonation types: modal; creaky represented in QZ orthography developed by Munro and Lopez (1997) as *v:*, breathy *vh*, and glottalized *v'*. The umlauted *ë* represents a high, mid-back, unrounded vowel, *y* represents a palatal glide; all other vowels are pronounced as in Spanish orthography. Consonants followed by a colon *c:* are retroflexed.

3. Following Kayne (1994), I assume that adjunction is movement to a specifier position. Following Cinque (1999), I assume (for the moment) that adverbs are specifiers of their projections.

4. There is evidence that negated expressions headed by *cëi'ty* undergo further movement after checking their features in NegP, much like that argued for constituents modified by adverbial or modal clitics. This comes from the fact that the negative head *-dya'* generally does not appear in negated clauses containing overt preverbal material, such as relative clauses (which have obligatory relative markers), *wh*-questions (*wh-*

movement is obligatory in QZ), and yes/no questions (which have overt, clause-initial question markers). The constraint against *-dya'* in these contexts can be considered an effect of the GDCF, which Koopman (1996) argues to hold only of overt lexical material: When negated expressions headed by *cëi'ty* appear clause-initially, they have raised out of NegP; thus, the head of NegP is the only overt constituent in NegP and is licit. Preverbal constituents such as relative markers, *wh*-words, and question markers, however, block subsequent movement of *cëi'ty* -VP out of NegP. In order for such structures to be licit, either the overt material of the head or specifier of NegP must be suppressed. Since the informational burden of the sentence is contained in the expression headed by *cëi'ty* in the specifier of NegP, *-dya'* in the head of NegP must thus be deleted.

5. A consequence of treating negated verbs as XPs is that the topmost negative morpheme–*cëi'ty* or *a'ti*–must be posited as base-generated directly above the negated constituent itself, rather than in the specifier of NegP. This is a desirable result because it reflects the fact that these negative elements actively select the type of constituents they may negate and determine the semantics of the resulting negative construction: *cëi'ty* may only precede verbs and express the negation of events; and *a'ti* may only precede focused constituents and provide constituent, rather than event, negation. Thus, the assumption that movement of all negated constituents into NegP is XP-movement–which therefore means verbs are XPs–captures the semantics of negation constructions more accurately than a verbal head-raising account.

6. Following the convention set forth in Munro and Lopez (1997) and Munro (1996), I list citation forms of QZ verbs with the habitual aspect marker.

7. Duffield (1994, 1995) proposes a similar account for Irish: He argues that sentences with sentence final adverbs are derived by raising the TP (containing the verb, subject, and object) to the left of the projection containing the adverb. This accounts for the sentence final ordering of adverbs without resorting to right adjunction, which would be inconsistent with the otherwise completely head-initial structure of Irish.

9

Locus Operandi

Ray Freeze and Carol Georgopoulos

In this chapter, we hope to provide new motivation for syntacticians to take a closer look at verb initial languages and, in particular, at VOS languages. Surface VOS languages are a distinct verb initial type, differing from VSO languages in many ways and posing different sets of questions. For example, VOS order presents no problem of composing an underlying VP, and many VOS languages are uniformly as left-headed as SOV languages are right-headed. A stronger sense of the properties of VOS languages can serve to round out many theories of syntactic phenomena. Recognition of VOS as a base order might strengthen analyses of VSO as a true (verb initial) base order in its own right, at least for some languages.

In this chapter we focus on locative constructions, which make robust distinctions between verb initial, V-final, and SVO order. Highlighting VOS languages, we show how the pervasive effects of locativity can illuminate very general issues in syntactic theory, such as those concerning phrase structure, agreement, and, especially, order. We conclude that verb initial order, along with SVO and SOV, is basic and underived.

We begin by identifying the *locative paradigm* as analyzed by Freeze (1992a). This paradigm is a set of derivationally related sentence forms commonly known as the predicate locative, the existential, and the possessive. The arguments in all three are location and theme. Freeze showed that the predicate locative construction (e.g., *The Jaguar is in the garage*), the existential (*There is a Jaguar in the garage*), and the possessive sentence (*Mary has a Jaguar*) are universally derived from a single underlying locative structure. Cross-linguistically, the predicate phrase in all three types is prepositional (or otherwise locative), and its arguments are location and theme. In the predicate locative, the theme argument is in subject position, while in the existential and possessive the locative phrase (the location or the possessor, respectively) is the subject. In some languages, the existential contains a locative proform (e.g., French *y*, Spanish *(ha)–y*, Arabic *fii*), and in relatively few languages the possessive sentence employs a 'have' copula. Both locative proform and 'have' form are argued to be lexicalizations of locative features.

From this unifying paradigm, which was based on data from dozens of languages and language types, two other interesting and previously unremarked generalizations emerged, both correlated to constituent order: According to Freeze (1992a), first, verb initial languages have no lexical 'have' form in possessives; and second, no SOV language has a locative proform in the existential.[1] The verb initial vs. verb final contrast uniting these two generalizations reveals the complementarity of the 'have' form (none in VSO/VOS) and the locative proform (none in SOV).[2] This raises the natural question: Are these two generalizations *conditioned* by constituent order? This question implicates another: *Does* base order vary among languages?

Among possible answers to these questions, two stand out. One is that there is one base order, and the 'have'/proform distribution arises in or as a consequence of the derivation of different surface orders. The other possibility is that the order variations are basic, and the lack of 'have' in verb initial orders and the lack of the proform in SOV order are properties (or even diagnostics) of the particular word orders. The second possibility allows for prior determinants of order, such as parametric settings.

We approach these alternatives by comparing the results of a movement approach that assumes a single base order (e.g., Kayne 1994) with the results of extending Freeze's (1992a) approach, which assumes that there are several possible base orders. Freeze (1992a) was productive in its ability to unify locative constructions universally and thereby to uncover the additional generalizations above. We show that this analysis has even further important consequences in providing strong support for the hypothesis that languages differ in their basic order. Specifically, we will argue that the 'have'/proform complementarity arises from basic differences in order. We show that the movement approach does not predict or account for the special properties of the various locative expressions, while these properties follow as unmarked options from the variant-base-order approach.

We focus on the Mayan languages (augmented by data from Austronesian) in constructing our arguments about verb initial languages. Mayan is verb initial and has no 'have'. SOV languages, those without an existential proform, are represented below primarily by Hindi, Mayo (Uto-Aztecan), and Japanese.

1.   The Locative Facts

This section is essentially a brief summary of the findings of Freeze (1992a).[3] Here we show the unity of locative expressions, without repeating much of the argumentation, which is extensive and can be found in the earlier article.[4]

First, consider the English examples in (1) and the Russian examples in (2). We claim that Russian represents the common (perhaps default) character of the locative paradigm cross-linguistically: The predicate locative presents the theme argument in subject position, and the existential and possessive have the locative phrase (the location or the possessor, respectively) in subject, and otherwise the three constructions vary minimally. English is exceptional in several respects.

(1) **English**
   a. The Jaguar is in the garage.   *predicate locative*
   b. There is a Jaguar in the garage.   *existential*
   c. Mary has a Jaguar.   *possessive*

(2) **Russian**
   a. Kniga   byla   na   stole.   *predicate locative*
      bookNOM-FEM was   on   tableLOC
      'The book was on the table.'

   b. Na stole   byla   kniga   *existential*
      on tableLOC   was   bookNOM-FEM
      'There was a book on the table.'

   c. U menja byla sestra.   *possessive*
      at I-GEN was sisterNOM
      'I had a sister.'

We make the common assumption that the arguments are initially projected within the predicate. Either argument may raise to subject. Usually, the definiteness of the theme argument determines the choice between a predicate locative structure and an existential structure: If the theme is definite, it raises to subject, yielding the predicate locative (2a); if the theme is indefinite, the locative raises to subject, yielding the existential (2b). We assume the usual distinction between overt morphological Case-marking and abstract Case: For example, raised locative subjects may bear inherent locative marking but receive structural nominative Case (see, e.g., Anderson 1988, Chomsky 1995).

The possessive is an existential as well (see Freeze 1992a:576); it also has a locative subject (the possessor is marked as a location), a locative copula, and a theme. In languages with more than one available possessive construction,[5] a possessor that is [+human] must be or is preferably subject. The predicate phrase in all cases is a PP.

Second, some languages (apparently few, from a cross-linguistic point of view) allow the bare location DP (the possessor) to be subject of a possessive, without marking it as locative or prepositional. In these cases the subject may be nominative, the theme appears as an object, and the copula appears as a 'have' lexical form. Possessive 'have' arises as follows: The "stranded" P left behind by the bare DP subject combines with sentential inflection, yielding 'have' (inflection + P = HAVE).[6] 'Have' is then one surface form of a locative copula. This description characterizes English (1c repeated below):

(1) c.'   Mary   has   a jaguar
     $[_{IP} ZP_{[location]i} [_{I'} Infl_{[+loc]}+P_j [_{PP} YP_{[theme]} [_{P'} e_j e_i]]]]$

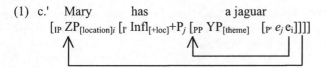

Third, this locative paradigm yields a locative proform in the existential of some languages. The proform co-occurs with a location argument elsewhere in the sentence, and itself is always either lexically locative or is an unmarked pronominal object of a preposition. French provides an example (lower case '*p*' = proform, capital P represents locative prepositions):

(3)   **French**
       Il *y* a   deux enfants dans l'auto.
       it *p* has two   children in   the.car
       'There are two children in the car.'

In (3), subject position is filled by dummy 'it'. The proform (*y* 'there') is not in subject position. The proform is obligatorily adjacent to Infl elements (see table 1 below), suggesting that it too is inflectional. Freeze (1992a, section 3) argues that the existential proform is a spellout of the [+loc] feature of Infl. We carry over that analysis here, and point out that the proform, cross-linguistically, is rare.

The structure below illustrates this type of existential, given for the sentence in (3):

(3')   Il   y a   deux enfants   dans   l'auto
        [$_{IP}$ ZP$_{[dummy]}$ [$_{I'}$ Infl$_{[+loc]}$ [$_{PP}$ YP$_{[theme]}$ [$_{P'}$ P   XP$_{[location]}$]]]]

The locative subject existential (as in, e.g., Russian) and the locative proform existential (e.g., French) are virtually the only possible forms; the exceptions to this are so rare as to probably lack a UG analysis.

One exception is English. Unlike existentials in most languages, the English existential has a lexically locative existential proform in subject position. Thus, the English existential (*There is a Jaguar in the garage*) is a rare and unrepresentative structure. Freeze (1992a) argues that the proform in this case is co-indexed with the locative phrase by predication, rather than being a lexicalization of [+loc]. Historically, this pronoun is 'it' even in English (and still is in Black English), and most other Germanic languages have an impersonal pronoun equivalent to 'it' in this position. See Visser (1963), as well as Freeze (1992a), for a much broader array of data, and for numerous arguments supporting the claims made here.[7]

2. Two New Locative Generalizations

In revealing the unity of the locative paradigm, Freeze recognized certain further generalizations which were not pursued in that paper. These generalizations can shed new light on issues of basic word order.

2.1 'Have' Lexicalizations

First, in contrast to SVO and SOV languages, there are no 'have' lexicalizations in the possessive sentences of verb initial languages. Compare the existential and the possessive in Yucatec (Mayan, VOS):[8]

(4) **Yucatec**

    a. yaan   huntul ciimin   ti? yukataan
       COP.LOC one   horse   P   Yucatan
       'There is a horse in Yucatan.'
       (Lit. 'In Yucatan is a horse.')

    b. yaan   huntul ciimin   ti? in-paapa.
       COP.LOC one   horse   P   my-father
       'My father has a/one horse.'
       (Lit. 'To my father is a horse.')

This is the representative pattern for verb initial languages: The possessive has the same form as the existential.

2.2 Locative Proform

Second, no SOV language has a locative proform in the existential. Compare existentials in Tongan (Austronesian, verb initial), Catalan (SVO), and Palauan (Austronesian, VOS), all of which have proforms, with Hindi, Mayo (Uto-Aztecan) and Japanese, all SOV (consistently right-headed) and without proforms (proforms are in italics below; Tongan and Palauan proforms are prepositional):

(5) **Tongan**

    ?oku   ?i   *ai*   ?ae   kurii ?i he poopao.
    PRES   P   3S   ABS.ART dog   P ART canoe
    'There's a dog in the canoe.'

(6) **Catalan**

    No   *hi*   ha peix al   menu d'avui.
    NOT [there] is fish on.the menu of today
    'Isn't there fish on today's menu?'

(7) **Palauan**[9]

    ŋ-ŋar *ŋii* a   bilis er   a   sers-ek.
    3S-be.P 3S NP dog   P   NP garden-MY
    'There is a dog in my garden.'

(8)   **Hindi**
       Kamree-mẽẽ   aadmii   hai.
       room-IN   man   COP(3S)
       'There is a man in the room.'

(9)   **Mayo**
       Howa-po hente a:ne.
       house-in people COP
       'There are people in the house.'

(10)   **Japanese**
       Kono kyooshitsu-ni   denki   dokei-ga   arimasu.
       this   classroom-DAT   electric   clock-NOM   COP
       'There is an electric clock in this classroom.'

The SOV languages all have a locative subject existential.

To sum up, verb initial languages have no 'have' possessive, and SOV languages have no proform existential. One may then ask whether the differences in constituent order are responsible for the distribution of locative (=possessive) 'have' and the locative (=existential) proforms. In pursuing this question, we must also consider the issue of whether there actually are any basic differences in order among the world's languages. We address these questions in the next section.

2.3 Empirical Basis of the Generalizations

It should be clear by now that we are assuming that languages differ in their order. We have taken the ordering specifications of these languages from the research of the linguists who have worked on them (including our own research on order; see also note 4). We don't repeat the arguments for various orders here. But our point of departure is not a set of word order claims, but rather a set of data-driven generalizations. It is the generalizations *themselves* that have classified these language types as verb initial, SOV, and so on. The class of languages none of whose members have an existential proform is precisely the class of languages described by their researchers as SOV; similarly languages with no 'have' form are verb initial. In section 4, below, we describe a third generalization, one that appears to pick out SVO order.

In our concluding section, we address the question of whether it is meaningful to posit underlying word order(s) at all. Here we proceed with the distinctions as we have found them.

3. Analysis

As Freeze (1992a) has shown and as we summarized above, the unmarked or default case for the existential/possessive is a locative sentence with a locative subject. Consequently, there is a locative feature in inflection, for all of the locative paradigm. This suggests specifier-head agreement when the subject is locative, and we henceforth assume that such agreement holds in such sentences. We will call this "locative agreement" (illustrated, e.g., in 11b below). The possessive variant with 'have' does not have a locative subject, since the subject is a bare DP location; the head P in these sentences moves to Infl, giving lexical 'have'. In this case, a [+loc] Infl does not have a [+loc] specifier, so there is no locative agreement. P may be thought of as a partial proxy for [+loc]: If it is on the subject, there may be locative agreement; if it combines with Infl, 'have' appears. See the trees in (12).

The SVO existential variant with a locative proform may or may not have a locative subject (see table 1 below); when it does, locative agreement holds. The proform itself, which, we recall, arises as a lexical spellout of [+loc], thus has a different distribution from locative subjects and also from agreement.

3.1 'Have'

Let us turn first to the generalization that verb initial languages (= predicate initial, in our case) have no 'have' possessive. We repeat the Yucatec (Mayan, VOS) example here, with a representative partial tree.

(11) a. **Yucatec**

yaan   huntul   ciimin   ti?   in-paapa
COP.LOC one   horse   P   my-father
'My father has a/one horse.'
(Lit. 'To my father is a horse')

b.

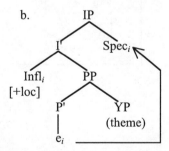

The locative copula is followed by the theme, then the location, which is raised out of the predicate to the (rightward) subject position. This then triggers locative agreement.[10] Since the subject is a raised locative phrase (P moves to

Spec with the location) and not a bare DP, 'have' is not possible, according to our analysis.

The alternative instantiated by verb initial languages is the unmarked one for us: The possessive is simply the locative existential, with the raised possessor as subject. Nothing more really needs to be said. The generalization about verb initial languages only seemed remarkable because we looked at it through SVO-colored glasses. The simplicity of the default case we have uncovered here is support for the correctness of our analysis in terms of UG.

But we can't resist the temptation to say more, so we observe also that if these languages were to opt for the more marked and relatively rare 'have' alternative, moving just the bare location nominal to subject, P would be stranded and forced to move to Infl, as described above. However, movement of P to Infl in these languages would be string-vacuous, violating the economy principle of Least Effort (Chomsky 1995). Since P and Infl don't meet, the morphological conditions for 'have' are not present. But since the same (least-effort) explanation does not work for SOV languages (which *may* have 'have'), we must assume that the *linear precedence* of the predicate head with respect to the locative argument in verb initial languages is also a factor. This same precedence condition is active in the distribution of the proform, so we will return to the issue of precedence in sections 4 and 5.

These suggestions may be seen more clearly in the following simplified trees, for each word order and alternative:[11]

(12)   a. VOS/VSO   b. SVO
          locative subject,   *bare DP subject,*
          no 'have'   *with 'have'*

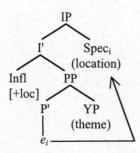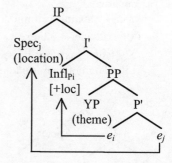

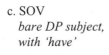

c. SOV
bare DP subject,
with 'have'

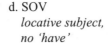

d. SOV
locative subject,
no 'have'

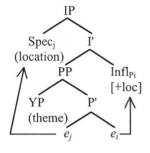

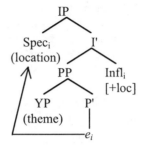

Why, then, does any language have 'have'?[12] Note, first, that 'have' subjects are not obliquely marked. This suggests that the diachronic motivation for 'have' formation may be the widespread historical tendency to disencumber the subject of morphological (oblique) marking when the possessive subject is [+human]. Such a subject is prototypical; extension of 'have' to [–human] subjects (as in *'The house has a roof'*) would then be by analogy. In the theory of locatives presented here, the most important difference between possessive and existential expressions is that in the former the location (possessor) is [+human]. Otherwise, as we have noted, most commonly the possessive and the existential are structurally identical.

Since only S-initial languages have 'have', removal of the preposition from a location subject can also be seen as part of the operation of fronting or "foregrounding" the argument that is designated subject. In structural terms, 'have' lexicalization can be seen as a prioritizing of abstract Case-marking over inherent Case-marking.

In contrast, many Austronesian languages are both verb initial (no 'have') and have focus-marking systems which provide alternative marking for the prominent or focused argument. This is a large topic which we don't pursue here, but it may be that 'have' is, at least diachronically, pragmatic.[13]

3.2 The Proform

We turn now to the second generalization, that SOV languages have no locative proform in the existential. Restated perhaps more clearly, locative proforms do not occur in languages in which inflection is final. In terms of our theory, this suggests that the [+loc] feature of inflection does not lexicalize as a proform unless inflection (and the proform) precedes the locative argument.[14] This restriction makes the proform case look like the clitic doubling case in Spanish: The clitic precedes and shares a theta-role with the postverbal phrase.

We do not analyze the proform as clitic doubling.[15] However, we do want to claim that it is clitic-like in that we believe it to be a second-position effect. In all cases that we know of, *the proform is in second position* (see the table below).[16]

Here is Freeze's table 4 (1992a), with subject positions aligned vertically and showing examples of proform existentials in SVO, VOS, and VSO languages. Note, inter alia, and as stated in note 2, VSO and VOS are indistinct with respect to the locative paradigm; see also our table 2 in section 4.4. The proform is in boldface (**p**); COP = copula; D = lexical dummy subject; e = empty subject position; L = Location; T = Theme. The shaded column represents subject position:

Table 1 *Position of existential proforms* (from Freeze 1992a: table 4)

Basic order	Example	Existential							
SVO	Finnish				L	COP	T		
	Russian				L	COP	T		
	Catalan				e	**p**	COP	T	L
	French				D	**p**	COP	T	L
VOS	Palauan	COP	**p**	T	L				
	Chamorro		COP	T	L				
VSO	P.Arabic	COP	**p**	T	L				
	Tagalog		COP	T	L				
SOV	Hindi				L	T	COP		
	Japanese				L	T	COP		

Here the second-position distribution of the proform is clear. We have argued elsewhere (see Freeze 1992b) that second position is a PF phenomenon, and we assume the same here.

No second-position effects are possible in locative predications in SOV order. The explanation for this is best couched in MP terms along with an added precedence condition. We claim that there is a difference between second position effects related to V-features on Infl (AgrS or T) and the second-position effect related to what we see as P-features on Infl; P-features belong to the locative subject. V-features are responsible for the movement of V to second position in some SOV languages, while the inflectional node bearing P-features can be checked by the subject *in situ*: In an SOV language with inflection to the right, the checking takes place to the right. The P-features of the subject are in fact invisible to V-movement or V-feature checking.

The proform must also *precede* the locative phrase; as table 1 shows, it only occurs when the locative subject is postposed. To us, this is a pure precedence effect, and we briefly broach a pragmatic explanation. Assuming that first position is prototypically a focus position ("announcing" the subject or topic), then second position announces sentential properties, such as predication type. If the proform is a second-position effect, announcing that the predicate is locative, the likelihood that it will be lexicalized is reduced if the locative subject is initial.

The conditions leading to lexicalization of the proform are thus extremely complex, suggesting that it should be rare, but not predicting that it is impossible. We have shown it to be rare, and we have found no cases of it in SOV languages. However, we cannot predict that it will never occur in this order type.

Note further, in table 1, that the distribution of the proform is unrelated to the distribution of locative subjects: Languages with one may or may not have the other. It should also be noted that, *within one order type*—e.g., SVO—several variants are possible: SVO order may or may not have a locative subject, and may or may not have the proform; the verb initial languages may or may not have the proform. Thus, there are subtypes within each language type. But table 1 also shows that the proform may not *follow* L. Therefore in particular verb initial languages the proform and a locative subject can co-occur, but in SVO languages they can't (the proform would *follow* the locative subject). These facts suggest that the second-position effect is a precedence phenomenon (linear only) which is, furthermore, sensitive to the order of constituents (see Freeze 1992a).

We show the possible positions of the proform in syntactic trees below, and its absence in SOV, without showing raised locative subjects.

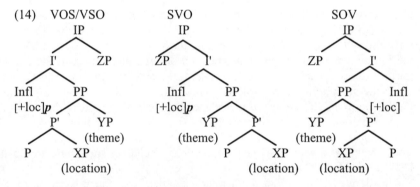

We hope the reader is not disappointed to find that such exotic facts as our two generalizations turn out to have such familiar explanations—that one arises from a default case, and the other is just a second-position effect in a new guise. These are precisely the results that we would wish—no new devices need to be proposed, and seemingly exotic variations are reduced to the familiar. That is, generative linguistic theory already encompasses these facts. However, allowance for variant orders is crucial to such simplifications. To put the facts most succinctly, you only have locative 'have' when the subject *precedes* Infl, and you only have the locative proform when the subject *follows* Infl.

Having accounted for our two order-based generalizations, we turn to another: Languages with SVO order do not even participate in these two generalizations. Does this mean that SVO order is irrelevant to the unified analysis of locativity?

4.   Views of Word Order: Antisymmetry vs. Directionality

Interestingly, SVO languages appear not to participate in the complementarity we have been discussing, since an SVO language (e.g., French) may have both a locative proform and a possessive 'have' form. This fact suggests that there are three order types for phrase structure—verb initial, SOV, and SVO—and we will in fact conclude this below.

At this point, we should consider an analysis of order that seems opposed to our approach, that of Kayne (1994).

4.1 Kayne's Antisymmetry

In current theory, parametric base variation in order is no longer taken for granted. Kayne (1994), for example, argues that SVO is the only order, for all languages, for all syntactic levels. Kayne's motivation is the goal of the most restrictive theory of syntax possible. Here we give a brief summary of his theory.

For Kayne, syntax is *antisymmetric* in the sense that the relation between phrase structure and linear order never varies; this is the *Linear Correspondence Axiom* (LCA). Syntax would be *symmetric* if the same hierarchical structure were allowed to yield symmetric opposing linear orders—e.g., VO and OV—but the formal statement of the LCA rules out ordered pairs of terminals that are mirror images of each other. For example, if the ordered pair of terminals <j,m> is in the maximal set of ordered pairs, there is no ordered pair <m,j>. Furthermore, the LCA maps to precedence (e.g., ordering j always before m for a given pair <j,m>), and other principles (e.g., binary branching and the H-C [head before complement] order) dictate that specifiers are always to the left. Thus, syntax is always H-C, and adjunctions, including specifiers, are on the left. This yields SVO order.

To derive SOV, VOS, and other surface orders, movement is necessary. For example, "VOS must have . . . VO moving as a unit leftward past S, or else V and O moving separately leftward past S" (Kayne 1994:36). SOV arises by movement of O to some specifier (to the left) of V. There is no rightward movement. Additionally, there is no "directionality parameter" responsible for ordering variations, given the results summarized here; only SVO is possible. SVO order is maintained at every level via the various functional heads and their specifiers, which provide landing sites for movement.

As stated above, Kayne's arguments are based on the (certainly valid) goal of constructing a restrictive theory of syntax. The theory of antisymmetry is provocative and as such has spurred much research. We will consider its adequacy in dealing with the facts at hand.

4.2 Head Directionality

In earlier versions of generative theory, languages were seen to conform to a head parameter that determines whether a head is initial or final in its phrase. Greenbergian generalizations about the differences and parallels between VO and OV languages were claimed to follow from this parameter, since languages (and phrases) could be either head-initial or head-final. Clearly, if all languages have the same base order, such a parameter does not exist, and surface variations in order are due to movement or other operations. Then the differences in properties of languages with contrasting orders must arise during or as a consequence of the operations deriving their surface order. This is essentially the claim that Kayne (1994) makes.

A recent study maintaining the head-parameter approach is found in Saito and Fukui (1998) (henceforth S&F). S&F is an attempt to analyze certain differences between English and Japanese via, in part, a version of head-parameter theory. They maintain that Japanese is head-final in its base order, English head-initial, and that the directionality of adjunction follows the head parameter: "An adjoined phrase follows the head in head-initial languages and precedes the head in head-final languages" (p. 449). Assuming that scrambling (in Japanese) and heavy-NP-shift (in English) are both instances of adjunction, this approach allows S&F to account, inter alia, for the leftward movement of scrambling in Japanese and the rightward movement of heavy-NP-shift in English. Thus, these so-called optional movements can be seen as compatible with X-bar theory:

(15)   (S&F's examples 16 and 18)
    a. *IP-adjunction scrambling*
      [$_{IP}$ Sono hon-o$_i$ [$_{IP}$ Mary-ga   [$_{VP}$ John-ni t_i watasita]]] (koto)
      that book-ACC   Mary-NOM   John-to   handed   fact
      '[$_{IP}$ That book$_i$ [$_{IP}$ Mary handed t_i to John.]]'

    b. *Heavy-NP-shift*
      [$_{IP}$ Mary [$_{VP}$ [$_{VP}$ handed t_i to John] [the book she brought back from China.]$_i$]]

Formally, S&F propose to incorporate the intuition behind the head parameter into Chomsky's (1994) theory of bare phrase structure by *ordering* the two elements combined by any Merge operation. That is, Merge for Chomsky does not order α and β below, while it does for S&F (their ex. (32)):

(16)   MERGE:
      Chomsky: *Saito and Fukui:*
      $K = \{ \alpha, \{ \alpha, \beta \} \}$ $K = \{ \gamma, <\alpha, \beta> \}$, where $\gamma \in \{ \alpha, \beta \}$
                          a. $\gamma = \alpha$: head-initial, left-headed
                          b. $\gamma = \beta$: head-final, right-headed

S&F suggest, however, that agreement may yield an exception to this directionality: in English, for example, agreement forces a specifier to left-adjoin to X', contrary to the head parameter. This is called the "directionality of agreement; . . . only a YP left-adjoined to a projection of X agrees with X" (p. 449 ff.).[17] Thus, since an agreeing specifier cannot be on the right, S&F do not recognize parametrically determined VOS order. In presenting arguments in favor of head directionality below, we will return to S&F's analysis— particularly their conclusion that, effectively, there are no VOS languages.

4.3 SVO and the Locative Paradigm

Consider now the contrast in options provided in Kayne's theory as opposed to the head-parameter theory, for example (16). Is there really any difference? Is the position that VOS/VSO is derived from SVO by movement different from positing "basic" VOS/VSO? In particular, can the distinctions in order revealed in the locative paradigm be derived equally well or better in Kayne's approach? We will argue that only the variant-base-order approach accounts for the differences among languages that we have described.

Our set of claims is that there are three base order types; that verb initial and SOV are polar opposites; and that SVO is a distinct type.[18] This set is the converse of Kayne's theory that SVO is the basic order type and the other orders are derived from it.[19] From Kayne's view, our generalizations must arise in deriving different surface orders, in such a way as to set apart SVO languages in just this way, even though SVO order remains the structurally defining order for all languages.

Does the failure of SVO languages to participate in the complementarity mean that SVO is basic? It may seem so at first, but in fact SVO is relevant to the complementarity, in a negative way: it is an order identified as distinct in order based properties from verb initial and verb final, just as verb initial and verb final have been shown to be distinct in properties from each other. The position of SVO in this order typology cannot be taken to indicate that all observed order types are derived from SVO, any more than the position of VOS in this typology can be taken to mean that the other types are derived from VOS. The following section provides an illustration of this by describing an SVO-particular limitation within the locative paradigm.

4.4 My-Helicopter-Is

K'ekchi? (Mayan, VOS) has yet another locative-possessive construction, which we have affectionately named the *My-helicopter-is* construction.[20] Here, the subject is a *possessed theme* (see Freeze 1992a for more detail):

(17) **K'ekchi?**

    wan   iʃ-soʔsol-tʃʼitʃʼ   li   iʃq.
    COP[+loc] 3s.GEN-dragonfly-metal the woman
    'The woman has a helicopter.' (Lit. 'The woman's helicopter is.')

The subject of (17) is 'the woman's helicopter', the possessed-theme argument. In addition, in (17), the copula is locative, the possessor of the subject is a location, the argument set is location and theme, and the semantics matches that of possessive sentences, not that of possessed NPs; the *theme* must be indefinite:

(17') ... [[the woman's]   helicopter   ] is.
        [+definite possr] [–definite theme]

Thus, the elements are the same as in the locative paradigm, and we assume constructions like (17) are part of the paradigm.[21] It is not a particularly rare construction cross-linguistically.

In Freeze's analysis of (17), adopted here, the predicate phrase is DP rather than PP, and the possessor is in the specifier of the theme nominal. This NP moves out of DP to the specifier of Infl.[22] For obvious reasons, given our analysis, no 'have' lexicalization occurs or is possible in this structure (there is no stranded P). Also, true to our analysis of the proform above, and consonant with the unity of the locative paradigm in general, it is interesting to find that the possessed-theme structure may contain the locative proform; the following Palauan (VOS, W. Austronesian) version is an example:

(18) **Palauan**

    a. ŋ-ŋar   ŋii a   berruk.
       3S-COP.P 3S NP raft-1S
       'I have a raft.'   (Lit. 'My raft is.')

    b. ŋ-ŋar   ŋii [a   berrul a   Sie me a Toki].
       3S-COP.P 3S NP raft-3S NP Sie and NP Toki
       'Sie and Toki have a raft.' (Lit. 'Sie and Toki's raft is.')

c.

The position of the proform shows it to be in second position, and to the left of the subject.[23] The possibility of the proform in this construction, and the fact that the theme is always indefinite, are further evidence that it is part of the locative paradigm, and more particularly, that it is an existential.

The interest of the structure in (17) and (18) for this chapter is that the possessed-theme-subject existential apparently does not occur in languages with SVO order (though it is found in SOV and verb initial orders). This finding suggests that SVO has no more privileged position the locative paradigm than verb initial and verb final order do.[24] If it can be maintained (and further research is needed on this point), it reinforces our general theme. Such order-based restrictions are, again, difficult to explain if all languages are basically SVO.

We conclude this section with table 2, which sums up our findings so far. Interestingly, as the table shows clearly, only verb initial languages have both the proform and the possessed-theme subject; SOV order does not allow the former, and SVO order does not allow the latter.

Table 2 *Correlation of order types and locative structures.*

	Existential/ Possessive Locative Construction	Possessive 'have'	Existential proform	Possessed -theme subject
VOS/VSO	yes	no	yes	yes
SVO	yes*	yes	yes*	no[+]
SOV	yes	yes*	no	yes*

* Do not co-occur in the same language; see also table 1.
[+] Further research needed.

5. Locatives and Ordering Parameters

To summarize to this point, we have identified properties of locative constructions that correlate with order. We have found restrictions that are specific to verb initial, verb final, and SVO orders. And we have asked if these facts militate in favor of one or another theory of order, or whether there is really any difference between them. In this section we attempt a definitive answer.

In a theory like that of Kayne (1994), one order—SVO—is basic; other surface orders are derived from it, but, crucially, SVO order is maintained in all syntactic structures in all languages at all levels. Therefore, the facts of the locative paradigm must be accounted for in terms of basically SVO structures, or in the derivation to each surface order. Other chapters in this volume, as well as Kayne himself, have shown how VSO and other orders may be derived from SVO. However, if verb initial and verb final languages have an abstract SVO order (specifiers to the left, complements to the right, all trees right-branching, etc.) at every syntactic level, they should still have the locative properties of an SVO language: They should all allow 'have' (P combined with inflection) and the proform existential[25] (lexicalization of [+loc] inflection), and the possessed-theme structure should not occur. But these predictions are patently not borne out. Furthermore, as we have shown, even SVO imposes limitations of its own on the locative paradigm—limitations not realized in other orders.

Let us pursue the hypothesis that the generalizations we describe can be accounted for in the derivation of the various surface orders. Take first the verb initial orders. Say VSO order is derived by movement of V, or movement of VP, to the left of the subject (e.g., Lee this volume, Travis and Rackowski, this volume, and Massam this volume); similarly for VOS. Underlyingly, however, all structures have SVO, right-branching structure. Now, as we have shown, 'have' lexicalizations are a property of subject initial (or specifier-initial) order; this order is constant throughout the derivation in the one-base-order theory. Yet 'have' is at some point ruled out—by what means? For us, the VOS/VSO facts are the default case, if VOS/VSO are base orders.

Further, say that SOV-Infl order (as, e.g., in Japanese) arises à la Kayne, by movement of the subject leftward out of the predicate, and of the object to the left of the verb (and perhaps movement of V to the left of inflectional elements) or movement of the object to some specifier preceding the verb. (Recall that only leftward movement is allowed in this theory.) Though the existential proform is a property of VO order, including SVO, it cannot surface in SOV order. In our theory, it is a lexicalization of a [+locative] Infl, when Infl precedes the location argument. Infl in derived SOV locatives still has such a feature, and in Kayne's theory SOV is *not* underlyingly head-final. Therefore, our explanation in terms of second position and the precedence of Infl does not carry over to *derived* SOV languages, and no other account in strictly SOV terms is available.

Continuing to entertain the derivational analysis, say that all VO orders have, or acquire, the possibility of a locative proform in second position (provided that they do not present a locative subject in first position), and verb initial and OV orders acquire the possibility of a possessed-theme existential, even though the underlying SVO order does not allow the latter. What mechanism of UG would give rise to the structure in (17)? Does the same mechanism, or a different one, ensure that 'have', though common in SVO, does not occur in the possessed-theme existential? (Note that this issue is not a straw man, since our analysis integrates the distribution of 'have' closely with the other locative facts.) Certainly, SVO base order does not allow this locative variation to be predicted.

If variations away from SVO order can be derived by different sets of movements, what ensures that different derivations yielding the same order will also yield the correct generalizations? For example, for Kayne, apparently, head-final languages are languages whose post-head complements move to the left; final complementizers result from movement of IP into specifier of C. SOV can also be derived in other ways. The base position of V does not change with respect to its phrase or its IP. The usual second-position effects should follow, contrary to fact.

Similarly, the theory of derived order should ensure that different derivations—SVO→VSO and SVO→VOS—will result in *uniting* VSO and VOS for purposes of the locative paradigm, while distinguishing them from subject initial orders. We believe this could be done in the derivational theory only in an extremely ad hoc way. While our approach does not provide a theoretical unification of VSO and VOS, verb initial orders are unified by the generalization about 'have' lexicalizations, and our account does not separate them.

We presume, in general, that the derivations suggested above could be complicated in some way so as to give an account of the facts. It would still be difficult to convincingly relate them to SVO order, however, since these facts concern variations based on order classes alone, not optional or dialectal variation, or relative positions of heads. We do not see how the generalizations described herein can be stated in terms of constituent order in Kayne's theory. Though second-position effects and lexicalizations of inflectional features may be universal, and even universally PF, effects, still an SVO structure cannot produce head-final effects, vary in weak to strong Infl features, predict lexicalization of [+loc] based on order, and so on. We won't even broach the problems that reconstruction would pose.

Such complications and limitations can be dispensed with in accepting the head-parameter theory, and the simple explanations it allows could be retained: 'Have' doesn't arise in verb initial order simply because these languages instantiate the default case: The subject is locative. The existential proform does not arise in V-final order essentially because the locative would precede it: It is a second-position effect correlated to the features of the subject.

Saito and Fukui (1998) retain the head-parameter theory, showing that it allows a simple and elegant account of various differences between Japanese and English. The results of applying the head-parameter theory to the variations in locatives are similar. S&F claim, however, that their theory has an exception in the case of agreement: Only leftward specifiers participate in specifier/head agreement. Had S&F recognized VOS languages, their argument for directionality of heads would have been stronger. We have shown in this article that VOS languages exist, have robust properties following from their order, and allow specifier/head agreement with a rightward specifier.

In order to account for the position of the specifier, we adopt the idea of the *specifier parameter* suggested in Georgopoulos (1991a,b); essentially, XP can be projected from combining a specifier and an X' in either order. Updating this approach to S&F's theory in (16) above, we simply allow γ to be either a specifier or a head; then the structure can be specifier-initial or specifier-final. This yields VOS as well as SOV and SVO orders (it also yields OVS, which may be eliminated on other grounds; *op.cit.*).

6. Conclusions

This chapter is based on a limited class of data—just the locative facts. The data set itself classified the facts into the various ordering types, and the data show, without stipulation, that precedence along with order is a strong motivating factor in this variety. But each order label (say VOS, SVO or SOV) is also a surrogate for an immense array of distinctive syntactic properties which goes way beyond the variation in locative constructions, some of which properties act to distinguish each type from the other types. The differences among these types were at one stage considered implications of different principles or different sets of parameter settings, and we have argued that this is still the correct approach. To propose that all these sets of properties are derived from some other set of properties (e.g., from SVO) is to suggest something that cannot be established on the basis of linguistic data. Though such an analysis would allow us to achieve an enviable level of abstraction, there is no way to show empirically that one order is a priori the first order. Thus, to opt for one or the other approach may reflect theoretical preference rather than empirical necessity.

To conclude, we have related the absence of 'have' in the locative paradigm of the verb initial type to the absence of 'there' forms in the SOV type, and related both to differences in underlying word order. We conclude that the various restrictions on locative expressions are to some extent *diagnostic* of underlying differences in word order.

Notes

1. Germanic is a separate case; most of its proforms are not locative; see section 3.6 of Freeze (1992a) and section 2 below.

2. We don't address the difference(s) between VSO and VOS, referring below to "verb initial" order. We have found no differences between them in the locative paradigm. That is, locatives in VSO languages look like locatives in VOS languages. See, e.g., tables 1 and 2 below.

3. The syntactic analysis that follows is in GB form; it could be translated into the Minimalist Program framework (Chomsky 1995) without substantive change (e.g., replace IP with AgrPs and TensePs, assume heads are taken fully inflected from the lexicon, expand trees and insert arguments via Merge, etc.). The precise syntactic framework chosen does not affect our analysis, as far as we can see, and we in fact do not include a lot of detail about particular derivations below.

4. Also see Freeze (1992a) for the data sources.

5. The world's languages present an intricate array of possessive forms, both internally and comparatively. One form may be used to signal inalienably possessed themes while another (or others) are used for various alienable classes, varying also by definiteness. See also section 4.4.

6. Incorporation of P with Inflection of course has language-particular morphological spellout.

7. Danish and Dutch may be exceptional in a way similar to English.

8. Although a subject initial language may or may not have 'have' (see Russian 2c above), no V-initial language has 'have' to our knowledge.

9. *a*, glossed 'np', is a nominal marker.

10. We note that VOS order in general, and specifier/head agreement with rightward subjects in particular, are exceptions to the analysis in Saito and Fukui 1998, many of whose other arguments we support. See section 4.2.

11. We use a VOS structure to represent V-initial languages, since the analysis of VSO vs. VOS is not at issue here. See also note 2. We also give the two possibilities for SOV, either 'have' or locative possessive. Tree (c) is the SOV 'have' tree, on which there is no locative agreement.

12. We include this brief historical excursus in the spirit of Weerman (1989)'s prologue:

"From the beginning of the generative tradition it has been suggested that historical linguistics might play an important role, . . . [W]e consider all stages of the languages we investigate as equivalent with respect to Universal Grammar."

13. Interestingly, the Austronesian languages that have 'have' are SVO.

14. The fact that a locative proform cannot follow the locative phrase suggests that it is not an anaphor or a pronoun in the sense of Binding theory.

15. It does not conform to the analysis of clitic doubling in any substantive way: it does not have ϕ features; as a spellout of a feature of Infl it is not co-indexed with any argument; it does not force prepositional case on any other argument; it occurs in languages without other clitic phenomena; and so on.

16. We adopt an analysis on which second position is Infl rather than C.

17. S&F leave open the question of how this limitation can be derived.

18. The claim that there are three basic order—VOS/VSO, SVO, and SOV—does not depend on analysis of the locative paradigm alone. Georgopoulos (1991a), for example, arrives at this conclusion from looking at precedence facts of VOS languages and the distribution of weak crossover.

19. Nothing in Kayne (1994) requires specifier before head and head before complement; in our reading of his arguments, only stipulation prevents spec from being adjoined to the right. Likewise, arguments used to derive the conclusion that the LCA maps to precedence are based on consideration only of right-branching trees with a prior SVO order (chapter 4).

20. This construction is also attested, inter alia, in Hindi, Turkish, Hungarian, and Luiseño (all SOV), Palauan (VOS, Western Austronesian), as well as K'ekchi?.

21. Some languages having this construction, e.g., Hindi, also have the locative-subject possessive. Choice of one over the other may depend on the distinction between alienable and inalienable possession: In Hindi, locative subjects occur with alienable possession while possessed-theme subjects occur with inalienable possession. K'ekchi? does not make this structural distinction: It has only the structure in (17).

22. See also Szabolcsi (1981) for a similar analysis of Hungarian.

23. There is some evidence that the Palauan proform has become part of the morphology of the locative copula, in which case it is parallel to the lexically locative copula *you* in Chinese, *may* in Tagalog (see Freeze 1992a).

24. If the SVO facts depend on the weak/strong feature of Infl, then locativity may not be implicated; then we would have to examine the strength of Infl in VOS/SOV in order to arrive at a full account. Alternatively, if this structure is conditioned by the adjacency of S and O (as in SOV and VOS), SVO order may lack the structure simply "by default." But we would not expect (two different kinds of) movement of an argument to *enable* a particular existential form.

25. As we suggested in section 1, and as Freeze (1992a) shows in detail, the English existential, with a proform in subject position, is an oddity among existential forms. English 'there' is not a spellout of [+loc] Infl.

10

Prosodic Conditions
on Anaphora and Clitics in Jakaltek

Judith Aissen

In studies which reach back more than twenty years, Colette Craig described certain disjoint reference effects in Jakaltek, a Mayan language spoken in the highlands of Guatemala (Craig 1977), and one of the rigid VSO languages in the family. These effects are induced by the presence of an overt pronominal element, as in (1), where the two instances of *ix* can only refer to different women (the genitive follows the head in Jakaltek).[1,2]

(1) Xkolwa *ix*   yinh [smi'   *ix*].
     helped NCL(she)   P   her.mother   NCL(her)
     'She[i] helped her[j/*i] mother.' [158]

The co-referential interpretation is expressed by omitting the second instance of the pronoun (this omission is represented throughout by Ø, glossed PRO). In fact, this is the only interpretation of (2).

(2) Xkolwa *ix*   yinh [smi'   Ø].
     helped NCL(she)   P   her.mother   PRO
     'She[i] helped her[i/*j] mother.' [158]

Craig considered at length the conditions which determine the distribution of the overt pronominal and Ø, and established that the two elements are in something approaching complementary distribution. With respect to examples like (1) and (2), Craig's key observation was that the covert form of the pronoun is required when it is *preceded* in some local domain by an antecedent. Conversely, the overt form of the pronoun is required when it is not. As a consequence, the first pronoun in (2) cannot be omitted.

In line with early transformational approaches, Craig conceived of the alternation between the overt and covert pronouns in terms of deletion. For her, the Ø form arose only at a late point in the derivation, as a consequence of deletion. Deletion was possible only if the pronoun was preceded by its

185

antecedent within some local domain, a domain which Craig characterized in terms of syntactic boundaries. The facts were reinterpreted by Hoekstra (1989) within the Binding theory. For Hoekstra, both the overt and covert forms were present throughout the derivation, but they were subject to different clauses of the Binding theory. Essentially, the overt form was analyzed as a pronoun, hence subject to condition B, while the covert form was analyzed as an anaphor, hence subject to condition A. Hoekstra argued more generally that the level at which the binding conditions hold should be parameterized, with surface structure the relevant level in Jakaltek. This conclusion was forced on him by his framework, which included the assumption that precedence is relevant only at superficial levels of representation. Both Craig and Hoekstra, then, attributed the fact that precedence was the critical relation between the pronoun and its antecedent, (rather than, say, c-command) to the fact that the alternation between Ø and the overt pronominals was determined at a superficial level of syntactic representation. It is true that if (surface) precedence is the relevant relation, then the conditions must hold at a very superficial level. But the fact that c-command apparently plays no role remains unexplained.

In the present chapter, I suggest that precedence plays the key role in licensing the Ø pronoun because the relevant conditions refer to prosodic structure, not syntactic structure. In prosodic structure, precedence is a meaningful relation between elements, while c-command is not. Support for the prosodic account will come from the fact that the domain in which Ø must find its antecedent likewise corresponds to a prosodic constituent, the intonational phrase. If this analysis is correct, it bears on the nature of the connection between phonology and syntax/semantics. The licensing conditions on Ø require access to prosodic structure; but at the same time, Ø is an anaphor, and as such, its presence restricts both the form and interpretation of the sentence in which it occurs. The licensing of Ø therefore appears to require some communication between the phonology and the level at which anaphoric relations are represented. For a conception of grammar like the Minimalist Program in which PF and LF are isolated (Chomsky 1995), such facts are problematic.

This work is based on the material and analyses of Jakaltek presented in Day (1973a), Datz (1980), and especially Craig (1977), which contains most of the analysis and data on which this chapter draws. It also draws on previous analyses of Jakaltek pronouns by Foley and Van Valin (1984), Hoekstra (1989), and Trechsel (1995) .

1.   Jakaltek Pronouns

Unlike most Mayan languages, Jakaltek has overt pronominal elements. These are drawn from a set of "noun classifiers which classify concrete objects and spiritual entities in twenty-four classes" (Craig 1986a:245); see also Day (1973b) and Craig (1977, 1986a, 1986b). Common classifiers include *naj*, used to classify male non-kin, *ix* for female non-kin, *ya'* for respected human, *ho'* for siblings, *no'* for animals, and *ixim* for corn and corn products.

The noun classifiers precede the nouns they classify, but they also occur self-standing with pronominal function[3]:

(3) a. naj Pel   'Peter'
     b. naj winaj   'the man'
     c. naj   'he'

Not all nouns are associated with classifiers. In particular, nouns denoting abstract and other non-concrete elements are not. Elements not associated with a classifier have no overt pronominal form, and pronominal reference back to such elements always involves a null pronoun. Following Wallace (1992), I assume that the classifiers belong to the category Determiner (D), where D may select an NP complement (Abney 1987). This makes sense of their capacity to both occur with a nominal complement and without. The other property of the pronominal classifiers which is relevant here is that they can be omitted. That is, reference back to an established discourse referent is sometimes accomplished with the overt classifier, and sometimes with Ø.

The following excerpt from Datz (1980:332-3) illustrates some of these properties. The protagonist (Ramon) is named at the start, in topic position. Subsequent references are either by the noun classifier *naj*, used for non-kin males, or by the null element Ø.

(4) Naj Ramon, kaw xtxumtxun sk'ul   *naj*   tzet
     NCL Ramon, very thought   his.stomach NCL$_{(his)}$ how

     chu   yelkanh *naj;* xtxumniloj *naj*   yijb'antoj
     could flee   NCL$_{(he)}$ he.thought NCL$_{(he)}$ he.accompany

     Ø   heb'   ix   yeskinahil skayehal yatut   Ø,
     PRO   PL   NCL$_{(them)}$ its.corner its.street his.house PRO

     mach xin yohtajoj heb' ix   yorona   tzetet lanhan
     not   they.know PL   NCL 'llorona' what   was

     xtxumtxun sk'ul   *naj*   yinh   Ø...
     thinking   his.stomach NCL$_{(his)}$ in.him PRO
     'Ramon, he wondered how he could escape; he decided to
     accompany them to the corner of the street of his house
     without the "lloronas" knowing what he was thinking. . .'

2. Problems with a Binding Account

Examples like (1)–(2), repeated below as (5a,b), illustrate the fact that the overt pronominal classifier is used when a pronoun has no local antecedent, and that Ø is used when it does. (In the examples which follow, italicized expressions are to be understood as co-indexed.)

(5) a. *Xkolwa *ix*   yinh [smi'   *ix*].
    helped   NCL$_{(she)}$ P   her.mother   NCL$_{(her)}$
    'She$_i$ helped her*$_i$ mother.' [158]

  b. Xkolwa *ix*   yinh [smi'   Ø].
    helped NCL$_{(she)}$ P   her.mother   PRO
    'She$_i$ helped her$_{i/*j}$ mother.' [158]

Following Reinhart (1983), and more specifically Trechsel (1995), I will assume here that the disjoint reference associated with the overt pronominal classifier is a pragmatic inference which follows from the speaker's failure to use the Ø form where s/he could have. I focus then on the licensing conditions associated with Ø. With Hoekstra (1989), we could say that Ø is an anaphor, subject to (some version of) condition A. Assuming that the domain for the binding conditions is at least the clause, (5b) is grammatical because Ø is bound; ((5a) is ungrammatical with co-reference because Ø could have been used, and was not). However, while Ø is an anaphor, in the sense that it must be anteceded locally, its properties do not follow from condition A.

    The first problem is that the notion of "bound" and "free" which is relevant here does not involve c-command, but precedence; that is, the overt form cannot be *preceded* by a co-indexed element within the relevant domain. That precedence, rather than c-command, is the operative notion is suggested by examples like (6)–(8), in which the second pronoun is not c-commanded by the preceding co-indexed element, yet Ø must be used if co-reference is intended. In (6), the antecedent is a genitive within the subject; examples (7)–(8) involve preposing of a focused prepositional phrase,[4] with the antecedent a genitive within the object of that preposition:

(6)   Xkolwa [yunin   *ix*]   yinh [s-mi'   Ø/**ix*].
    helped her.child NCL$_{(her)}$ P   her.mother   PRO /NCL$_{(her)}$
    'Her$_i$ child helped her$_i$ mother.' [161]

(7)   [Boj smam   *naj*]   xtoyi Ø/**naj*.
    with his.father NCL$_{(his)}$ went PRO /NCL$_{(he)}$
    'It's with his$_i$ father that he$_i$ went.' [163]

(8)   [Sat [stx'at   *naj*]]   xhwayi Ø/**naj*.
    on   his.bed NCL$_{(his)}$ sleeps PRO /NCL$_{(he)}$
    'It's on his$_i$ bed that he$_i$ sleeps.' [161]

However, since genitives are known to take scope over the structure c-commanded by the NP or PP in which they are contained (Reinhart 1987), examples like (6)–(8) are not necessarily compelling. These might still be amenable to an account of Ø as bound variable anaphora. But there are examples in which the antecedent is much more deeply embedded, e.g., within a relative clause on a preposed object[5]:

(9) [Ixim ixim k'ochb'il yu *ix*]   xitoj   Ø   yinh molino.
     NCL corn shelled   by NCL$_{(her)}$ she.took PRO to   mill
     'It is the corn that she$_i$ had shelled that she$_i$ took to the mill.' [167]

In the face of this apparent indifference to hierarchical structure, there are two possible conclusions. One is that the structural relation between Ø and its binder is characterized in syntactic terms, but the relevant notion is precedence rather than c-command; the other is that this relation is not characterized in syntactic terms. Hoekstra (1989) takes the first tack. Because his discussion is embedded in a framework in which precedence is a property only of superficial levels of syntactic structure, Hoekstra concludes that the Binding theory is parameterized as to the level at which it holds, and that in Jakaltek, it holds at S-structure.[6]

As support for this interpretation of the facts, Hoekstra (1989) observes that reconstruction is irrelevant to the distribution of the pronominal classifiers and Ø (see also Craig 1977:163). As illustration, consider (10) which shows that if co-reference is intended, the first instance of the pronoun must be overt and the second Ø. Thus, of the four possible outcomes, only one is grammatical, that in which the first pronoun is overt and second is covert:[7]

(10) Yinh molino xitoj   *ix*/*Ø   [ixim k'ochb'il yu Ø/*ix].
      to   mill   2s.took NCL$_{(she)}$/PRO corn   shelled by PRO/NCL$_{(her)}$
      'To the mill she$_i$ took the corn that she$_i$ had shelled.' [167]

However, if the object is fronted for focus, the pronoun that must be covert in (10) comes to be first, and must now be overt; the pronoun that must be overt in (10) comes to be second and may now be covert, as in (9). If the conditions determining the distribution of Ø could be satisfied through reconstruction, the version in (11), where Ø is followed by *ix*, would be grammatical.

(11) *[Ixim ixim k'ochb'il yu Ø]   xitoj   *ix*   yinh molino.
      NCL corn shelled   by PRO she.took NCL$_{(she)}$ to   mill
      *'It is the corn that she$_i$ had shelled that she$_i$ took to the mill.'

But (11) is impossible. The fact that it is provides further corroboration that what is relevant here is surface precedence, and shows that any Binding theory account must be parameterized to a very superficial level of structure, per Hoekstra. So far, then, it seems possible to sustain a syntactic account of the distribution of Ø, as long as reference to precedence is permitted. However, when we turn to the question of the *domain* within which Ø is licensed, the syntactic account becomes less plausible.

Within the typology of Reuland and Koster (1991), Ø would not qualify as a short-range anaphor. Unlike the reflexive anaphor in Jakaltek, which is strictly clause-bounded (and must be anteceded by the subject) (Craig 1977:217, 362), Ø can be bound from outside the minimal clause, and across an intervening subject[8]:

(12) Xil   *ix*   [$_{VP}$ hawilni   *Ø*].
      she.saw NCL$_{(she)}$ you.look PRO
      'She$_i$ saw you looking at her$_i$.' [168]

(13) Xil   *ix*   [hawatx'en   skamixh   *Ø*].
      she.saw NCL$_{(she)}$ you.make   her.blouse PRO
      'She$_i$ saw you make her$_i$ blouse.' [169]

However, it might qualify as a medium-range anaphor. Reuland and Koster (1991) propose that medium-range anaphors satisfy two conditions: First, the domain within which they are bound coincides with the minimal domain of tense (or inflection) containing the anaphor; and second, the binder is a subject. However, neither of these properties holds for Jakaltek Ø. With respect to domain, there is an interesting range of cases in which it looks likes the domain within which Ø is bound does coincide with tense (cf. Foley and Van Valin 1984, esp. p. 298, table 12). The examples in (12)–(13), which allow binding across a subject, involve tenseless complements, while CP complements and adjuncts, which are inflected for tense, are barriers to binding of Ø:

(14) Chal   *naj*   [$_{CP}$ chub'il   chuluj   *naj/*Ø*].
      he.says NCL$_{(he)}$ that   will.come   NCL$_{(he)}$/PRO
      'He$_i$ says that he$_i$ will come.' [172]

(15) Chin=tzotel tet *ix*   an [yunhe sta'wi *ix*   wet   an].
      I.talk   to NCL$_{(her)}$ 1S so.that answers NCL$_{(she)}$ to.me 1S
      'I will talk to her$_i$ so that she$_i$ will answer me.' [280]

But setting the binding domain for Ø as the minimal tensed domain faces a serious obstacle: That Ø within a tensed relative clause can be bound from outside the relative clause:

(16) Xa'   *ix*   hune' kamixhe$_i$ [stz'isa   *Ø*   t$_i$]
      she.gave NCL$_{(she)}$ a   shirt   she.sewed PRO   t$_i$

      tet snoh   *Ø*.
      to   her.brother PRO
      'She$_j$ gave a shirt that she$_j$ had sewed to her$_j$ brother.' [165]

(17) Mat yohtajoj *ix*   naj$_i$ [xmaqni t$_i$ Ø yul parke].
     not she.knows NCL$_{(she)}$ NCL$_{(he)}$ WH.hit t$_i$ PRO in   park.
     'She$_j$ doesn't know the man that hit her$_j$ in the park.' [165]

(18) Xchiwa   sk'ul   *ya'*   yinh ni'an unin$_i$
     was.angry her.heart NCL$_{(her)}$ at   little child

     [xpohnitoj t$_i$ [sxih   Ø]].
     broke   t$_i$ her.pot PRO
     'She$_j$ was angry at the child who broke her$_j$ pot.' [166]

Examples like these indicate that the minimal domain of tense is not the correct characterization of the domain within which Ø must be bound.

Nor is it the case that the antecedent for Ø must be a subject. A number of earlier examples show this for cases in which Ø and its antecedent are clause-mates (e.g., 6–9). But even when they are not clause-mates, the antecedent need not be subject. Example (18), where the antecedent is grammatically genitive, is one case; example (19) is another:

(19) Xkin=b'ey wila' [yatut$_i$ *naj*
     I.went   I.see his.house NCL$_{(his)}$

     [swatx'e [sk'ahol Ø   ] t$_i$]].
     he.made   his.son PRO
     'I went to see his$_j$ house that his$_j$ son made.' [166]

In sum, the relation between Ø and its antecedent is constrained by none of the properties which typically constrain the relation between a medium-range anaphor and its binder—the antecedent need not c-command Ø, the antecedent need not be a subject, and the two may be members of separate tensed domains. Taken together, these facts suggest that a binding condition which is defined over syntactic structure is not correct. In the following section, I argue that there is a straightforward *prosodic* characterization of the domain in which Ø must be bound.

3. The Intonational Phrase as 'Binding' Domain

The basic proposal is that Ø must find an antecedent within the intonational phrase that contains it.[9]

(20) CONDITION ON Ø:
      The anaphor Ø must be co-indexed with a nominal which precedes it within the same intonational phrase.

In Aissen (1992), an algorithm for deriving intonational phrasing from phrase structure in Jakaltek was proposed to account for a different set of facts, discussed below in section 4. This algorithm depended crucially on the fact that CP complements obligatorily extrapose in Jakaltek (Craig 1977:248). Thus, normal order is VSOX, but when O is a CP, it follows adverbials:

(21) Xal naj tet anma   yul parke ewi
      said he to people in park yesterday

      [chub'il chim huluj naj presidente konhob'].
      that   may come the president village
      'He said to the people in the park yesterday that the president may come to the village.'

In contrast, relative clauses and tenseless complements do not extrapose:

(22) Xitij   [naj   ah   hoyom [x'apni yet   qani
      he.brought NCL$_{(he)}$ from T.S.   arrived when last night

      boj   sk'ahol Ø]] ixim.
      with his.son PRO corn
      'The [man] from Todos Santos [who came last night with his son] brought corn.' [194]

(23) X'okkanh [ha=loq'ni ha=cheh]   yinh ha=k'ul.
      entered you.buy your.horse in   your.stomach
      'You decided to buy yourself a horse.' [255]

I will not review the algorithm proposed in the earlier article except to say that it involved alignment of the right edge of an ungoverned maximal projection with the right edge of an intonational phrase. Under the phrase-structural assumptions of that article (which still seem reasonable), extraposed clauses and topics were not governed. What that algorithm achieved, and what must be achieved by any such algorithm, is a division of the sentence into (potentially) three spans, each corresponding to a separate intonational phrase: the topic, the body of the clause (containing the focus, core arguments, relative clauses, and tenseless complements), and what we might term the tail, consisting of any (extraposed) CP complement or subordinate adverbial clause.

(24)

TOPIC	BODY	TAIL (Extraposed CP)

Day's description of Jakaltek (1973) provides phonological evidence that each of these spans corresponds to a separate prosodic constituent. He distinguishes several forms of juncture, including one which corresponds to what I call *intonational phrase*:

> The juncture ≠ sets off some major constituents from the remainder of the sentence, . . . Its occurrence with some constituents is optional. The more important the syntactic separation, the more likely that it will be marked by ≠. At some syntactic breaks ≠ is accompanied by a contour. [p. 20]

Relevant here are those instances of ≠ that are accompanied by contour (contour is indicated phonetically by a change in pitch on the last stressed syllable before the juncture). It is precisely those breaks that are accompanied by contour that mark the boundaries of the domain relevant to the distribution of the overt pronoun and its covert counterpart.

Day's description supports the spans that are identified in (24). It makes clear that topics and extraposed and adjunct clauses constitute their own intonational phrases (pp. 22–23, 87–88, 103), while relative clauses, tenseless complements, and preverbal focus do not (pp. 72, 84–87, 89). All three of the latter constructions are subsumed in larger intonational phrases.

How these three spans might correspond to the syntactic representation is shown in figure 1, following the phrase-structural assumptions of Aissen (1992). The topic (see Jelinek, this volume, for a different view of topic and focus) is adjoined to the root node; the focus occupies specifier of IP, and extraposed CPs are adjoined to VP.[10]

Figure 1

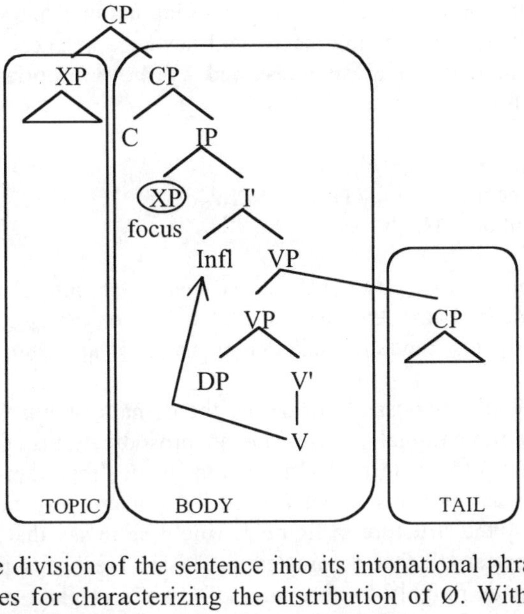

The division of the sentence into its intonational phrases provides the right structures for characterizing the distribution of Ø. Within a simple sentence, reference back to an antecedent within the same sentence can always be accomplished by Ø, as in examples (2) and (5)–(8). The Ø form is possible because a simple sentence falls under a single intonational phrase. Within a relative clause or a tenseless (non-extraposed) complement, reference back to an antecedent outside that clause may also be accomplished by Ø, as in examples (12)–(13), (16)–(18). Again, this is true because such structures are part of larger intonational phrases, and as long as the antecedent is contained within that larger intonational phrase, reference back to it by Ø will be possible. Since extraposed and adjunct CPs constitute their own intonational phrases, reference back to an antecedent outside the CP always requires the overt pronominal; see (14)–(15).

There are differences in the prosodic relation of the topic and focus to the rest of the clause, and these differences generate a set of predictions concerning Ø. As noted above, the topic constitutes its own intonational phrase, while the focus is subsumed into a larger intonational phrase. Under the prosodic account developed here, (20) predicts that Ø within the body of the clause can be anteceded by a nominal within the focus. That this is true is shown by examples (8)–(9), repeated below:

(25)   [Sat [stx'at   *naj*]]ⱼ   xhwayi Ø   tⱼ.
       on his.bed NCL(his)   sleeps   PRO
       'It's on hisᵢ bed that heᵢ sleeps.' [161]

(26)   [Ixim ixim k'ochb'il yu *ix*]ⱼ   xitoj   Ø   tⱼ yinh molino.
       NCL   corn shelled   by NCL(her) she.took PRO to   mill
       'It is the corn that was shelled by herᵢ that sheᵢ took to the mill.' [167]

However, since the topic is contained in a separate intonational phrase from what follows, Ø within the body of the clause will never be anteceded by the topic. Accordingly, the topic is always resumed by the appropriate overt pronominal classifier (if one exists), as in (27)–(28):

(27)   *Naj pel*   [smaq   *naj/*Ø*   ix].
       NCL Peter   he.hit NCL(he)/ PRO   NCL(her)
       'Peterᵢ, heᵢ hit her.' [12]

(28)   *Wal naj tz'um*   *wex*   xin, [xal   ya'   mame tet *naj*   ta...]
       but NCL leather   pants   ENC he.said NCL father to NCL(him) that...
       'But Leather Pantsᵢ, the father said to himᵢ that ...' [Datz 1980, 374]

I conclude, then, that it is possible to define the domain within which Ø must be bound as the intonational phrase—i.e. in prosodic terms. Can this domain be defined in syntactic terms? One would expect that it might be possible, since intonational phrasing is determined by syntactic structure. One possibility, suggested by the structure in figure 1, would be to say that Ø must be bound within the lowest CP that dominates it. This is Trechsel's proposal (1995), and it corresponds roughly to an update of Craig's original proposal, which was stated in terms of syntactic boundaries. Such an account makes most of the same predictions as the prosodic account. The two accounts might make different predictions about relative clauses, depending on whether they are CPs or not. If they are, then the syntactic account makes the wrong prediction (see examples 16–18), while the prosodic account makes the right prediction. Relative clauses in Jakaltek contain no overt relative pronoun or complementizer, so it is not clear whether they are CPs or not; Trechsel (1995) assumes they are not.

However, even if the syntactic account is descriptively adequate, it seems less satisfactory on several fronts than the prosodic account. To judge from Reuland and Koster (1991), setting the binding domain for Ø as the lowest CP which contains it neither aligns Jakaltek with other well-known cases, nor does it make any sense of the fact that this binding is blind to hierarchical structure and sensitive rather to precedence. In contrast, defining the domain prosodically suggests a way to understand the importance of precedence, and the irrelevance of c-command. While hierarchical syntactic structure, as constituted by the c-command relations among elements of various categories, is relevant to the determination of prosodic phrasing, once that phrasing is determined, c-command and category type become irrelevant, and what is left as the audible form of syntactic structure is precisely precedence and phrasing. Thus, characterizing the domain condition on Ø in prosodic terms predicts exactly what is found: The domain corresponds to a prosodic constituent, and the relevant relation is precedence, not c-command. A characterization of the domain in syntactic terms (minimal containing CP) still leaves the irrelevance of c-command without any explanation.

There is further evidence that the domain in which Ø is licensed corresponds to a prosodic constituent: This same domain defines the host for the enclitic *an*, a clitic which occurs optionally in sentences containing a first person pronoun.

4.   Intonational Phrase as Host for Encliticization

The clitic *an* is subject to two licensing conditions, one prosodic and one syntactic: It attaches to the right edge of a prosodic domain; and it occurs only in domains which contain a first person pronoun.[11] The intonational phrase is the relevant domain for both conditions. The grammatical function of the licensing pronoun is irrelevant, and *an* may be located far from the position canonically associated with that function. The examples in (29) illustrate *an* licensed by a first person which is, respectively, subject, object, and genitive. Here, the agreement morphology associated with the licensor is italicized; first and second person pronouns usually do not occur overtly, but are cross-referenced on governing heads. Cross-hatch indicates an intonational phrase boundary.

(29) a. Xk*in*=to   hawatut   *an*. #
   I.went   your.house   1ST
   'I went to your house.' [278]

    b. Xk*in*=hawil   tx'onhb'al   *an.* #
       you.saw.me   market   1ST
       'You saw me in the market.' [278]

    c. Xkam   *hin*cheh   *an.* #
       died   my.horse   1ST
       'My horse died.' [277]

Craig (1977) defined the distribution of *an* in terms of the same syntactic boundaries which she saw as relevant to the distribution of Ø and the overt classifiers. However, that the position of *an* should be defined phonologically, rather than syntactically, is suggested by Day (1973a:56), who calls *an* a "sentence clitic" which occurs "only before contour". The term "sentence clitic" is a misnomer, since *an* frequently occurs *internal to* what we would term a sentence on syntactic grounds. In Aissen (1992), *an* is analyzed as a clitic which attaches to the right edge of an intonational phrase, subject to the condition that that phrase contain a first person pronoun (the licensor). While *an* is optional when the first person licensor is singular, it is obligatory when the licensor is first person plural exclusive, and impossible when the licensor is first person plural inclusive (Craig 1977:277). Thus, *an* has two functions, one prosodic, the other semantic: It demarcates the right edge of an intonational phrase, and it distinguishes first person plural exclusive from inclusive.

    Since simple clauses form a single intonational phrase, *an* occurs sentence-finally in examples like (29). More complex examples confirm that the domain in which *an* must find its licensor coincides exactly with the domain in which the covert anaphor, Ø, must find its antecedent.

    In structures containing tenseless complements and relative clauses, *an* occurs at the right edge of the sentence, even when its licensor occurs in the main clause:

    (30) *tenseless complement*
         Xil   wanab'   [$_{VP}$hawek'   yul kaya] *an.* #
         she.saw my.sister   you.pass   in   street 1ST
         'My sister saw you go by in the street.' [279]

    (31) *relative clause*
         *W*ohtaj naj$_i$ [xul t$_i$ ewi]   *an.* #
         I.know   NCL$_{(he)}$ came   yesterday 1ST
         'I know the man who came yesterday.' [279]

By hypothesis, this is true because the whole sentence falls under a single intonational phrase, and *an* is licensed at the right edge of that intonational phrase. Example (32) illustrates rather dramatically the fact that *an* occurs sentence-finally even when its licensor is located within a sentence-internal relative clause:

(32) Xitoj   [ya' komam   [xhmunla yinh *hin* mam]]
      he.sent   NCL older.man works   for   my father

[no' chech [i'o' ixim   ixim   tinanh]] *an*. #
NCL   horse carry NCL   corn   today   1ST
'The old man who works for my father sent the horse to carry
the corn today.' [279]

Here again, this complex sentence falls under a single intonational phrase, so
that *an* is prosodically licensed; it is also syntactically licensed, since that
intonational phrase contains a first person pronoun. Examples (30)–(32) parallel
(12)–(13) and (16)–(18) above in which the Ø anaphor within a tenseless
complement or a relative clause finds its antecedent in the matrix clause.

The facts are different in the case of extraposed complements and adjunct
clauses. When the main clause contains a first person, then any *an* which it
licenses must occur *before* the extraposed complement (33) or adjunct (34),
rather than sentence-finally:

(33) Xwal tet naj   (*an*) # [CP chub'il ch'ahtoj naj
      I.say to NCL(him) 1ST   that   climb.up NCL(he)

swi' te' nhah] (**an**). #
its.top NCL house 1ST
'I told him to climb on the roof.' [281]

(34) Lanhan *hin*tx'ahni xil qape   (*an*) # [yet   xkach=huli] (**an**). #
      ASP   I.wash   NCL clothes 1ST   when you.came   1ST
      'I was washing clothes when you came.' [280]

These examples fall under two intonational phrases, with the break marked
exactly by the position of *an*. The *prosodic* licensing condition is satisfied by the
ungrammatical examples, but the *syntactic* condition is not, since the second
intonational phrase does not contain a first person. These examples parallel
(14)–(15) above, which show that the Ø anaphor within an extraposed clause
cannot be anteceded by an element within the main clause, since the two are not
within the same intonational phrase.

As expected, if the antecedent for *an* is within the extraposed clause, then
an occurs sentence-finally:

(35) Xal   naj   # [chubil x'apni *hin* mam *watut]   *an*. #
      he.said NCL(he)   that   arrived my father my.home 1ST
      'He said that my father had arrived at my house.' [284]

In this case, both licensing conditions are satisfied. (See also example (15), in
which *an* is licensed twice, in distinct intonational phrases.)

The differences seen earlier between topic and focus are replicated in the distribution of *an*. If the topic contains a first person, then *an* is licensed but occurs between the topic and the remaining sentence. Since this position coincides with an intonational phrase break, *an* is licensed here prosodically:

(36) *W*uxhtaj   *an* # [sloq'   ho'   no' cheh k'ej'inh tu'].#
      my.brother 1ST he.brought NCL$_{(he)}$ NCL horse black   that
      'My brother, he bought that black horse.' [280]

Note that the pronoun which resumes the topic (*ho '*) must be overt, because its antecedent is located in a different intonational phrase.

However, when the focus contains a first person, *an* occurs not immediately following the focus, but at the first intonational phrase break following the focus:

(37) [Ha' [*hin* mam]$_i$] xal   naj   *an* # [chubil x'apni   t$_i$]. #
      FOC   my father   he.said NCL$_{(he)}$ 1ST that   arrived
      'It is my father that he said had arrived.' [283]

Example (37) is particularly interesting because the focus is extracted from the embedded (extraposed clause). Nonetheless, it is contained within the first intonational phrase, not the second, and it is this that determines which intonational phrase hosts cliticization of *an*.[12]

I conclude, then, that the domain which Craig established as relevant to the distribution of the pronominal classifiers and Ø corresponds to a prosodic domain—exactly the domain that determines the position and distribution of *an*. This predicts certain interactions between pronoun realization and *an*. In a sequence of clauses like that of (38), in which the first clause contains a first person and a third person, the presence of *an* between the two clauses signals the edge of an intonational phrase; accordingly, reference in second clause back to the same third person will require an overt classifier.

(38) [....third person$_i$...] *an* # [.....NCL$_i$..]#

Examples (15) and (36) above conform to this prediction. So does the text example in (39), where the pronoun *ix* 'she' in the second clause is anteceded by *ix yajaw kusina*, 'the cook' in the first:

(39) Chi*n*to *w*ala' tet ix yajaw   kusina-h   *an* #
      I.go   I.talk to NCL mistress kitchen   1ST

      [ta   swatx'e ix   hawan]. #
      that   she.make NCL$_{(she)}$ your.medicine
      'I'm going to tell the cook$_i$ that she$_i$ make medicine for you (lit. your medicine).' [Datz 1980:407]

It appears, then, that the domain in which *an* is licensed coincides with that in which Ø must be bound. While it is of course possible that the two domains accidentally coincide, the position taken here is that they coincide because the distribution of both *an* and Ø is defined over the same prosodic domain. The position and distribution of *an* and the alternation between Ø and the overt pronominal classifiers work together to mark the chunking of discourse into intonational phrases.

5. Conclusion

The proper account of the covert anaphor Ø in Jakaltek requires simultaneous reference to two kinds of information, prosodic and syntactic. The need to refer to prosodic structure in an account of Jakaltek Ø could be satisfied quite directly within a model like the Minimalist program by assuming that Ø arises through deletion of a pronominal classifier at PF. This deletion, which represents a return to Craig's original analysis, might be analogized to the PF deletion which Chomsky envisages for ellipsis (1995:202ff.). However, PF cannot be the only level involved. Deletion depends on co-indexation, and the relevant indices are not present in prosodic structure. They are present at LF, and this implies the need for some communication between PF and LF.

The Jakaltek material thus provides support for the view that the phonology and syntax cannot be entirely isolated from one another, and further, that the interaction is not limited to the construction of prosodic structure on the basis of a syntactic representation. What is required is not wholesale access to the phonology, but just access to prosodic structure, and this is consistent with the suggestion of Zec and Inkelas (1990) that such communication be mediated exactly by prosodic structure.

Acknowledgments

Thanks to Sandra Chung, Andrew Carnie, and an anonymous reviewer for comments on an earlier version of this article, and to James McCloskey and Daniel Büring for discussion. I am especially grateful to Victor Montejo (University of California, Davis) for clarifying a number of questions, and for help with several examples. An earlier version of some of this material was presented to the Yale Linguistics Colloquium in 1990.

Notes

1. Unless otherwise noted, all page references are to Craig (1977). Throughout, orthography has been changed from original sources to conform with that put forth by Academia de las lenguas mayas (1988). However, word boundaries in the original sources are retained. Unfamiliar symbols may include {tx, tx', x} which represent a series of retroflex consonants, {ch, ch', xh}, a series of palatal consonants, the velar nasal {nh} and the velar fricative {j}. Abbreviations which appear in glosses are: ASP: aspect;

ENC: enclitic; FOC: focus marker; NCL: noun classifier; P: preposition; PL: plural: PRO: Ø anaphor; 1ST: 1st person enclitic. The symbol = links prosodically distinct words which are glossed as a unit.

2. In Jakaltek, verbs are rigidly classified as transitive or intransitive. Transitive verbs agree with both subject and object through a system of agreement which is organized along ergative lines in tensed clauses, and along what has been called "extended ergative" in untensed clauses. That is, the ergative markers are extended to intransitive subjects in untensed clauses. Furthermore, nouns agree with their possessors. Morphological analysis of words is not provided, but nouns and verbs which contain an agreement marker are glossed with the corresponding pronoun (e.g., *smi'* 'her.mother' in (1) and *xitoj* 'she.took' in (9)). In tensed clauses with third person subjects, this distinguishes transitive from intransitive verbs, since third person intransitive subjects are not cross-referenced. Thus, *xitoj* in (9), glossed 'she.took', is transitive, while *xkolwa* in (1), glossed 'helped', is intransitive.

3. The classifiers are glossed throughout by NCL, regardless of function. An English translation is given in parentheses for classifiers in pronominal function.

4. The verbs in (7)–(8) end in the terminal element *-i*, which appears only before contour; if the overt subject pronoun were possible in these examples, *-i* would not appear, yielding *xto* and *xhway*.

5. According to Victor Montejo, the second pronoun in (9) may also be overt (i.e., *ix*).

6. In what follows, I continue to refer to the relation between Ø and the expression which licenses it—e.g., *ix* in 9—as *binding*, and I use the term *antecedent* interchangeably with *binder*.

7. Thanks to Victor Montejo, who confirmed that (10) is ungrammatical if the first pronoun is covert; likewise (11).

8. According to Craig (1977), the Ø form in (13) can be replaced by the overt form of the pronoun without resulting in disjoint reference. Craig attributes this to two factors: The fact that the pronoun is a genitive, and the fact that it is located within a different clause than its antecedent. Some speakers also allow the overt pronoun in (12).

9. There is one regular exception to this which refers to the grammatical function of Ø. Craig (1977) notes that Ø in genitive function can find its antecedent outside the domain which she identifies as relevant to Ø, and the texts of Datz (1980) confirm this. When Ø occurs in object function in the second of two coordinate clauses, it is sometimes omitted if its antecedent has parallel function in the first coordinate clause (Craig 1977:169ff).

10. Extraposed CPs might be adjoined higher.

11. I treat *an* here not as the first person pronoun itself, but as an element which must be licensed by the presence of a first person pronoun somewhere within the relevant domain. Two problems arise if *an* itself is interpreted as the first person (argumental) pronoun. First, *an* may co-occur with the lexeme which is usually considered the first person pronoun, *hayin* 'I'. Second, in domains containing several first person pronouns (e.g., analogues of 'I went to my house'), only one instance of *an* is ever possible.

12. In Aissen (1992), I considered the question whether the constituent to which *an* attaches could be defined syntactically, and concluded that it could not. This conclusion depends crucially on where the extraposed clause attaches.

11

Animacy Hierarchies and Sentence Processing

Seth Minkoff

This chapter offers an explanation for the well-known observation that, in certain languages but not in others, the acceptability of any particular subject-object pairing in an unmarked[1] transitive active declarative clause is determined according to a criterion along the lines of (1), by which an argument's degree of animacy is determined by an animacy hierarchy minimally along the lines of (2). (See, for example, Hale 1973, Creamer 1974, and Witherspoon 1977.)

(1)   The subject of any transitive verb must be at least as animate as its object.

(2)   human > animal > plant > mineral

An example of a language that obeys (1) is Mam-Maya.[2] In Mam, sentences like (3a–c) are acceptable because, in each case, the subject is at least as animate as the object, as required by (1).[3]

(3) a Ø-Ø-t-il   qya   tx'yan.
       DC-ABS3S-ERG3S-see   woman   dog
       'The woman saw the dog.'

   b. Ø-Ø-kub'   t-b'ajsa-'n   tx'yan   k'uul
       DC-ABS3S-DIR   ERG3S-kill-TV+DIR   dog   plant
       'The dog killed the plant.'

   c. Ø-Ø-kub'   t-b'ajsa-'n   k'uul   ab'j[4]
       DC-ABS3S-DIR   ERG3S-destroy-TV+DIR   plant   rock
       'The plant destroyed the rock.'

In contrast, sentences like (4a–c) are unacceptable, as indicated by the symbol #, because in each case the subject is less animate than the object, contra the requirements of (1):

(4) a. #Ø-Ø-t-il   tx'yan   qya.
     DC-ABS3S-ERG3S-see   dog   woman
     'The dog saw the woman.'

    b. #Ø-Ø-kub'   t-b'ajsa-'n   k'uul   tx'yan.
       DC-ABS3S-DIR   ERG3S-kill-TV+DIR   plant   dog
       'The plant killed the dog.'

    c. #Ø-Ø-kub'   t-b'ajsa-'n   ab'j   k'uul.
      DC-ABS3S-DIR   ERG3S-kill/destroy-TV+DIR   rock   plant
      'The rock destroyed/killed the plant.'

An example of a language that seems exempt from (1) is English. English sentences are acceptable whether they satisfy (1), as in (5–6), or not, as in (7–8):

    (5)   The woman saw the dog.
    (6)   The dog killed the plant.
    (7)   The dog saw the woman.
    (8)   The plant killed the dog.[5]

In this work, I offer an answer to the following question: Why does (1) seem to determine the acceptability of subject-object pairings in Mam but not in English?

I will argue that, contra the spirit of proposals by authors including Hale (1973), Creamer (1974), England (1991), and Witherspoon (1977), where (1) is grammaticalized, the answer to this question is to be found in the way the human language processor interacts with certain independent properties of syntax.

Section 1 argues that, on the reasonable assumption that the processor is subject to what I shall call the *Base Generation Bias* (9) (following the spirit of Bever 1970 and Tabossi et al. 1994, among others), Mam and English differ in terms of when each allows the processor to determine which argument is the subject.

    (9)   BASE GENERATION BIAS (BGB):
        All other factors being equal, considerations of frequency of occurrence cause the language processor to prefer a base generated analysis of any declarative sentence.[6,7]

First, English is verb medial and does not allow *pro*-drop of the leftmost argument (the subject, as it happens). Either of these facts alone is sufficient to enable the processor of an English sentence to determine which NP is the subject after identifying just one NP; by contrast, Mam is verb initial and does allow *pro*-drop of the leftmost argument (the subject). These two facts together conspire to prevent the processor from determining which NP is the subject until it has identified both the subject and object NPs.

Next, section 2 argues that the processor is innately structured to obey the *Graded Animate Agent Preference* (10).

(10)   GRADED ANIMATE AGENT PREFERENCE (GAAP):
The more animate a potential agent, the more highly the human language processor values the interpretation that assigns it the agent role (absent any reason to do otherwise).

The content of (10) reflects previous findings that the processor prefers to analyze animate NPs as agents and subjects. (See, for example, Clark 1965, Johnson 1967, Bever 1970, Jarvella and Sinnott 1972, Itagaki and Prideaux 1985, McDonald, Bock, and Kelly 1993, Trueswell, Tanenhaus, and Garnsey 1994, and McRae, Spivey-Knowlton and Tanenhaus 1998.) Moreover, it is reminiscent of Clark and Begun's (1971) finding that the acceptability of subjects of transitive verbs patterns according to the hierarchy in (11), with human nouns being the most acceptable subjects, and abstract mass nouns being the least acceptable subjects.

(11)   human nouns > animal nouns > concrete count nouns > concrete mass nouns > abstract count nouns > abstract mass nouns

The GAAP differs from Clark and Begun's proposal in two important respects. First, it operates in terms of animacy, and therefore accords "plant nouns" a status distinct from other concrete count nouns (see (2)). Second, as I will argue below, it entails that the hierarchy of noun types should influence decisions that the language processor makes regarding which NP is likely to be an agent and therefore, in many cases, a subject.

Section 3 argues that (1) is obeyed by Mam, and flouted by English, because of how the BGB and the GAAP interact with the distinct timings of subject determination for each of these languages—that is, with the fact that the processor determines the subject after identifying just one NP in English, but both NPs in Mam. Whether or not a language obeys (1) turns out to follow not from how any rule of grammar addresses the animacy of subjects versus objects but, instead, from how innate properties of the processor interact with independent syntactic variables of verbal position (verb initial/final vs. verb medial) and *pro*-drop.

1.   The Difference between English and Mam

The difference between English and Mam observed above—namely, that Mam obeys (1) and English does not—correlates with the fact that, given an unmarked transitive active declarative sentence (henceforth a "transitive sentence"), the processor cannot determine which argument is the subject as quickly for Mam as it can for English.

Given the BGB (9), when the processor analyzes an English transitive sentence such as (12), or indeed any transitive sentence in any language that is verb medial or forbids *pro*-drop of the leftmost argument (henceforth, "leftmost *pro*-drop"), the processor can determine which NP is the subject before it identifies the second (i.e., rightmost) argument.

(12)   The dog saw the woman.

Suppose, on the one hand, that the order of arguments is, like that of English, subject-before-object. First, if this language is verb medial, then, once the processor identifies the verb—which is to say, before it identifies the second argument—it knows that the subject must be the argument preceding the verb. This holds true even if the language allows leftmost *pro*-drop since, if the processor identifies no argument preceding the verb, it will know that the sentence must have a *pro* subject. Second, if this language forbids leftmost *pro*-drop, then, as soon as the processor identifies the first argument—once again, before it identifies the second argument—it knows this argument must be the subject. Obviously, this holds true even if the language is not verb medial. Suppose, on the other hand, that the language's word order is object-before-subject. If this language is verb medial, then, once the processor identifies the verb—once again, before it identifies the second argument—it knows that the subject must be the argument following the verb; if no such argument can be identified, it posits a *pro* subject. If this language forbids leftmost *pro*-drop, then, as soon as the processor identifies the first argument—before it identifies the second argument—it knows the subject must be the second argument. Returning now to the case in point, since English is verb medial and forbids leftmost *pro*-drop, it follows that, even before the argument *the woman* is identified, the processor can tell that the subject of (12) is *the dog*. Broadly put, the syntactic properties of English allow the processor to determine the subject "earlier" rather than "later."[8]

In contrast, Mam is a verb initial language, and it allows leftmost *pro*-drop. Therefore, the leftmost argument (the subject, as it happens) in any Mam transitive sentence may be either overt as in (13a), or covert as in (13b).[9,10]

(13) a. Ø-Ø-t-il   qya   ab'j.
        DC-ABS3S-ERG3S-see   woman   rock
        'The woman saw the rock.'

     b. Ø-Ø-t-il   *pro* ab'j.
        DC-ABS3S-ERG3S-see   *pro* rock
        'She/he/it saw the rock.'

When the processor analyzes a Mam transitive sentence like (13a), or indeed any transitive sentence in any verb initial language that allows leftmost *pro*-

drop, the processor cannot determine which argument is the subject until it has identified both arguments, assuming again the BGB (9). Suppose, on the one hand, that the language's word order is, like that of Mam, subject-before-object. Here, verb initiality and the permissibility of leftmost *pro*-drop combine to guarantee that, before the processor identifies the second argument, it cannot know which argument is the subject. This is so because, without *pro*-drop, the subject will be the first argument identified, and with *pro*-drop, it will be the second; furthermore, since the language is verb initial, the processor cannot use an argument's position relative to the verb to determine whether it is the subject, as it can in English. Suppose, on the other hand, that the language's word order is object-before-subject. Here, verb initiality and the permissibility of leftmost *pro*-drop once again combine to guarantee that, before the processor identifies the second argument, it cannot know which argument is the subject. This is so because, without *pro*-drop, the subject will be the second argument identified, and with *pro*-drop, it will be the first; and, once again, the language's verb initiality prevents the processor from using an argument's position relative to the verb to determine whether it is a subject. Returning now to the case in point, when the processor of the Mam sentence (13a) is at the point of having identified *qya*, but not *ab'j*, the status of *qya* is ambiguous, forcing a postponement of the determination of subjecthood until more information is available. Broadly put, the syntactic properties of Mam force the processor to determine the subject later rather than earlier.[11]

2. The Graded Animate Agent Preference

I will argue that the difference in the timing of subject determination in English and Mam combines with the effects of the GAAP to cause Mam to obey (1), and English not to. This argument first requires a closer look at the GAAP.

The GAAP claims that the processor is innately configured so that it values any interpretation that assigns the agent role to any NP that might bear it, and that this value is proportional to the animacy of the NP in question. The processor's predilection for agency can be seen in English sentences like (14a–14c):

(14) a. Mary hit John.
 b. Mary hindered John.
 c. Mary helped John.

In each of these examples, *Mary* can be interpreted either as an agent—that is, as causing intentionally the event in which she participates—or else as a mere causer, that is, as causing the event in which she participates with no intention of doing so.[12] In each case, the processor prefers the agent reading, as can be seen by the contrast that arises when (14a–c) are continued as in (15a–c) vs. (16a–c).

(15) a. Mary hit John, but/and it was an accident.

   b. Mary hindered John, but/and it was an accident.
   c. Mary helped John, but/and it was an accident.

(16) a. Mary hit John, #but/and it was on purpose.
   b. Mary hindered John, #but/and it was on purpose.
   c. Mary helped John, #but/and it was on purpose.

On the one hand, in (15a–c) the conjunction *but* is acceptable because the assertion of accidentalness contrasts with the agency that the processor presumes on the part of *Mary*; on the other hand, in (16a–c) the conjunction *but* sounds odd (as indicated by the symbol #) because the assertion of purpose, as opposed to accidentalness, does not contrast with Mary's presumed agency. The contrast between (15) and (16) arises because the processor prefers to assign the agent role.[13] (Of course, the acceptability of (15a–c) also demonstrates that the processor can forgo agency when given the right kind of additional information.) Finally, the obligatory non-agentivity of (17a–c) makes it obvious that the processor's preference for agency depends upon the argument in question being animate:

(17) a. The wind hit John.
   b. The wind hindered John.
   c. The wind helped John.

Next, it seems that the processor not only prefers to assign the agent role but also that the value that it places on this assignment increases with the animacy of the argument in question. The demonstration of this point first requires some discussion of an interaction between agency and *self-NP* binding.

As noted in Minkoff (1994), after Chomsky (1977), when a subject intervenes between a *self-NP* and its antecedent, the acceptability of the sentence degrades more severely if the intervenor happens to be an agent, as in (18a–b), than if it happens not to be, as in (19a–b)[14]:

(18) a. *Mary caused us to strike herself.
   b. *Mary made the people bear down on herself.

(19) a. ?Mary caused lightning to strike herself.
   b. ?Mary made the vices bear down on herself.

It is clear that agency, not animacy, is the true culprit in the acceptability alternation seen here. For example, imagine that (18a–b) describe situations in which Mary makes the intervening subject act by physically manipulating it in some relevant way; for instance, suppose that, in (18a), Mary grabs our fists and forces them against her; and that, in (18b), she pulls the people up against her. In this case, the intervening subjects cease to be agents, and now the sentences become more acceptable, as is indicated in (20a–b). This makes it clear that intervening agency, not animacy, is what degrades sentences like (18a–b).

(20) a. ?Mary caused us to strike herself (by forcing our fists against her).
   b. ?Mary made the people bear down on herself (by forcing them up against her).

Of course, sentences like (18)–(20) are more complex than sentences like (14)–(17). However, the point is that in each case the processor treats a subject intervening between a *self-NP* and its antecedent in the same way that it treats the subjects of (14)–(17). When these subjects are animate, as in (18), it prefers to assign them the agent role, just as it does in (14); and when there is reason to withhold this agentive assignment, as in (20), it can do so, just as it does in (15).

Returning now to the task of showing that the processor's valuation of agency increases with the animacy of the argument in question, note first that the behavior of sentences like (21)–(24) shows that (18b) and (19b) (repeated as (21) and (24)) are at the extreme ends of a spectrum whose middle range includes, at least, sentences like (22) and (23).

(21)   ?Mary made the vices bear down on herself.
(22)   ??Mary made the Venus fly traps bear down on herself.
(23)   (*)Mary made the dogs bear down on herself.
(24)   *Mary made the people bear down on herself.

The pattern in these sentences seems to be that acceptability degrades progressively as the animacy of the intervening subject increases. Given that it is intervening agency, not animacy, that is incompatible with *self-NP* binding—see the discussion of (18)–(20)—the progressive degradation of (21)–(24) must be due to the fact that, as the animacy of the intervening subject increases, the processor values ever more highly the agentive interpretation. In particular, it seems that, because the intervening subject is located between a *self-NP* and its antecedent, its animacy causes the processor to experience conflicting impulses: to assign the agent role, as the GAAP impels it to do, or not to assign it, in order to render the binding relation acceptable. Moreover, as the intervening subject's animacy increases, the GAAP causes the processor to increasingly value assignment of the agent role, bringing these impulses increasingly into conflict; and this, in turn, makes the sentence harder to process, and hence less acceptable.[15] Thus, the progressive degradation of (21)–(24) suggests that the processor obeys the GAAP.

3.   The Effect of the BGB and the GAAP on English and Mam

Now the differing behaviors of English and Mam fall out automatically from how the BGB and the GAAP interact with differences in the timing of subject determination.

On the one hand, given a transitive sentence of Mam, or of any verb initial language that allows leftmost *pro*-drop, the processor cannot determine the subject until it has identified both NPs and therefore it must consider whether the subject relation is to be fulfilled by the subject NP, or by the object NP. Until the processor makes its decision, both NPs represent potential subjects and, therefore, potential agents. This has the consequence in turn that, whenever such a sentence violates (1), the BGB and the GAAP impel the processor toward mutually incompatible analyses, making the sentence unacceptable. Consider, for example, what happens when the processor analyzes (25), which violates (1) since its object, *qya*, is more animate than its subject, *tx'yan*:

(25)   #Ø-Ø-t-il   tx'yan   qya.
       DC-ABS3S-ERG3S-see   dog   woman
       'The dog saw the woman.'

Here, the BGB will guarantee that the processor must assign the subject relation to *tx'yan*, not *qya*. However, since the processor cannot determine the subject until it has identified both NPs, it is forced to consider whether the subject relation should be fulfilled by *tx'yan* or *qya*. Until the processor makes its decision, both these NPs represent potential subjects, and hence potential agents.[16] Therefore, the GAAP requires the processor to assign two values: a greater value to the interpretation that assigns the agent role to the more animate argument, *qya*, and a lesser value to the interpretation that assigns the agent role to the less animate argument, *tx'yan*. In other words, on account of the GAAP, the processor prefers to assign the agent role to *qya*, not *tx'yan*. This means that the BGB and the GAAP, respectively, impel the processor toward mutually incompatible interpretations: One assigns the subject relation to *tx'yan*, and another assigns the agent role to *qya*; and the incompatibility of these interpretations is what renders (25) unacceptable. Broadly put, the syntactic properties of Mam, or of any verb initial leftmost *pro*-drop language, guarantee that, whenever the object of a transitive sentence is more animate than its subject, the BGB and the GAAP will interact in a way that makes the sentence unacceptable.[17]

On the other hand, given a transitive sentence of English, or of any language that either is verb medial or forbids leftmost *pro*-drop, the processor can determine the subject after identifying only the first NP, and therefore it never has to consider whether the subject relation might be fulfilled by the object; at all times the true subject is perceived as the only potential subject, and hence as the only potential agent. This has the consequence that, even when such a sentence violates (1), the BGB and the GAAP impel the processor toward mutually compatible analyses, enabling the sentence to be acceptable. Consider, for example, what happens when the processor analyzes (26), which violates (1) since its object, *the woman*, is more animate than its subject, *the dog:*

(26)   The dog saw the woman.

Here, the BGB guarantees that the processor must assign the subject relation to *the dog*, not *the woman*. Moreover, since the processor can determine the subject after identifying only the first NP, it never has to consider whether the subject relation might be fulfilled by *the woman*; *the dog* at all times represents the only potential subject, and hence the only potential agent. Therefore, the GAAP requires the processor to assign a value just to the interpretation that assigns the agent role to *the dog*, not *the woman*. This means that the BGB and the GAAP, respectively, impel the processor toward mutually compatible interpretations: one assigns the subject relation to *the dog*, and another assigns the agent role to *the dog*; and the compatibility of these interpretations is what enables (26) to be acceptable. Broadly put, the syntactic properties of English, or of any verb-medial or non-leftmost-*pro*-drop language, guarantee that, even when the object of a transitive sentence is more animate than its subject, the BGB and the GAAP will interact in a way that enables the sentence to be acceptable.

4. Conclusion

In this work, I have argued that whether or not a language obeys (1) is determined by whether its syntactic characteristics permit the processor to determine the subject of a transitive sentence after identifying just one NP, as in English, or both NPs, as in Mam. In the former case, the BGB and the GAAP impel the processor toward mutually compatible interpretations, resulting in acceptability, irrespective of whether the sentence obeys or flouts (1). In the latter case, the BGB and the GAAP impel the processor toward mutually compatible interpretations, resulting in acceptability, if the sentence obeys (1); and toward mutually incompatible interpretations, resulting in unacceptability, if the sentence flouts (1). If the proposed analysis is correct, then—contra the spirit of proposals by authors including Hale (1973) and Creamer (1974) for the case of Navajo, and England (1991) for various Mayan languages—(1) has no status as a rule or principle, linguistic or otherwise, but, instead, is merely a list of results that fall out from the way in which innate properties of the processor interact with an array of independent syntactic facts.[18]

Finally, if the arguments in this work are correct, then, as indicated in note 11, the processor's determination of subject should be delayed until both arguments are identified, not just for any verb initial language that allows leftmost *pro*-drop but, instead, for any verb peripheral (i.e., either verb initial or verb final) language that does so. Therefore, all such languages should obey (1), ultimately for the same reasons that Mam does. I expect to test this prediction in future research.

Notes

1. I assume that a clause is unmarked only if all of its arguments are in their base generated positions.

2. I am most grateful to B'aayil, Eduardo Perez, whose patience and insight have been invaluable to the field work on which this article is based.

3. Here and throughout this work I employ the following abbreviations: Ø=zero morpheme; DC = distant completive; ABS = absolutive; 3 = third person; S = singular; ERG = ergative; DIR = directional; TV+DIR = suffix for transitive verb-plus-directional

4. This sentence is felicitous, for example, when it refers to a circumstance in which a plant's roots grow into a rock, causing it to crumble.

5. This sentence is felicitous, for example, when it refers to a circumstance in which a dog is killed by a poisonous plant that it has eaten.

6. I assume that declaratives occur in base generated form more often than not, so that such a reading will be favored by considerations of frequency of occurrence.

7. If a factor is present that favors a non-base generated reading, I assume the processor will abandon the Base Generation Bias. For example, if the first phrase of an English sentence is an NP with topic stress, I assume that, during the processing of the sentence, the processor will use this cue to establish a preference for the topicalized reading.

8. Note that I am assuming that something along the lines of (i) must be true.

    (i)   Given the assumption of a base generated sentence, the language processor decides that an argument is a subject as soon as it has sufficient evidence to make this decision.

9. For the sake of exposition, I assume that the covert NP is a *pro*; no argument made in this work depends upon this assumption.

10. It also is possible for the object to be covert, as in (i), and for both the subject and object to be covert as in (ii).

    (i)   Ø-Ø-t-il   qya   *pro.*
        DC-ABS3S-ERG3S-see   woman *pro*
        'The woman saw her/him/it.'

    (ii) Ø-Ø-t-il   *pro pro.*
        DC-ABS3S-ERG3S-see   *pro pro*
        'she/he/it saw her/him/it.'

11. In general, the processor's determination of the subject should be similarly delayed for any "verb peripheral" (i.e., either verb initial or verb final) language that allows leftmost *pro*-drop: In all such languages, the processor will be unable to use either the verb or the leftmost argument as a means of determining whether the subject will be the first argument it identifies, or the second one; in all cases, the processor will only be able to determine subjecthood once it identifies both arguments. I expect to examine this matter in future research.

12. On the "causer" reading of (14a–c), Mary's thematic role is identical to that of the wind in (i)–(iii).

    (i)   The wind hit John.
    (ii) The wind hindered John.
    (iii) The wind helped John.

13. Since agency commonly entails subjecthood, I suspect that there is no independent motivation for a preference on the part of the processor for assigning subjecthood on the basis of animacy. This suspicion is bolstered by the contrast between (i) and (ii), in which the processor prefers to assign agency, but apparently not subjecthood, to the animate object of the *by*-phrase.

(i) John was helped by Mary, but/and it was an accident.
(ii) John was helped by mary, #but/and it was on purpose.

14. See Minkoff (1994) for an explanation of the relative acceptability of sentences like those in (19a–b) in terms of a theory of "logophoric binding"; also, see especially note 98 of that work for a possible explanation for the relative degradation of sentences like (18a–b).

15. The wording of the GAAP makes it possible for one effectively to "short-circuit" the processor's impulse to increase the value it places on the agentive interpretation by supplying a sentence with additional content that implies that the argument in question is not an agent; this occurs in (15a–c) and (20a–b) in the text. An interesting question is why one can short-circuit the processor's *pro*-agency impulse with sentences like these, but not with sentences like (18) and (22–24), in which one might have imagined that the long-distance-bound *self-NPs* would "clue the processor in" on the fact that the intervening subjects must not be agents. Apparently, the GAAP allows the impulse in question to be canceled for the sake of avoiding a contradiction (namely, that a given NP both is and is not an agent) within the propositional content of the sentence itself; but it does not allow this impulse to be canceled for the sake of rescuing grammaticality. In other words, the GAAP is sensitive to linguistic, but not metalinguistic, information. I leave this matter for future research.

16. In other words, both *tx'yan* and *qya* represent potential subjects, and hence potential agents, during the interval that begins when the processor has identified both NPs, and ends when the processor determines which of these NPs is the subject.

17. An anonymous reviewer suggests that, if the arguments made here are correct, then speakers should not merely find (25) unacceptable: They should be unable to say which NP is the subject. While I have no data that would indicate whether speakers are confused in this way, I do not see why they necessarily should be. The claim I make is that (25) is unacceptable because, at the moment at which the processor has to choose the subject, it is torn between opposing interpretations. It is possible that the processor's dilemma lasts long enough to produce the observed unacceptability, but passes by the time the speaker introspects to answer the question "Which NP is the subject?" If this is the case, then speakers' conscious knowledge of Mam word order might lead them to say that *tx'yan* is the subject, fully aware of the sentence's unacceptability, but unaware of how the matter of subjecthood has hung so recently in the balance.

18. It also follows from this proposal that (1) cannot be a reflection of cultural rules or metaphysical propositions associated with a particular world view, contra the spirit of Witherspoon's (1977) arguments for the case of Navajo; at the deepest level of its etiology, (1) reflects universal traits of human biology, not individual traits of culture.

Furthermore, I suspect that disparate cultures will show little or no variation even with respect to (2), the animacy hierarchy of which the processor—specifically, the GAAP—makes use. The plausibility of cross-cultural accord on (2) is suggested (though clearly not proven) by the fact that, as far as the current investigation finds, the animacy hierarchy is identical for English—see (21)–(24)—and for Mam, two languages whose speech communities differ widely with respect to beliefs concerning what is and is not animate. (For example, many speakers of Mayan languages differ from most speakers of North American English in that they believe that all elements of the universe are alive in equal measure.)

Further, one can imagine that two cultures might differ with respect to how animate (that is, how strongly predisposed toward agency) they deem some particular entity to be and, therefore, with respect to what rank it occupies in the hierarchy (2). For example, two cultures could disagree about the powers inherent in a virus, leading one to accord this organism the animacy status of a plant, and the other to accord it the animacy status of a mineral. However, I suspect that variations in (2) are minimal if they exist at all, and are due to differences between what individual speakers know about particular types of organisms, rather than to any deeper differences between cultural world views. (In fact, it seems likely that significant differences in world view may not be reflected in the animacy rankings of which unconscious linguistic processes make use. For example, Minkoff, in progress, demonstrates that K'ichee'-Maya speakers who believe that all elements in the universe are alive nonetheless structure certain binding phenomena around the same dichotomy between living and non-living things as do speakers of English who embrace no such "animist" beliefs.) Ultimately, I suspect that the animacy hierarchy reflects an underlying system of conceptual distinctions that are themselves innate, and therefore inaccessible to cultural manipulation.

12

Predicate Raising in Lummi, Straits Salish

Eloise Jelinek

Lummi belongs to the North Straits Salish group of languages or dialects, spoken in the northwest coast area of North America. The architecture of the Lummi clause closely follows information structure. There is a focus position adjoining C, to which the predicate raises, placing it in sentence initial position. Lummi is a "polysynthetic" or *pronominal argument* language (Jelinek 1984, 1995) that manifests the following typological parameter:

(1) In pronominal argument languages, there is a strict mapping between argument structure and information structure.

Information structure refers to the organization of the clause with respect to presuppositional (familiar) material vs. information new to the discourse (Diesing 1992, Diesing and Jelinek 1995). In pronominal argument languages, only pronouns—either definite discourse anaphors or variables bound by a quantifier—serve as arguments. These pronominal arguments are always backgrounded. New information appears in lexical items. In contrast, "isolating" or lexical argument languages (English, for example), show a wide range of constituents in argument positions: pronouns, indefinite nouns, quantified NPs and clauses. Thus, entirely new information can be introduced in an argument position, and this new information carries focus.

1. Type-Theoretic Properties and Type Shifting

Linguistic expressions have been classified on the basis of whether they refer, predicate, or quantify:

(2)   *Expression*   *Semantic type*   *Function*
       a. pronouns; proper names   <e>   referential
       b. indefinite nouns   <e,t>   predicative
       c quantified NPs   <(e,t)t>   quantificational

Pronouns and proper names are used to refer to individuals; predicates assign properties to individuals (*man, dog*); and quantified NPs may include a quantifier and the predicate providing the restriction on that quantifier (*all men, every dog*).

Partee (1987) argues for the view that NPs in English do not correspond to a single semantic type, but frequently show "type-shifting" across their various uses. That is, a linguistic expression can serve any of the functions listed in (2) in different contexts, according to regular interpretive principles and compositional rules. It is easy to see how common nouns can vary in interpretation in this way. Compare the uses of *dogs* in (3):

(3) a. The dogs are outside.   *referential*
     b. Fido and Rover are dogs.   *predicative*
     c. Dogs are loyal companions.   *quantificational (generic)*

Proper names are most commonly simple referring expressions, except for contexts where a determiner is present:

(4)   Do you know the "Howard" who sits next to me in English class?

In (4), we see contrastive focus on *Howard* (**this** Howard rather than any other person of that name.) Kiss (1998) draws attention to the important contrast between two levels of focus. There is "information" (or *default*) focus, which is associated with new information; and, "identificational" (or *contrastive*) focus, which is quantificational in nature. Contrastive focus picks out a particular subset from a presupposed set of individuals:

(5) a. *default focus (new information)*
        Fido belongs to +Howard.   *default focus (new info.)*

     b. *contrastive (quantificational) focus*
        i. Fido belongs to **Howard**.
        ii. It's **Howard** that Fido belongs to.

In (5a), we see default information focus, marked with the + sign; in (5b,i), the speaker uses a marked intonation contour to point out that the dog is the property of Howard, as opposed to other members of a set of presupposed dog-owners. Kiss notes that in Hungarian and many other languages, clefts (5b,ii) are used for contrastive focus.

Pronouns can also be type shifted and used contrastively:

(6) a. *referential 'you'*
      I saw you.

     b. *quantificational "**you**"*
        i. It was **you** that I saw.
        ii. The **you** I used to know would never have done such a thing.

2. Pronominal Argument Languages and Type Shifting

Pronominal argument languages do not allow the kind of "type-shifting" or flexibility in the interpretation of nominals and pronouns that we see in (3-6). These languages show a strict mapping between linguistic form, semantic type, and information structure:

(7)

Expression	Type	Function	Information structure
a. Pronouns	<e>	referential	backgrounded
b. Lexical item	<e,t>	predicative	default focus
	<(e,t),t>	quantificational	contrastive focus

In pronominal argument languages, pronouns serve only as backgrounded referring expressions, or as variables bound by a quantifier; these two uses of pronouns seem to be language-universal. In these languages, lexical items are predicates or quantifiers, and receive either default or contrastive focus. We will see that there is some type-shifting in the functions of lexical items, but type-shifting in what may serve as an argument is excluded. In Minimalist terminology, the semantic content of the features defining this mapping is:

(8) a. Arguments have only ϕ-features, that is, semantic features characteristic of pronouns: person, number, and the like.
     b. Predicates and quantifiers have λ (lexical semantic) features.

Numerous and powerful consequences for the syntax follow from the constraint stated in (1), producing a cluster of parametric properties shared by pronominal argument languages. These include:

(9) a. Pronominal arguments are morphologically incorporated, since free-standing pronouns would be lexical items subject to focus.
     b. There are no lexical items in A-positions, since lexical items are confined to predicative or quantificational functions.
     c. There is no determiner quantification, since there are no lexical items in A-positions.
     d. Word order does not reflect grammatical relations; it marks information structure.

e. There are no embedded clauses, only adjoined subordinate clauses.

The grammaticalization of information structure in pronominal argument languages makes it necessary to refer to this level of the grammar in order to give an adequate account of the morphology and syntax. Information structure cannot be assigned to an extra-grammatical discourse level in these languages.

3. The Predicate and the Clitic String

A feature that is crucial to the syntax of the Straits Salish languages is the presence of a second position ("Wackernagel") clitic string, including clitics marking mood, tense/aspect, modality, and the subject:

(10) a. [čey]=lə'=sən.   b. [čey]=sə'=sx^w .
     work=PAST=NOM1S   work=FUT=NOM2S
     'I worked.'   'You will work.'

The predicate is marked as new information by virtue of its sentence-initial position, and gets word stress; the clitics are presuppositional, backgrounded and unstressed.[1]

3.1 Composition of the Predicate

The predicate includes functional projections marking transitivity and voice, where direct arguments check Case. These elements are auxiliaries or "light verbs."

3.1.1   Transitivity

[±Transitive] is overtly marked. The root may be followed by one of a set of transitivizers where the volitionality or success of the agent (traditionally called "control" in Salish studies) is marked:

(11)   *t = 'control' TRANS*
        [t'əm'-*t*-óŋəł]=lə=sx^w.
        hit-C:TRANS-ACC1P=PAST=NOM2S
        'You hit us (on purpose).'

(12)   *n(əx^w) = 'non-control' TRANS*
        [t'əm'-*n*-óŋəł]=lə'=sx^w.
        hit-NC:TRANS-ACC1PL=PAST=NOM2S
        'You hit us (accidentally).' or: 'You finally managed to hit us.'

3.1.2   Internal Arguments

A transitivizer entails an internal argument. In the examples here, clitics are
marked with an equal sign, while affixes to the root are marked with a hyphen.
The root plus its affixes forms a *phonological word*—shown in brackets in
(10)–(14)—which is the domain of word stress.

(13)   [leŋ-t-óŋəɫ]=lə'=sxʷ.
         see-C:TRANS-ACC1PL=PAST=NOM2S
         'You looked at us.'

When no phonologically overt pronoun follows TRANS, a third person absolutive
argument is entailed, as in (14) below. These Ø third person absolutive
arguments are definite and referential, when no nominals are present. The
reading in (14b) is excluded.

(14)   [leŋ-(í)t-Ø]=lə'=sxʷ.
         see-C:TRANS-ABS3=PAST=NOM2S
    a. 'You looked at him/it.'
    b. *'You looked at somebody/something.'[2]

3.1.3   The Voice Projection and 'External' Arguments

Above the transitive projection is the voice projection (active, passive, middle,
anti-passive, etc.), where the subject appears (Kratzer 1993). In (15), the passive
suffix -ŋ marks the subject as *affected*, and derives an intransitive construction;
it is mutually exclusive with an ergative or accusative pronoun. The passive
marker is also integrated into the predicate word; in (15) it receives word stress.

(15)   t'əm'-t-(í)ŋ=lə'=sən   ('ə   cə   swəy'qə).
         hit-C:TRANS-PASS=PAST=NOM1S   OBL   DET   male
         'I was hit (by the man).'

Note that the transitivizer still marks the volitionality of the "implicit" agent in
(15). Passives are derived from transitives. This agent may optionally be
identified in an oblique nominal adjunct, as shown. In middles (16), -ŋ also
marks the subject as affected, but no distinct agent is presupposed in the absence
of the transitivizer.

(16)   so'k'ʷ-(í)ŋ=lə'=sxʷ.
         bathe-MID=PAST=NOM2S
         'You bathed.'

In sum, the lexical root, containing λ features, combines with the TRANS marker and the pronoun marking an internal argument to compose the new information, a phonological word, that is predicated of the subject. In Straits, information new to the discourse is never introduced in an argument position, only as a predicate, an adverbial, or an adjunct.

The predicate+Infl clitic complex contains all the direct arguments, which are exclusively pronominal affixes with φ-features. Lexical items, including proper names and quantifiers, as well as clauses, cannot appear in A-positions. It is important to note that there are no independent pronouns with which the pronominal arguments could agree, ruling out the possibility that these incorporated pronouns are non-argumental agreement features.

3.2 Predicate Raising

Mood, which marks a clause as finite, is initial in the clitic string. I identify this mood projection as C (see Hendrick, this volume, and Massam, this volume, for related discussion of inflection in C). The question particle ə appears in C in yes/no questions. In main clauses, the predicate word, a phonological unit which includes the functional projections and any internal argument, raises to adjoin the clitic string at a focus position adjoining C, where it checks mood (see Aissen, this volume, for a related discussion of focushood and topichood in Jakaltek).

(17) a.

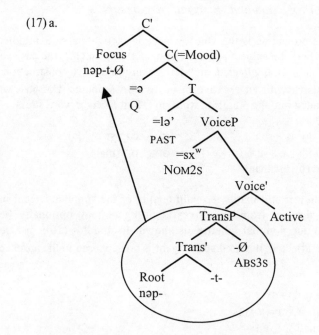

b. nəp-t-Ø=ə=lə'=sx^w?

    advise-C:TRANS-3ABS=Q=PAST=NOM2S

    'Did you advise him?'

The voice projection is last in the predicate word. The value of voice marks the theta-role of the subject clitic (Kratzer 1993) which checks "external" Case (Nominative or Absolutive) at this projection. Since the transitivizers and the internal argument they introduce are incorporated into the predicate word, it is this entire word, rather than a lexical head, which raises to the focus position as new information. The internal argument is presuppositional, but it is part of the new information in this context.

3.3 Serial Predicates: Evidence for Raising

Evidence for the raising analysis is provided by complex or serial predicates. In these complexes, every word carries a primary stress. Only the first word of the complex predicate raises to adjoin C; the second remains *in situ*, with the attached TransP and voice head. In (18) below, with the complex predicate 'come see', there is only one clause; there is just one clitic string, and no subordinate clause marking.

(18) a.

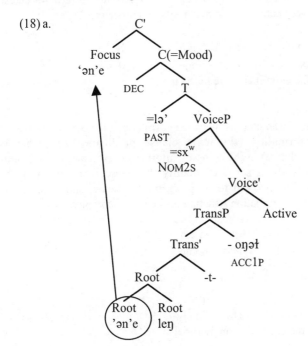

b 'ən'e=lə'=sx^w   leŋ-t- oŋəł.
come=PAST=NOM2S see-C:TRANS-ACC1P
'You came to see (i.e., visited) us.'

The initial root in serial predicates is limited to directionals and adjectivals (Jelinek 1995). Passive takes scope over the entire complex. (Note that (19) does not mean 'You came to be seen. . . '.)

(19) 'ən'e=lə'=sx^w   leŋ-t-ŋ   ('ə   cə   swəy'qə).
      come=PAST=NOM2S see-C:TRANS-PASS   OBL DET male
      'You were "come-to-see-ed" (i.e. visited) by the man.'

4. Adjoined Subordinate Clauses

Lummi has a variety of adjoined subordinate clause types, including "internally headed" relative clauses. The structure of Infl in relatives differs from main clauses. There is no mood C; the question particle is excluded, but tense/aspect/modality may be marked. The relative clause C is the determiner, a proclitic which binds a third person argument of the relativized predicate. This variable is the "head" of the relative, which is co-referent with a main clause pronoun. With serial predicates, both lexical roots remain below C:

(20) si'em=lə'=Ø   cə   'ən'e leŋ-t-oŋəł.
      noble=PAST=ABS3   DET   come see-C:TRANS-ACC1P
      'It was a/the chief that came to see us.'

There is no overt copula is any paradigm in Straits. DPs never appear in sentence-initial position. The contrast between (21a) and (21b) below is a matter of what is new information (the main clause predicate), and what is presuppositional (the relative) in the complex information structure of the multi-clause construction. Relatives serve to identify the referent of a main clause pronoun. Each clause has its own focus peak, the predicate, and each clause participates in the larger information structure of the whole complex.[3]

(21) a. qiləs=lə'=Ø   cə   si'em.
        lonely=PAST=ABS3   DET   noble
        'He was lonely, the chief.'

     b. si'em=lə'=Ø   cə   qiləs.
        noble=PAST=ABS3   DET   lonely
        'He was a/the chief, the lonely [one].'

Straits relatives are typically "anti-topics" (Lambrecht 1994). Anti-topics (so-called right-detached nominals) are adjuncts that serve to reactivate in the discourse the familiar referent of a main clause pronoun, as in (22). They are backgrounded or presuppositional with respect to the main clause.

(22)   a. He's a good guy, your brother.

      b. **Non-standard French**
         Pierre il   la-voit, Marie.
         Pierre, he her-sees, Marie
         'Pierre, he sees her, Marie.'

Straits has the following relative clause subtypes:

(23)   cə leŋ-t-ən   'the one that I see'   *Patient-headed*
       cə leŋ-t-oŋəł 'the one that sees us'   *Agent-headed*
       cə čey   'the one that works'   *Subject-headed*

Other examples of subject-headed relatives:

(24)   cə leŋ-t-ŋ   'the one that is seen' (passive subject)
       cə 'əy'   'the [one that is] good'
       sə nə-ten   'the.FEM my mother'
       cə ŋən'   'the many'
       sə Lena   'the.FEM Lena (proper name)'

Any open class root can appear as lexical head of either a main clause or a relative clause. Proper names also appear with determiners. The determiner/complementizers are demonstratives that do not mark number, but mark gender, proximity, and visibility. The default reading of relatives is definite, but they may type shift to receive indefinite readings in certain contexts. Some deictic roots can receive either a locative or an existential interpretation:

(25)   ni'=Ø   cə sčeenəx^w.
       LOC=ABS3 DET salmon
      a. 'It's there, the fish.'   (locative; definite)
      b. 'There's (a/some) fish.'   (existential; indefinite)

On the indefinite reading, the absolutive argument of the main clause and the co-indexed head of the non-restrictive relative are interpreted as free variables which receive default existential closure (Heim 1982).[4] In these constructions, the relative is linked to the main clause absolutive pronoun by predication, and has focus. New referents are introduced as intransitive subjects, in presentational sentences.

(26)   le'=č'ə=Ø   ə   cə sweləx   cə swi'qoəł   'i' . . .
       LOC=EVID=ABS3 OBL DET Orcas Island DET young man   CONJ
       'There reportedly on Orcas Island was a young man, and. . . '

Transitive objects may also be coindexed with a nominal on an indefinite reading. Finally, main clause roots may undergo this same type-shifting, and be read as indefinites, as in (20) above.

5. The Person-Deictic Roots

If arguments in Straits are restricted to pronouns that are confined to the transitive and voice functional projections, then certain problems for the grammar must follow:

(27) a. How are pronominal referents to be focused, since affixes and clitics cannot have focus?
   b. How are oblique pronominal objects to be expressed?

These problems are solved by the use of a set of "person-deictic" roots, which are used to mark contrastive focus. Compare:

(28) a. leŋ-n-oŋəs=lə'=sən.
       see-NC:TRANS-ACC2S=PAST=NOM1S
       'I saw you.'

   b. nək^w=yəx^w=lə'=Ø   cə leŋ-n-ən.
       YOU=CONJECT=PAST=ABS3   DET see-NC:TRANS-SUBORD1S
       'It must have been **you**, the one I saw.'

In (28a), the pronominal arguments are referential; in (28b), the deictic root provides contrastive focus on a person referent. Similarly:

(29) a. k^{w}əniŋ-t-oŋəs=lə'=sən.
       help-C:TRANS-ACC2S=PAST=NOM1S
       'I helped you.'

   b. k^{w}əniŋ-t-Ø=lə'=sən   sə   nək^w.
       help-C:TRANS-ABS3=PAST=NOM1S DET.FEM   YOU
       'I helped **you** (the one who is **you**).'

With these deictic roots, person and number are lexical semantic (λ) features. These roots do not match the pronominal arguments in morphological shape. Like all lexical roots, they occur only as lexical heads, either of finite clauses

(28b), or under the scope of a determiner (29b). The paradigm of these demonstrative roots is:

(30)

Person	1	2	3
singular	'əs	nək^w	nił
plural	niŋəł	nək^{w}iliyə	nəniłiyə

Compare this paradigm with the Case-marked pronominal arguments:[5]

(31) a. *Nominative clitics*

	singular	plural
1	=sən 'I'	=ł 'we'
2	=sx^w 'you'	= sx^w-hela 'you.PL'

b. *Accusative suffixes*

	singular	plural
1/2	-oŋəs 'you/me'	-oŋəł 'us'

c. *Ergative suffix*

	singular/plural
3	-s 'he/they'

d. *Absolutive*

	singular/plural
3	Ø

The form *sx^w-hela* includes a collective marker. There is also a reflexive suffix -oŋət which occurs with subject pronouns of any person or number.

The person-deictic roots exclude first or second person subject or object pronominal arguments; they are third person lexical roots.

(32) a. *nək^w=sx^w sə   nə-ten.
        YOU=NOM2S   DET.FEM   my-mother

    b. *k^{w}əniŋ -t-oŋəs=sən   sə   nək^w.
        help-C:TRANS-ACC2S=NOM1S   DET.FEM   YOU

They are also used for oblique person referents:

(33)   t'əm'-t-ŋ=sən   'ə cə nək^w.
       hit-C:TRANS-PASS=NOM2S   OBL DET YOU
       'I was hit by *you*.'

The fact that the person-deictic roots are third person rules out the possibility that the Straits Salish pronominal arguments could constitute agreement with "dropped" person-deictic roots.[6]

6. The Absence of Determiner Quantification

Across languages, some determiner quantifiers occur with a noun serving as the restriction on the quantifier: *all men, every man.* The quantifier states a relation between the sets which represents the restriction and scope of the quantifier. Straits has no quantifiers of this kind; quantifiers are lexical roots, predicates or adverbs. The contrast between strong and weak quantifiers is syntactically overt in an interesting way.

Weak quantifiers (cardinality expressions) in Straits are ordinary open class roots. In many languages of Native America, numerals are verb-like in syntax.

(34)   ŋən'=ɬ.
       many=NOM1P
       'We are many.'

This syntactic distribution of the weak quantifiers is in keeping with their semantic function: They assign the attribute of number to a set.

Strong quantifiers in Straits are limited to unselective adverbials, as defined by Lewis (1975). A strong quantifier cannot be a predicate, the sole lexical root in a clause. Strong quantifiers state a relation between two presupposed sets of individuals. The Straits adverbial quantifiers have a special "link" syntax; they appear in clause-initial position, linked to the main clause root by a conjunctive particle *'əw'*. They are followed by the clitic string, showing that, as the first word in the predicate complex, they raise to the Focus position adjoining C.[7] They have contrastive focus. Example (35) is a yes/no question, showing that the focused adverbial quantifier has raised to C.

(35) a.

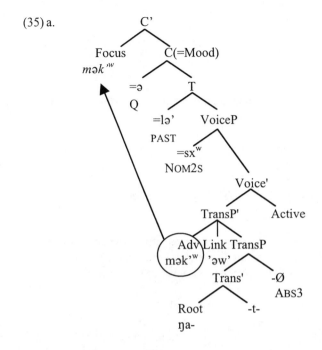

b. mək'ʷ=ə=lə'=sxʷ   'əw'   ŋa-t-Ø?

    ALL=Q=PAST=NOM2S   LINK   eat-C:TRANS-ABS3

    'Did you eat it up completely/eat all of them?'

Since the strong quantifiers are not linked to an argument position, they are unselective in scope:

(36) mək'ʷ=sə'=Ø   'əw' p'əq'   cə sp'eqəŋ.

    ALL=FUT   (x) LINK white (x)   DET flower (x)

    Q   Nuclear Scope Restrictive Clause

    'The flowers will be all white.'

    a. '*All* the flowers will be white.'

    b. 'The flower(s) will be *completely* white [not particolored].'

Example, (37) also shows the variability in scope of the adverbial:

(37) mək'ʷ=ł   'əw' ŋa-t-Ø.

    ALL=NOM1P LINK   eat-C:TRANS-ABS3

    a. 'We ate it up *completely*/ate *all* of them.'

    b. '*All* of us ate it/them.'

Another example of an unselective adverbial quantifier:

(38)   λ'e'=sən   'əw'   t'əm'-t-Ø.

    ADDL-NOM1S   LINK   hit-C:TRANS-ABS3   (ADDL = "additionally")

    a. 'I hit him again.'

    b. 'I also hit him.'

Within relative clauses, the strong quantifier also manifests variable scope, which is evidence of its adverbial character:

(39)   cə   mək'ʷ   p'əq'

    DET ALL   white

    'those that are all white'

    a. 'the completely white one(s); not parti-colored.'

    b. 'the set all members of which are white; no red ones.'

Wh-words in Straits show the same syntax as other lexical roots. They can appear as the lexical head of a main clause (40a) or a DP (40b), when they may be read as indefinite quantifiers. They never appear in A-positions:

(40) a. steŋ=lə'=Ø?   b. cə   steŋ

      what/thing=PAST=ABS3   DET what/thing

      'What was it?'   'the thing, something'

Jelinek (1998) shows that there is no *wh*-movement in Lummi that is distinct from the predicate-raising to Focus that is common to all clauses.

    Some open-class roots can be type raised to function as an adverbial quantifier, with the "link" syntax.

(41) a. ŋən'=sxʷ.   b. ŋən'=sxʷ   'əw'   łčikʷəs.

      big/many=NOM2S   big=NOM2S   LINK   tired

      'You're big.'   'You're very tired.'

In (42), an adverbial quantifier is type lowered and transitivized:

(42)   mək'ʷ-t-Ø=yəq=sxʷ.

    all-C:TRANS-ABS3=MODAL=NOM2S

    'Wish you would take them all/"total" them.'

And relatives can be type shifted in definite and indefinite readings.

7.   Other Evidence on the Adjunct Status of Nominals

Relative clauses in Lummi are anti-topics attached to the clause at C', in an A-bar position. When a single relative is adjoined to the clause, it is interpreted as co-referent with the absolutive argument.[8]

(43) a. ye'=ə=lə=Ø   cə   swəy'qə'?   S
      leave=Q=PAST=ABS3   DET male   /\
      'Did he leave, the man?'   C'   Adjunct

   b. kʷəniŋ-t-s=lə'=Ø   sə   steni'.
      help-C:TRANS-ERG3=PAST=ABS3 DET.FEM female
      'He helped her, the woman.'

   c. kʷəniŋ-t-Ø=lə'=sxʷ   sə   steni'.
      help-C:TRANS-ABS3=PAST=NOM2S DET.FEM female
      'You helped her, the woman.'

In (43a) and (43b), the anti-topic adjunct is co-referent with the external argument, the absolutive pronoun, which is topical. In (43a), this pronoun is the intransitive subject; in (43b), it is a patient. When a first or second person subject pronoun is present, as in (43c), the nominal is necessarily co-indexed with the non-topical third person absolutive.

Typically, no more than one (non-oblique) adjunct appears in a sentence, outside of elicited contexts. In the unusual sentences with more than one anti-topic, either may be interpreted as co-referent with the Absolutive pronoun; the adjunct order is free:

(44)   kʷəniŋ-t-s=lə'=Ø   sə   steni' cə swəy'qə'.
      help-C:TRANS-ERG3=PAST=ABS3 DET.FEM female DET male
   a. 'The woman helped the man.' *or*
   b. 'The man helped the woman.'
      [x helped y, man$_{x/y}$, woman$_{x/y}$]

With passive, two adjuncts are more acceptable, and there is no ambiguity, since one of the adjuncts is oblique. However, the order of the adjuncts is again free.

(45) a. kʷəniŋ-t-ŋ=Ø   sə   steni' 'ə cə swəy'qə'.
      help-C:TRANS-PASS=ABS3 DET.FEM female OBL DET male
      'She was helped, the woman, by the man.'

   b. kʷəniŋ -t-ŋ=Ø   'ə cə swəy'qə' sə steni'.

The free order of the adjuncts is evidence that neither is in an A-position. Pragmatic factors, of course, would render implausible some interpretations of a transitive sentence with two nominals (in either order):

(46)   leŋ-t-s=Ø   cə   swəy'qə'   cə   snəxʷəł.
       see-C:TRANS-ERG3=ABS3   DET male   DET canoe
       a. 'The man saw the canoe.'
       b. ## 'The canoe saw the man.'

Other evidence that the DPs are adjuncts to the clause can be drawn from complex sentences, where we do not see the expected constraints on co-reference across clauses that would apply if the DPs were arguments. In (47), the DP follows the predicate of the subordinate temporal clause, yet is co-indexed with the third person pronominal subject of both clauses.

(47)   qə'q'enəł=Ø   'ał   š-šət-ŋ-s   cə   'əs'eləxʷ.
       slow=ABS3   CONJ   NOM-walk-MID-SUBORD3   DET elder
       a. 'He is slow when he walks, the old man.'
       b. ## 'He is slow when the old man walks.'

The temporal conjunction marks the two events in this complex sentence as simultaneous. If the DP were in an A-position in the temporal clause, and thus not an adjunct to the complex sentence, we would have no account of the co-reference of the main and subordinate clause subjects and the DP adjunct.

8.   Obligatory "Dative Shift"

I turn now to a new line of evidence bearing on the question of pronominal arguments: the constraints on the distribution of Case on semantic goals seen in these languages. Many languages, for example English, have constructions where goals may have either structural or inherent (oblique) Case (i.e., "dative shift").

(48) a. George gave a paper to the +teacher.
     b. George gave the teacher a +paper.

(The + sign marks normal default focus.) Bresnan (1982) notes that the animacy of goals plays a role in the dative alternation. Compare:

(49) a. I sent a letter to +George.
     b. I sent George a +letter.

(50) a. I sent a letter to +Dallas.
     b. #I sent Dallas a +letter.

Example (50b) is excluded unless reference is made to a person or group (not a place) named Dallas. Animate goals are affected in a way that inanimate destinations are not. Note that the same applies to benefactives:

(51) a. I mixed a drink for +George.
b. I mixed George a +drink.

(52) a. I mixed a dressing for the +salad.
b. #I mixed the salad a +dressing.

Basilico (1998) provides an interesting new perspective on dative movement, in terms of information structure. He argues that when the goal or benefactee is raised, it is backgrounded (or "topicalized" within the VP), while the theme is given focus as the new information. Note that animate obliques are usually familiar, while inanimate obliques are frequently new information. The constraints on "dative movement" in English shown in (51) and (52) exploit the feature of animacy.

Since pronouns in English can type shift to a contrastive use, they can undergo dative movement or not, depending on which argument the speaker elects to focus. Dative movement backgrounds oblique arguments, but in English we can use intonation contrasts to do the same work:

(53) a. I sent a **letter** to you.   *referential "you"*
b. I sent you a **letter**.

(54) a. I sent a letter to **you**.   *contrastive "YOU"*
b. I sent **you** a letter.

In (54b) contrastive focus overrides the effect of dative movement. Given these facts, what should we predict about dative movement in pronominal argument languages? We have seen that in pronominal argument languages, pronouns are always backgrounded, while lexical items always have one kind of focus or the other. Therefore, we must predict that there can be no "optional" dative movement in these languages. The speaker can't choose whether or not to background a pronoun or an NP. Dative movement should be strictly grammaticalized. This is exactly what we find.

We have seen that Straits has only two direct argument positions, introduced at the voice and transitive projections. The pronominal arguments appear only at these projections; there are no prepositions that take pronominal objects (Jelinek 1997). There is just one preposition, the oblique marker ʼə, which occurs only with nominals. Therefore, Straits has no ditransitive constructions in the usual sense. For example, with the stem ʼoŋəs-t, the root 'give+C:TRANS', the direct object pronoun represents the animate recipient, which is promoted (in Relational Grammar terms) to accusative Case. The item exchanged may be optionally identified in an oblique adjunct.

(55)   ʼoŋəs-t-oŋəɫ=ləʼ=sx^w   (ʼə cə sčeenəx^w).
      give-C:TRANS-ACC1P=PAST=NOM2S   OBL DET salmon
      'You gifted us ([with] a/the salmon).'

In the corresponding passive, the recipient is promoted to subject:

(56) 'oŋəs-t-ŋ=ł   ('ə cə sčeenəxʷ).
      give-TRANS-PASS=NOM1P   OBL the salmon)
      'We were gifted (with the salmon).'

As always with passives, an optional oblique agent may be included. Adjunct order is free. Again, there are pragmatic constraints on plausible readings.

(57) 'oŋəs-t-ŋ=sxʷ   ('ə   cə sčeenəxʷ) ('ə   cə si'em).
      give-TRANS-PASS=NOM2S (OBL DET fish)   (OBL DET chief)
      a. 'You were gifted (with the fish) (by the chief).'
      b. ##'You were gifted (with the chief) (by the fish).'

Reading (57b) is rejected as implausible. The structure is:

(58)

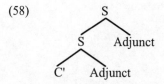

Many Salish languages have an applicative transitivizer. Montler (1986) identifies a transitivizer in Saanich, a North Straits dialect, which marks the syntactic direct object as a benefactee:

(59) k'ʷə́n-sí-sə=sən.
      look-BENEFACTIVE-OBJ2S=SUBJ1S
      'I looked for you (on your behalf).'

Montler notes that this could be used, for example, to report that the speaker looked over a boat that the hearer is thinking about buying.
    With respect to inanimate goals, destinations cannot be represented by a pronoun. They can be expressed in oblique nominals:

(60) ye'=Ø   'ə cə swi'iłč.
      go=ABS3   OBL DET lake
      'He went to the lake.'

There are also constructions in which inanimate destinations are expressed as lexical roots plus one of two directional prefixes:

(61) a. λ'i-xʷotqəm=sən.   b. čə-xʷotqəm=sən.
        to-Bellingham=NOM1S   from-Bellingham=NOM1S
        'I [am going] to Bellingham.'   'I [am] from Bellingham.'

Here is a directional in an irrealis clause, with a loanword from English:

(62)   se'e-t-ŋ=sən   kʷ   λ'i-tawən-ən.
       tell-TRANS-PASS=NOM1S   DET   to-town-IRR1
       'I was told [to go] to town.'

In sum, animate goals and benefactees are backgrounded direct object pronouns; inanimate goals are oblique nominals, which receive focus. The speaker can use a deictic root—not a subject or object argument—to place contrastive focus on a person referent.

9. Conclusions

Straits Salish conforms to the definition of pronominal argument languages given above:

(1) In pronominal argument languages, there is a strict mapping between argument structure and information structure.

When only pronouns or variables can serve as arguments, lexical items are restricted to serving as predicates or quantifiers, and by definition are new information with some degree of focus. If arguments cannot receive focus, there can be no determiner quantification; strong quantifiers mark contrastive focus, and weak quantifiers are simple predicates. The feature that characterizes these languages is the fact that there is no type shifting of the kind seen in languages where almost anything—pronouns, NPs, predicates, quantifiers and clauses—occur in argument positions, and *any* constituent, even some affixes, can be given contrastive focus via intonation.

Diesing's (1992) Mapping Hypothesis claims that by the level of Logical Form, presuppositional NPs appear above the VP, while indefinites, new information, are in the VP, where they are subject to existential closure (Heim 1982). Diesing and Jelinek (1995) extended this schema to account for the raising of object pronouns to an aspectual projection in IP, in languages with object clitics.[9] What I am concerned with here is an additional parametric feature, that which defines pronominal argument languages. In these languages, direct arguments are definite pronouns, discourse anaphors, or variables bound by a quantifier. The pronouns appear at functional projections in the inflectional component of the clause. As a result:

(63) In pronominal argument languages, the distribution of old and new information in the clause is
     a. consistent with the Mapping Hypothesis, and
     b. uniformly overt at spell-out, not delayed until LF movement.

In the Minimalist framework, this distribution can be stated in terms of checking "strong" features—pronoun, predicate, and (strong) quantifier. Languages vary in how information structure is mapped into the clausal architecture. In languages where focus, including contrastive focus, is marked via stress and intonation rather than in the morphosyntax, we do not see focus movement of this kind. In Lummi, there is an overt Focus position above C, to which the verb, predicate, or other focused item raises, deriving its predicate initial character.

Acknowledgments

I thank Emmon Bach, Andrew Barss, David Basilico, Andrew Carnie, Dick Demers, Molly Diesing, Terry Langendoen, Tim Montler, Barbara Partee, Montserrat Sanz, and Mary Willie for comments and help. None of these is responsible for any errors or omissions. The analysis given here is based on field work on Lummi and Samish/Malahat between 1982 and 1988, supported in part by the Wenner-Gren Foundation and the American Philosophical Society. I am greatly indebted to Dick Demers, a collaborator in work on Straits, who generously made available to me his field notes from over two decades of work on Lummi. I follow the classification of the Straits Salish group given in Montler 1996: Northern Straits comprises a group of related dialects including Lummi, Saanich, Samish, Songish, and Sooke; Klallam is less closely related. The Northern Straits dialects share major syntactic properties, and from what I have been able to determine from the publications of colleagues working on Straits, the analysis I propose here applies generally to the other Northern Straits dialects as well.

Notes

1. Some modal and aspectual notions are marked in adverbial particles or lexical roots (Montler 1986; Jelinek and Demers 1994). These constituents, unlike the clitics, have focus. Reduplication of the root is extensively employed to mark various aspectual and other quantificational notions (Jelinek and Demers 1997).

2. There is an ergative split: first and second person pronouns are nominative/accusative, while third person pronouns are ergative/absolutive. Third person ergative is an overt internal argument. Nominative first and second person pronouns are "external", following the PAST clitic as in (14); in (i) below, the "internal" ergative -*s* pronoun precedes the PAST clitic.

(i)   leŋ-t-s=lə'=Ø.
        see-C:TRANS-ERG3=PAST=ABS3
        'He looked at him/it.'

The absolutive (third person intransitive subject or transitive object) is the only null pronoun in any paradigm. There is an anti-passive suffix that can follow the root to describe an intransitive "activity". Montler (1986) gives the following minimal pair in Saanich, another North Straits Salish language:

(ii) a. t'əmət sən   'I figured it out.'   *transitive*
      b. t'əm'-el's sən 'ał. 'I'm just guessing.'   *intransitive*

(iia) contains the *-t-* control transitivizer; (iib) has the activity or anti-passive *-el's* suffix, and an adverbial particle *'aɬ* 'just'.

3. A formal approach to the study of the information structure of complex sentences has been developed by linguists of the Prague School. See Hajičová (1983), and other work by Hajičová and Petr Sgall.

4. In languages where determiners mark definiteness, the determiner fixes the reading of an NP. However, there is ambiguity or type shifting of the kind seen with Straits DPs, in the interpretation of bare plural nouns in English. Bare plurals have no determiner, and may be read as definite and referential, or as indefinites providing the restriction on a generic quantifier, as in example (3) above (see Diesing 1992).

5. These pronominal arguments undergo some morphophonological changes in aspectual alternations.

6. These roots undergo various derivational and inflectional processes. In irrealis clauses, third person subject inflection is **overt**.

i) čte-t-ŋ=sən kw nək^{w}-əs.
ask-TRANS-PASS=NOM1S DET be.you-IRR3
'I was asked if it was ***you***.'

ii) xən-ŋ=Ø cə Bill k^{w} 'əs-əs.
do/act-MID=ABS3 DET Bill DET be.me-IRR3
'Bill acted for ***me***. (in my place; acting as if he were me)'

7. There are extensive parametric differences across the members of the large Salishan family. In the Interior Salish languages, in contrast to the Straits dialects, we find (a) no second position clitic string including the subject; (b) free-standing pronouns; (c) determiner quantification; (d) DP occurring initially in the clause; and (e) no link syntax for the strong quantifiers. Many of these languages also lack Ergative Case. Lummi has a person hierarchy, not discussed here for lack of space, that is not manifested in most of the Interior languages. See Levine (1984) on argument structure in Kwakwala, a non-Salish language of the Northwest Coast area, for evidence that some of the parametric properties considered here are areal in distribution.

8. See Gerdts (1988) for a discussion of the "one-nominal interpretation" rule in Halkomelem Salish.

9. There is a subclass of lexical argument languages, the subject-agreement object clitic languages, such as Arabic and the Romance languages. In these languages also the object clitics cannot receive contrastive stress. However, these languages also have NPs in A-positions that receive focus, and consequently lack the cluster of syntactic properties listed in (10). Jelinek and Willie (1996) and Willie and Jelinek (in press) argue that Navajo is a pronominal argument language. In both Straits Salish and Navajo, verbs of speech have a special syntax where quoted material is simply directly adjoined, like the other subordinate clause types (temporal, irrealis, etc.). Partee (1973) identifies quotative constructions of this kind in universal grammar, and Munro (1982) addresses the question of the low transitivity of verbs of speech across languages.

References

Abney, Steven (1987) *The English Noun Phrase in Its Sentential Aspect*. Ph.D. dissertation, MIT.

Academia de las lenguas mayas (1988) *Documento de referencia para la pronunciación de los nuevos alfabetos oficiales*. Instituto Indigenista Nacional, Guatemala City.

Adger, David (1996) Aspect, Agreement and Measure Phrases in Scottish Gaelic. In Robert Borsley and Ian Roberts (eds.), *The Syntax of the Celtic Languages: A Comparative Perspective*. Cambridge University Press, Cambridge. pp. 200–222.

Aissen, Judith (1992) Topic and Focus in Mayan. *Language* 63:43–80.

Alexiadou, Alexis and Elena Anagnostopoulou (1998) Parameterizing AGR: Word Order, V-Movement and EPP-Checking. *Natural Language and Linguistic Theory* 16:491–539.

Anderson, Stephen (1981) Topicalization in Breton. *Berkeley Linguistics Society* 7:27–39.

—— (1982) Where's Morphology? *Linguistic Inquiry* 13:571–612.

—— (1984) Kwakwala Syntax and the Government-Binding Theory. in *The Syntax of North American Indian Languages. Syntax and Semantics* 16:21–75. Academic Press, New York.

—— (1988) Morphological Theory. In Fredrick J. Newmeyer (ed.), *Linguistics: The Cambridge Survey*, vol 1. pp. 146–191. Cambridge University Press, Cambridge.

—— (1993) Wackernagel's Revenge: Clitics Morphology and the Syntax. *Language* 69:68-98.

Anderson, Stephen and Sandra Chung (1977) On Grammatical Relations and Clause Structure in Verb Initial Languages. In Peter Cole and Jerrold Sadock (eds.), *Grammatical Relations, Syntax and Semantics* 8:1–25. Academic Press, New York.

Aoun, Joseph and Elabbas Benmamoun (1999) Gapping, *PF* Merger and Patterns of Partial Agreement. In Elabbas Benmamoun and Shalom Lappin (eds.), *Fragments: Studies in Ellipsis and Gapping*. pp. 175–220. Oxford University Press, Oxford.

Aoun, Joseph, Elabbas Benmamoun, and Dominique Sportiche (1994) Agreement, Word Order, and Conjunction in Some Varieties of Arabic. *Linguistic Inquiry* 25:195–220.

Awbery, Gwenllian M. (1976) *The Syntax of Welsh: A Transformational Study of the Passive*. Cambridge University Press, Cambridge.

—— (1977) A Transformational View of Welsh Relatives. *Bulletin of the Board of Celtic Studies* 27:155–206.

Baker, Mark (1985) The Mirror Principle and Morphosyntactic Representation. *Linguistic Inquiry* 16:373–416.

—— (1988) *Incorporation: A Theory of Grammatical Function Changing*. University of Chicago Press, Chicago.

Barbiers, Sjef (1995) *The Syntax of Interpretation*. Ph.D. Dissertation, University of Leiden.

235

Basilico, David (1998) Object Positions. *Natural Language and Linguistic Theory* 14:541–595.

Bauer, Winifred (1997) (with William Parker, Te Kareongawai Evans and Te Aroha Noti Teepa) *The Reed Reference Grammar of Māori.* Reed Publishing, Auckland.

Benmamoun, Elabbas (1992) Structural Conditions on Agreement. *Proceedings of NELS* 22:17–32. GLSA, University of Massachusetts, Amherst.

Bergin, Osborn (1938) On the Syntax of the Old Irish Verb. *Ériu* 12:197–214.

Berman, Ann (1974) On the VSO Hypothesis. *Linguistic Inquiry* 5:1–38.

Bever, Thomas G. (1970). The Cognitive Basis for Linguistic Structures. In J. R. Hayes (ed.), *Cognitive Development of Language,* pp. 277–360. John Wiley and Sons, New York.

Bhatt, Rakesh and James Yoon (1991) On the Composition of COMP and Parameters of V-2. *Proceedings of WCCFL* 10:41–52. CSLI, Stanford University, Stanford CA.

Bobaljik, Jonathan and Andrew Carnie (1996) A Minimalist Approach to Some Problems of Irish Word Order. In Ian Roberts and Robert Borsley (eds.), *The Syntax of the Celtic Languages,* pp. 223–240. Cambridge University Press, Cambridge.

Bobaljik, Jonathan and Höskuldur Thráinsson (1998) Two Heads Aren't Better than One. *Syntax* 1.1:37–71.

Borer, Hagit (1986) I-Subjects. *Linguistic Inquiry* 17:375–416.

—— (1995) The Ups and Downs of Hebrew Verb Movement. *Natural Language and Linguistic Theory* 13:527–606.

Borsley, Robert (1990) A GPSG Approach to Breton Word Order. In Randall Hendrick (ed.), *The Syntax of the Modern Celtic Language: Syntax and Semantics* 23:81–96. Academic Press, San Diego.

Borsley, Robert, Maria-Luisa Rivero, and Janig Stephens (1996) Long Head Movement in Breton. In Ian Roberts and Robert Borsley (eds.) *The Syntax of the Celtic Languages.* pp. 53–74. Cambridge University Press, Cambridge.

Bowers, John (1993) The Syntax of Predication. *Linguistic Inquiry* 24:591–656.

Bresnan, Joan (1974) The Position of Certain Clause-Particles in Phrase Structure. *Linguistic Inquiry* 5:614–619.

—— (1982) *The Mental Representation of Grammatical Relations.* MIT Press, Cambridge, MA.

Carney, James (1978) Aspects of Archaic Irish. *Éigse* 17:417–435.

Carnie, Andrew (1993) Nominal Predicates and Absolutive Case Marking in Irish. In Colin Phillips (ed.), *Papers on Case and Agreement II: MIT Working Papers in Linguistics* 19:89–130.

—— (1995) *Non-Verbal Predication and Head Movement,* Ph.D. Dissertation, MIT.

Chapin, Paul G. (1974) Proto-Polynesian *ai. *Journal of the Polynesian Society* 83:259–307.

Choe, Hyon-Sook (1987) An SVO Analysis of VSO Languages and Parameterization: A Study of Berber. In Mohammed Guerssel and Kenneth Hale (eds.), *Studies in Berber Syntax. MIT Lexicon Project Working Paper* 14:121–158.

Chomsky, Noam (1977) *Essays on Form and Interpretation,* North Holland, New York.

—— (1981) *Lectures on Government and Binding.* Foris. Dordrecht.

—— (1986) *Barriers.* MIT Press, Cambridge MA.

—— (1991) Some Notes on the Economy of Derivation and Representation. In Robert Freidin (ed.), *Principles and Parameters in Generative Grammar.* pp 417–454. MIT Press, Cambridge.

—— (1993) A Minimalist Program for Linguistic Theory. In Kenneth Hale and Samuel J. Keyser (eds.), *The View From Building 20.* pp. 1–49. MIT Press, Cambridge, MA.

—— (1994) Bare Phrase Structure. *MIT Occasional Papers in Linguistics 5.* Cambridge, MA.

—— (1995) *The Minimalist Program*. MIT Press, Cambridge, MA.

—— (1998) Minimalist Inquiries: The Framework. *MIT Occasional Papers in Linguistics 15*. Cambridge, MA.

Chung, Sandra (1970) *Negative Verbs in Polynesian*. Ms., University of California, Santa Cruz.

—— (1976) An Object Creating Rule in Bahasa Indonesia. *Linguistic Inquiry* 13:39–77.

—— (1983) The ECP and Government in Chamorro. *Natural Language and Linguistic Theory* 1:209–244.

—— (1990) VPs and Verb movement in Chamorro. *Natural Language and Linguistic Theory* 8:559–620.

—— (1996) Surface Word Order in Two Polynesian Languages. Presented at the Verb Initial Reading Group, University of California, Santa Cruz.

Chung, Sandra and James McCloskey (1987) Government, Barriers and Small-clauses in Modern Irish. *Linguistic Inquiry* 18:173–237.

Cinque, Guglielmo (1999) *Adverbs and Functional Heads: A Cross-Linguistic Perspective*. Oxford University Press, Oxford.

Clack, Susan (1994) A Consideration of V2 in Relation to Middle Welsh. In Ian Roberts (ed.), *Research Papers in Welsh Syntax. Bangor Research Papers in Linguistics* 5:38–77.

Clark, Herbert. H. (1965) Some Structure Properties of Simple Active and Passive Sentences. *Journal of Verbal Learning and Verbal Behavior* 4:365–370.

Clark, Herbert. H. and Begun, Jeffrey S. (1971) The Semantics of Sentence Subjects. *Language and Speech,* 14:34–46.

Clark, Ross (1976) *Aspects of Proto-Polynesian*. Linguistic Society of New Zealand, Auckland.

Cole, Shari and Vitolia Kulatea (1996) *Tau Koloa Fakamotu ha Niue: Tau Koloa Laufa (Cultural Crafts of Niue: Pandanus Weaving)*. Government of Niue and Institute of Pacific Studies, Alofi.

Craig, Colette G. (1977) *The Structure of Jacaltec*. University of Texas Press, Austin, Texas.

—— (1986a) Jacaltec Noun Classifiers. *Lingua* 70:241–284.

—— (1986b) Jacaltek Noun Classifiers: a Study in Language and Culture. In Colette G. Craig (ed.), *Noun Classes and Categorization*. pp 263–294. John Benjamins. Amsterdam.

Creamer, Mary H. (1974) Ranking in Navajo Nouns. *Diné Bizaad Náníl'ííh (Navajo Language Review)* 1:29–38. Center for Applied Linguistics, Arlington, Virginia.

Datz, Margaret J. Dickeman. (1980) *Jacaltec Syntactic Structure and the Demands of Discourse*. Ph.D. dissertation, University of Colorado, Boulder.

Day, Christopher (1973a) *The Jacaltec Language*. Bloomington: Indiana University Press.

—— (1973b) The Semantics of Social Categories in a Transformational Grammar. In Munro Edmonson (ed.), *Meaning in Mayan Languages,* pp. 85–106. Mouton, The Hague.

de Caen, Vincent (1995) *On the Placement and Interpretation of the Verb in Standard Biblical Hebrew Prose*. Ph.D. dissertation, University of Toronto.

de Haan, Ger J. and Fred Weerman (1986) Finiteness and Verb Fronting in Frisian. In Hubert Haider and Martin Prinzhorn (eds.), *Verb Second Phenomena in Germanic Languages*. pp. 77–110. Foris, Dordrecht.

den Besten, Hans (1981) On the Interaction of Root Transformations and Lexical Deletive Rules. *Groninger Arbeiten zur Germanistischen Linguistik* 20:1–78.

—— (1983) On the Interaction of Root Transformations and Lexical Deletive Rules. In Werner Abraham (ed.), *On the Formal Syntax of Westgermania*, pp. 47–131. John Benjamins, Amsterdam.

Déprez, Viviane and Kenneth Hale (1986) Resumptive Pronouns in Irish. *Proceedings of the Harvard Celtic Colloquium* 5:38–48.

Desbordes, Yann (1983) *Petite grammaire du breton moderne.* Mouladuriou Hor Yezh Lesneven.

Diesing, Molly (1992) *Indefinites.* MIT Press, Cambridge, MA.

—— (1996) Semantic Variables and Object Shift. In Höskuldur Thráinsson, Samual D. Epstein and Steven Peter (eds.) *Studies in Comparative Germanic Syntax, vol.2,* pp. 66–84. Kluwer, Dordrecht.

—— (1997) Yiddish VP Order and the Typology and Object Movement in Germanic. *Natural Language and Linguistic Theory* 15.2:369–427.

Diesing, Molly and Eloise Jelinek (1995) Distributing Arguments. *Natural Language Semantics* 3:123–176.

Doherty, Cathal (1996) Clausal Structure and the Modern Irish Copula. *Natural Language and Linguistic Theory* 14:1–46.

Doron, Edit (1990) VP-ellipsis in Hebrew. Unpublished ms. Hebrew University of Jerusalem.

—— (1996) The Predicate in Arabic. In Jacqueline Lecarme, Jean Lowenstamm, and Ur Shlonsky (eds.), *Studies in Afroasiatic Grammar*, pp. 77–87. Holland Academic Graphics, The Hague.

—— (1999) V-movement and VP-ellipsis. In Elabbas Benmamoun and Shalom Lappin (eds.), *Fragments: Studies in Ellipsis and Gapping.* pp. 124–140. Oxford University Press, Oxford.

—— (to appear) Word Order in Hebrew. In Jacqueline Lecarme, Jean Lowenstamm and Ur Shlonsky (eds.) *Studies in Afroasiatic Grammar II*, Holland Academic Graphics, The Hague.

Doron, Edit and Caroline Heycock (1999) Filling and Licensing Multiple Specifiers. In David Adger, Susan Pintzuk, Bernadette Plunkett and Georges Tsoulas (eds.), *Specifiers: Minimalist Approaches.* Oxford University Press, Oxford.

Duffield, Nigel (1991) *Particles and Projections.* Ph.D dissertation, University of Southern California, Los Angeles.

—— (1994) Are You Right? On Pronoun-Postposing and Other Problems of Irish Word-Order. *Proceedings of WCCFL* 13:221–237. CSLI, Stanford University, Stanford, CA.

—— (1995) *Particles and Projections in Irish Syntax.* Kluwer, Dordrecht.

—— (1996) On Structural Invariance and Lexical Diversity. In Robert Borsley and Ian Roberts (eds.), *The Syntax of the Celtic Languages. A Comparative Perspective,* pp. 214–240. Cambridge University Press, Cambridge.

Emonds, Joseph (1976) *A Transformational Approach to English Syntax.* Academic Press, New York.

—— (1978) The Verbal Complex V-V in French. *Linguistic Inquiry* 9:151–175.

—— (1980) Word Order and Generative Grammar. *Journal of Linguistic Research* 1:33–54.

England, Nora (1991). Changes in Basic Word Order in Mayan Languages. *International Journal of American Linguistics* 57:446–486.

Ernst, Thomas (1998) The Scopal Basis of Adverb Licensing. In Puis N. Tamanji and Kiyomi Kusumoto (eds.), *Proceedings of NELS* 28:127–142. GLSA, University of Massachusetts, Amherst.

Eska, Joseph (1994) Rethinking the Evolution of Celtic Constituent Configuration. *Münchener Studien zur Sprachwissenshaft* 55:7–39.

—— (1996) On Syntax and Phonology within the Early Irish Verbal Complex. *Diachronica* 13:225–257.

Farkaş, Donka and Draga Zec (1995) Agreement and Pronominal Reference. In Guglielmo Cinque and Giuliana Giusti (eds.), *Advances in Roumanian Linguistics,* pp. 83–101. John Benjamins, Amsterdam.

Fassi Fehri, Abdelkadar (1989) Generalized IP Structure, Case and VS Word order. *MIT Working Papers in Linguistics* 10:75–113.

—— (1993) *Issues in the Structure of Arabic Clauses and Words.* Kluwer, Dordrecht.

Foley, William A. and Robert Van Valin (1984) *Functional Syntax and Universal Grammar.* Cambridge University Press, Cambridge.

Freeze, Ray (1992a) Existentials and Other Locatives. *Language* 68:553–595.

—— (1992b) Is There More to V2 than Meets the I? *Proceedings of NELS* 22:151–164.

Gazdar, Gerald, Ewan Klein, Geoff Pullum, and Ivan Sag (1985) *Generalized Phrase Structure Grammar.* Blackwell, Oxford.

Gensler, Orin (1991) *A Typological Evaluation of Celtic/Hamito-Semitic Syntactic Parallels.* Ph.D. dissertation, University of California, Berkeley.

George, Ken and George Broderick (1993) The Revived Languages: Modern Cornish and Modern Manx. In Martin J. Ball and James Fife (eds.), *The Celtic Languages,* pp. 644–664. Routledge, London.

Georgopoulos, Carol (1991a) Canonical Government and the Specifier Parameter: An ECP Account of Weak Crossover. *Natural Language and Linguistic Theory* 9:1–46.

—— (1991b) *Syntactic Variables: Resumptive Pronouns and A Binding in Palauan.* Kluwer, Dordrecht.

Gerdts, Donna (1988) *Object and Absolutive in Halkomelem Salish.* Garland, New York.

Gesenius, Friedrich H.W. (1910) *Hebrew Grammar.* E. Kautzsch (ed.), 2nd English edition revised by A.E. Cowley, Clarendon Press, Oxford.

Gillies, William (1993) Scottish Gaelic. In Martin J. Ball and James Fife (eds.), *The Celtic Languages,* pp. 145–227. Routledge, London.

Government of Niue (1982) *Niue: a History of the Island* The Institute of Pacific Studies of the University of the South Pacific and Government of Niue, Alofi.

Gramadeg Cymraeg Cyfoes (1976) (*Contemporary Welsh Grammar*). D. Brown ai Feibion Cyf., Cowbridge.

Green, Anthony (1995) *Old Irish Verbs and Vocabulary,* Cascadilla Press, Somerville, MA.

Greenberg, Joseph (1963) Some Universals of Grammar with Particular Reference to the Order of Meaningful Elements. In Joseph Greenberg (ed.) *Universals of Language,* pp. 58–90. MIT Press, Cambridge, MA.

Greene, David (1977) Archaic Irish. In Rolf Ködderitzsch and Karl Horst Schmidt (eds.), *Indogermanisch und Keltisch,* pp. 11–33. Reicher and Verlag, Wiesbaden.

Gregor, Douglas B. (1980) *Celtic: A Comparative Study of the Six Celtic Languages: Irish, Gaelic, Manx, Welsh, Cornish, Breton Seen against the Background of their History, Literature, and Destiny.* Oleander Press, Cambridge, MA.

Grimshaw, Jane (1990) *Argument Structure.* MIT Press, Cambridge, MA.

—— (1994) Minimal Projection and Clause Structure. In Barbara Lust, Margarita Suñer, and John Whitman (eds.), *Heads, Projections and Learnability,* pp. 75–84. Lawrence Erlbaum Associates, Hillsdale, New Jersey.

Guilfoyle, Eithne (1987) Parameters and Functional Projection. *Proceedings of NELS* 18:193–207. GLSA, University of Massachusetts, Amherst, MA.

—— (1990) *Functional Categories and Phrase Structure Parameters.* Ph.D. dissertation, McGill University, Montréal.

—— (1993) Non-finite Clauses in Modern Irish and Old English. *Proceedings of the 29th Regional Meeting of the Chicago Linguistic Society,* pp. 199–214.

—— (1997) The Verbal Noun in Irish Non-finite Clauses. In Vera Capková and Anders Ahlqvist (eds.) *Dán do Oide, Essays in Memory of Conn Ó Cléirigh,* pp. 187–200. Institiúid Teangeolaíochta Éireann, Dublin.

—— (in press) Tense and N-features in Modern Irish and Early Child Grammars. In Usha Lakshmanan (ed.), *Minimalist Approaches to Language Acquisition,* Kluwer, Dordrecht.

Guilfoyle, Eithne, Henriette Hung, and Lisa Travis (1992) Spec of IP and Spec of VP: Two Subjects in Austronesian Languages. *Natural Language and Linguistic Theory* 10:375–414.

Haegeman, Liliane (1991) *Introduction to Government and Binding Theory.* Blackwell, Oxford.

—— (1995) Root Infinitives, Tense and Truncated Structures in Dutch. *Language Acquisition* 4:205–255.

Hajičová, Eva (1983) Topic and Focus. *Theoretical Linguistics* 10:268–276.

Hale, Kenneth (1973). A Note on Subject-Object Inversion in Navajo. in Braj B. Kachru et al. (eds.), *Issues in Linguistics: Papers in Honor of Henry and Renée Kahane,* pp. 300–309. University of Illinois Press, Urbana.

—— (1989) Incorporation and the Synthetic Verb Forms in Irish, Unpublished ms. MIT, Cambridge, MA.

—— (1990) Some Remarks on Agreement and Incorporation. *Studies in Generative Grammar* 1:117–144.

Hale, Kenneth and Samuel Jay Keyser (1991) On the Syntax of Argument Structure, *Lexicon Project Working Paper* 34, MIT, Cambridge, MA.

Hamiora, Angeline (n.d.) *Ko e Pusi* (a children's reader). Learning Media, Ministry of Education, Wellington, New Zealand.

Harley, Heidi (1995) *Subjects, Events and Licensing.* Ph.D. dissertation, MIT, Cambridge, MA.

Harlow, Stephen (1981) Government and Relativisation in Celtic. In Frank Heny (ed.), *Binding and Filtering,* pp. 213–254. Croom Helm, London.

—— (1992) Finiteness and Welsh Sentence Structure. In H. G. Obenauer and Anne Zribi-Hertz (eds.), *Structure de la phrase et théorie du Liage.* Presses Universitaires de Vincennes, Paris. pp 93–119.

Hatav, Galia (1997) *The Semantics of Aspect and Modality; Evidence from English and Biblical Hebrew.* John Benjamins. Amsterdam.

Hayes, Bruce (1989) The Prosodic Hierarchy in Meter. In Paul Kiparsky and G Youmans (eds.), *Rhythm and Meter,* pp. 201–260. Academic Press, San Diego.

Heim, Irene R. (1982) *The Semantics of Definite and Indefinite Noun Phrases.* Ph.D. dissertation, University of Massachusetts, Amherst, MA.

Hendrick, Randall (1988) *Anaphora in Celtic and Universal Grammar.* Kluwer, Dordrecht.

—— (1991) The Morphosyntax of Aspect. *Lingua* 85:171–210.

—— (1994) The Brythonic Copula and Head Raising. In David Lightfoot and Norbert Hornstein (eds.), *Verb Raising,* pp. 163–188. Cambridge University Press, Cambridge.

Higginbotham, James and Gillian Ramchand (1996) The Stage-Level/Individual Level Distinction and the Mapping Hypothesis. *Oxford University Working Papers in Linguistics, Philology and Phonetics* 2:53–84.

Hoekstra, Eric (1989) A Parameter for Anaphor Binding: The Case of Jacaltec. In L. Marácz and P. Muysken (eds.), *Configurationality: The Typology of Asymmetries.* Foris, Dordrecht.

Hohepa, Patrick (1969) *Not* in English and *kore* and *eehara* in Māori. *Te Reo* 12:1–34.

Holmberg, Anders (1997) The True Nature of Holmberg's Generalization. *Proceedings of NELS* 27:203–217. GLSA, University of Massachusetts, Amherst, MA.

Holmberg, Anders and Christer Platzack (1988) *On the Role of Inflection in the Syntax of the Scandinavian Languages.* Oxford University Press, Oxford.

Hung, Henriette (1988*) Derived Verbs and Nominals in Malagasy.* Unpublished ms. McGill University.

Iatridou, Sabine and Anthony Kroch (1992) The Licensing of CP Recursion and Its Relevance to the Germanic Verb-Second Phenomenon. *Working Papers in Scandinavian Syntax* 50:1–24.

Itagaki, Nobuya and Gary D. Prideaux (1985). Nominal Properties as Determinants of Subject Selection. *Lingua* 66:135–149.

Jarvella, Robert J. and Joan Sinnott (1972). Contextual Constraints on Noun Distributions to Some English Verbs by Children and Adults. *Journal of Verbal Learning and Verbal Behavior* 11:47–53.

Jelinek, Eloise (1984) Empty Categories, Case, and Configurationality. *Natural Language and Linguistic Theory* 2:39–76.

—— (1995) Quantification in Straits Salish. In Emmon Bach, Eloise Jelinek, Angelika Kratzer and Barbara Partee (eds.), *Quantification in Natural Languages,* pp. 487–541. Kluwer, Dordrecht.

—— (1997) Prepositions in Northern Straits Salish and the Noun/Verb Question. In Ewa Czaykowska-Higgins and M. Dale Kinkade (eds.), *Salish Languages and Linguistics.* pp. 325–346. Mouton, The Hague.

—— (1998) *Wh*-Clefts in Lummi (North Straits Salish). Paper presented at WECOL, Arizona State University, Tempe.

Jelinek, Eloise and Richard Demers (1994) Predicates and Pronominal Arguments in Straits Salish. *Language* 70:697–736.

—— (1997) Reduplication as a Quantifier in Salish. *International Journal of American Linguistics* 63.3:302–315.

Jelinek, Eloise and Mary Willie (1996) Psych Verbs in Navajo. In Eloise Jelinek, Sally Midgette, Keren Rice and Leslie Saxon (eds.), *Athabaskan Language Studies: Essays in Honor of Robert W. Young,* pp. 15–34. University of New Mexico Press, Albuquerque.

Johnson, Michael. G. (1967). Syntactic Position and Rated Meaning. *Journal of Verbal Learning and Verbal Behavior* 6:240–246.

Joüon, Paul (1923) *Grammaire the Hébreu Biblique.* Institut Biblique Pontifical, Rome.

Kaplan, Tami (1991) A Classification of VSO Languages. *Proceedings of ESCOL* 91:198–209.

Kaulima, Aiao, and Clive H. Beaumont (1994) *A First Book for Learning Niuean.* Clive H. Beaumont and Daisy J.M. Beaumont, Ranui, Auckland.

Kayne, Richard (1969). *The Transformational Cycle in French Syntax,* Ph.D. dissertation, MIT, Cambridge MA.

—— (1994) *The Antisymmetry of Syntax. Linguistic Inquiry Monograph 25.* MIT Press, Cambridge, MA.

—— (1998) Overt and Covert Movement. *Syntax* 1.2:128–191

Keenan, Edward (in press) Morphology is Structure: a Malagasy Test Case. In Ileana Paul, Vivianne Phillips, and Lisa Travis (eds.), *Formal Issues in Austronesian Linguistics.* Kluwer, Dordrecht.

Kiss, Katalin E. (1998) Identificational vs. Information Focus. *Language* 74:245–273.

Koopman, Hilda (1984) *The Syntax of Verbs.* Foris, Dordrecht.

—— (1996) The Spec-Head Configuration. In Edward Garrett and Felicia Lee (eds.), *Syntax and Sunset. UCLA Working Papers in Syntax and Semantics* 1:37–64.

Koopman, Hilda and Dominique Sportiche (1991) The Position of Subjects. *Lingua* 85:211–258.

Koopman, Hilda and Anna Szabolcsi (1997) The Hungarian Verbal Complex: Complex Verb Formation as XP Movement. Unpublished ms., University of California, Los Angeles.

Kornfilt, Jaklin (1985) *Case Marking, Agreement and Empty Categories in Turkish.* Ph.D. dissertation, Harvard University.

Koster, Jan (1978) Why Subject Sentences Don't Exist. In S. J. Keyser (ed.), *Recent Transformational Studies in European Languages*, pp. 53–64. MIT Press, Cambridge, MA.

Kratzer, Angelika (1993) On External arguments. In *Functional Projections, University of Massachusetts Working Papers in Linguistics* 17:103–130.

—— (1996) Severing the External Argument from its Verb. In Johan Rooryck and Laurie Zaring (ed.), *Phrase Structure and the Lexicon*, pp. 109–138. Kluwer, Dordrecht.

Kroeger, Paul (1990) The Morphology of Affectedness in Kimaragang Dusun. Presented at Stanford University.

Krupa, Victor (1982) *Languages of Asia and Africa.* vol 4: *The Polynesian Languages.* Routledge and Kegan Paul, London.

Ladusaw, William (1979) *Polarity Sensitivity as Inherent Scope Relations.* Garland, New York.

Laka, Itziar (1991) *Negation in Syntax: On the Nature of Functional Categories and Projections.* Ph.D. dissertation, MIT, Cambridge MA.

Lambrecht, Knud (1994) *Information Structure and Sentence Form.* Cambridge University Press, Cambridge.

Lane, Chris (1978) *Niuean Field Notes.* Unpublished ms. Victoria University of Wellington, New Zealand.

Larson, Richard (1988) On the Double Object Construction. *Linguistic Inquiry* 19:335–393.

—— (1990) Double Objects Revisited: Reply to Jackendoff. *Linguistic Inquiry* 21:589–563.

Lazard, Gilbert, and Louise Peltzer (1991) Predicates in Tahitian. *Oceanic Linguistics* 30:1–31.

Lee, Felicia (1996) Aspect, Negation, and Temporal Polarity in Zapotec. In Brian Agbayani and Sze-Wing Tang (eds.), *Proceedings of WCCFL* 15:305–320. CSLI, Stanford University, Stanford, CA.

—— (forthcoming) *Antisymmetry and the Syntax of San Lucas Quiaviní Zapotec.* Ph.D. dissertation, University of California, Los Angeles.

Legate, Julie (1997) *Irish Predication: A Minimalist Analysis.* MA thesis, University of Toronto.

Lehmann, R.P.M. and W.P. Lehmann (1975) *An Introduction to Old Irish.* Modern Language Association, New York.

Levin, Juliette and Diane Massam (1984) Surface Ergativity: Case-/Theta Relations Reexamined *Proceedings of NELS 15:*286–301. GLSA, University of Massachusetts.

—— (1986) Classification of Niuean verbs: Notes on Case. In Paul Garaghty, Lois Carrington, and S. A. Wurm (eds.), *FOCAL I: Papers from the Fourth International Conference on Austronesian Linguistics*, pp. 231–244. Pacific Linguistics C–93. Canberra: Australian National University.

Levin, Saul (1971) *The Indo-European and Semitic Languages.* SUNY Press, Albany, New York.

Levine, Robert (1984) Empty Categories, Rules of Grammar, and Kwakwala Complementation. In E.-D. Cook and Donna Gerdts (eds.), *The Syntax of Native*

American Languages. Syntax and Semantics, 16:215–245. Academic Press, San Diego.

Lewis, David (1975) Adverbs of Quantification. In Edward L. Keenan (ed.) *Formal Semantics of Natural Language,* pp. 3–15. Cambridge University Press, Cambridge.

Mackinnon, Roderick (1971) *Gaelic.* David McKay, New York.

Marantz, Alec (1984) *On the Nature of Grammatical Relations.* MIT Press, Cambridge, MA.

Massam, Diane (1996) Predicate Fronting in Niuean. In *Proceedings of the 1996 Canadian Linguistics Association Annual Meeting, Calgary Working Papers in Linguistics,* pp. 247–256.

—— (1998a) *Aki* and the Nature of Niuean Transitivity. In *Oceanic Linguistics* 37:12–28.

—— (1998b) Niuean Noun Incorporation: Not Nouns, Not Incorporation. Presented at AFLA V, University of Hawaii. Ms., University of Toronto.

Massam, Diane and Caroline Smallwood (1997) Essential Features of Predication in English and Niuean. In *Proceedings of NELS* 27:236–272. GLSA, University of Massachusetts, Amherst.

May, Robert (1985) *Logical Form.* MIT Press, Cambridge, MA.

McCloskey, James (1978) Stress and Syntax in Old Irish Compound Verbs. *Texas Linguistic Forum* 10:58–71.

—— (1979) *Transformational Syntax and Model Theoretic Semantics.* Reidel, Dordrecht.

—— (1980) Is There Raising in Modern Irish? *Ériu* 31:59–99.

—— (1983) A VP in a VSO language. In Gerald Gazdar, Geoff Pullam, and Ivan Sag (eds.), *Order Concord and Constituency.* Foris, Dordrecht.

—— (1986) Inflection and Conjunction in Modern Irish. *Natural Language and Linguistic Theory* 4:245–281.

—— (1990) Resumptive Pronouns, A-bar Binding and Levels of Representation in Irish. In Randall Hendrick (ed.), *The Syntax of the Modern Celtic Languages. Syntax and Semantics* 23:199–248. Academic Press, San Diego.

—— (1991) Clause Structure, Ellipsis, and Proper Government in Irish. In *The Syntax of Verb Initial Languages: Lingua Special Edition* 85:259–302.

—— (1992) Adjunction, Selection and Embedded Verb Second. Ms. University of California at Santa Cruz.

—— (1996a) Subjects and Subject Positions. In Robert Borsley and Ian Roberts (eds.), *The Syntax of the Celtic Languages,* pp. 241–283. Cambridge University Press, Cambridge.

—— (1996b) On the Scope of Verb Movement in Irish. *Natural Language and Linguistic Theory* 14:47–104.

—— (1997) Subjecthood and Subject Positions. In Liliane Haegeman (ed.), *Elements of Grammar: Handbook in Generative Grammar,* pp. 197–236. Kluwer, Dordrecht.

McCloskey, James and Kenneth Hale (1984) On the Syntax of Person-Number Inflection in Modern Irish. *Natural Language and Linguistic Theory* 1:487–533.

McCone, Kim (1987) *The Early Irish Verb.* An Sagart, Maynooth.

—— (1994) An tSean-Ghaeilge agus a Réamhstair. In Kim McCone, Damian McManus, Cathal Ó Háinle, Nicholas Williams, and Liam Breatnach (eds.), *Stair na Gaeilge* pp. 61–220. Roinn na Sean-Ghaeilge, Coláiste Phádraig, Maigh Nuad.

McDonald, Janet L., Kathryn Bock and Michael H. Kelly (1993). Word and World Order: Semantic, Phonological and Metrical Determinants of Serial Position. *Cognitive Psychology,* 25:188–230.

McEwen, James M. (1970) *Niue Dictionary.* Dept. of Māori and Island Affairs, Wellington, New Zealand.

McRae, Ken, Michael J. Spivey-Knowlton, and Michael K. Tannenhaus(1998) Modeling the Influence of Thematic Fit (and Other Constraints) in On-Line Sentence Comprehension. *Journal of Memory and Language* 38.3:283–312.

Minkoff, Seth. (1994). *How Some So-called "Thematic Roles" That Select Animate Arguments are Generated, and How These Roles Inform Binding and Control.* Doctoral Dissertation, MIT.

Mohammed, Mohammed (1988) On the Parallelism between IP and DP. *Proceedings of WCCFL* 7:241–254. CSLI, Stanford University, Stanford, CA.

—— (1990) The Problem of Subject-Verb Agreement in Arabic: Towards a Solution. In Mushira Eid (ed.), *Perspectives on Arabic Linguistics I,* pp. 95–125. John Benjamins, Amsterdam.

Montler, Tim (1986) *An Outline of the Morphology and Phonology of Saanich, North Straits Salish. University of Montana Occasional Papers in Linguistics* 4, University of Montana, Missoula.

—— (1996) Languages and Dialects in Straits Salishan. Presented at the 31st ICSNL, University of British Columbia, Vancouver, B.C.

Moreshet, Menachem (1967) hanasu hakodem lishney nosim bilshon hamikra. *Leshonenu* 31:1–10.

Moritz, Luc, and Daniel Valois (1994) French Sentential Negation and LF Pied-Piping. *Linguistic Inquiry* 25:667–707.

Munro, Pamela (1982) On the Transitivity of Say Verbs. In Paul Hopper and Sandra Thompson (eds.), *Studies in Transitivity. Syntax and Semantics 15:*301–317. Academic Press, New York.

—— (1996) Making a Zapotec Dictionary. *Dictionaries* 17:131–155.

Munro, P. and F. Lopez (with R. Garcia and O.V. Méndez) (1997) *Dicyonaary X:te:en Di:izh Sah Sann Luuc: San Lucas Quiaviní Zapotec Dictionary. Diccionario Zapoteco de San Lucas Quiaviní.* Unpublished ms. University of California, Los Angeles.

Myhill, John (1985) Pragmatic and Categorial Correlates of VS Word Order. *Lingua* 66:177–200.

Nash, Leá and Alain Rouveret (1997) Proxy Categories in Phrase Structure Theory. *Proceedings of NELS* 27:287–307. GLSA, University of Massachusetts, Amherst, MA.

Nespor, Marina and Irene Vogel (1986) *Prosodic Phonology.* Foris, Dordrecht.

Nilsen, Oystein (1998) The Syntax of Circumstantial Adverbials. M.phil. thesis, University of Tromsø, Norway.

Noonan, Máire (1994) VP-Internal and VP-External AgrO Phrase: Evidence from Irish. *Proceedings of WCCFL* 13:318–334. CSLI, Stanford University, Stanford, CA.

Ó Se, Diarmuid (1987) The Copula and Preverbal Particle in West Kerry Irish. *Celtica* 19:98–110.

—— (1990) Tense and Mood in Irish Copula Sentences. *Ériu* 41:62–75.

Ó Siadhail, Mícheál (1980) *Learning Irish.* Dublin Institute for Advanced Studies, Dublin.

Ouhalla, Jamal (1993) Subject-Extraction, Negation and the Anti-Agreement Effect. *Natural Language and Linguistic Theory* 11:477–518.

—— (1994) Verb Movement and Word Order in Arabic. In David Lightfoot and Norbert Hornstein (eds.) *Verb Movement,* pp. 41–72. Cambridge University Press, Cambridge.

Partee, Barbara (1973) The Syntax and Semantics of Quotation. In Stephen Anderson and Paul Kiparsky (eds.), *A Festschrift for Morris Halle* pp. 410–418. Holt, Rhinehart and Winston, New York.

—— (1987) Noun Phrase Interpretation and Type-Shifting Principles. In Jeroen Groenendijk, Dick De Jongh, and Martin Stokhof (eds.), *Studies in Discourse Representation and the Theory of Generalized Quantifiers.* GRASS 8:115–143. Foris, Dordrecht.

Pearce, Elizabeth (1997) Negation and Indefinites in Māori. in Danielle Forget, Paul Hirschbühler, France Martineau and María-Lusia Rivero (eds.), *Negation and Polarity: Syntax and Semantics,* pp. 271–288. John Benjamins, Amsterdam.

—— (forthcoming) The Syntax of Genitives in the Māori DP. In Diane Massam and Barry Miller (eds.), *Topics in Austronesian Syntax: The Canadian Journal of Linguistics,* special issue.

Pearson, Matthew (1998) Two Types of VO Languages. Unpublished ms., University of California, Los Angeles.

Pensalfini, Robert (1995) Malagasy Phrase Structure and the LCA. In Robert Pensalfini and Hiroyuki Ura (eds.), *Papers on Minimalist Syntax. MIT Working Papers in Linguistics* 27: 209–221.

Pesetsky, David (1995) *Zero Syntax: Experiencers and Cascades.* MIT Press, Cambridge, MA.

Pintzuk, Susan (1991) *Phrase Structures in Competition: Variation and Change in Old English Word Order.* Ph.D. dissertation, University of Pennsylvania, Philadelphia.

Platzack, Christer (1986a) Comp, Infl, and Germanic Word Order. In Lars Hellan and Kirsti K. Christensen (eds.), *Topics in Scandinavian Syntax,* pp. 185–234. Reidel, Dordrecht.

—— (1986b) The Position of the Finite Verb in Swedish. In Hubert Haider and Martin Prinzhorn (eds.), *Verb Second Phenomena in Germanic Languages,* pp. 27–47. Foris, Dordrecht.

—— (1986c) A Survey of Generative Analyses of the Verb Second Phenomenon in Germanic. *Nordic Journal of Linguistics* 8:49–73.

—— (1987) The Scandinavian Languages and the Null Subject Parameter. *Natural Language and Linguistic Theory* 5:377–401.

—— (1995) The Loss of Verb Second in English and French. In Adrian Battye and Ian Roberts (eds.), *Clause Structure and Language Change.* pp. 200–226. Oxford University Press, Oxford.

Pollock, Jean-Yves (1989) Verb Movement, Universal Grammar and the Structure of IP. *Linguistic Inquiry* 20:365–424.

Potter, Brian (1995) Minimalism and the Mirror Principle. In *Proceedings of the North East Linguistics Society* 26:289–302.

Press, Ian (1986) *A Grammar of Modern Breton.* Mouton de Gruyter, Berlin.

Pyatt, Elizabeth (1992) Incomplete Subject Raising and Welsh Word Order. *Proceedings of the Harvard Celtic Colloquium* 12:135–165.

—— (1996) *An Integrated Grammar of the Syntax, Morphology and Phonology of Celtic Mutations.* Ph.D. dissertation, Harvard University.

Rackowski, Andrea (1998) Malagasy Adverbs. In Ileana Paul (ed.) *The Structure of Malagasy, Volume 2,* pp. 11–33. *UCLA Occasional Papers in Linguistics.* Los Angeles.

Reinhart, Tanya (1983) Coreference and Bound Anaphora: A Restatement of the Anaphora Questions. *Linguistics and Philosophy* 6:47–99.

—— (1987) Specifier and Operator Binding. In Eric J. Reuland and Alice G. B. ter Meulen, (eds.) *The Representation of (In)definiteness.* MIT Press Cambridge, MA. pp. 130–167.

Reinhart, Tanya and Eric Reuland (1993) Reflexivity. *Linguistic Inquiry* 24:657–720.

Reuland, Eric and Jan Koster (1991) Long-distance Anaphora: an Overview. In Jan Koster and Eric Reuland (eds.), *Long-distance Anaphora,* pp.1–25. Cambridge University Press, Cambridge.

Rex, Leslie, Tongakilo Togia Viviani, Ahetoa, Aue, Hafe Vilitama, Ikipa Togatule, and Tahafa Talagi (eds.) (undated) *Everyday Words and Phrases in English and Niuean.* University of the South Pacific, Niue Centre, Alofi, Niue.

Rivero, Maria-Luisa (1991) Long Head Movement and Negation: Serbo-Croatian vs. Slovak and Czech, *Linguistic Review* 8:319–351.

—— (1993) Finiteness and Second Position in Long Head Movement Languages: Breton and Slavic, Ms., University of Ottawa.

—— (1994) Clause Structure and V-movement in the Languages of the Balkans. *Natural Language and Linguistic Theory* 12:63–120.

Rizzi, Luigi (1990) *Relativized Minimality.* MIT Press, Cambridge MA.

—— (1993/4) Some Notes on Linguistic Theory and Language Development. *Language Acquisition* 3:371–395.

—— (1997) The Fine Structure of the Left Periphery. In Liliane Haegeman (ed.), *Elements of Grammar: Handbook of Generative Grammar,* pp. 281–338. Kluwer, Dordrecht.

Rizzi, Luigi and Ian Roberts. (1989) Complex Inversion in French. *Probus* 1:1–30.

Roberts, Ian (1993) *Verbs and Diachronic Syntax.* Kluwer, Dordrecht.

—— (1994) Two Types of Head Movement in Romance. In David Lightfoot and Norbert Horstein (eds.), *Verb Movement,* pp. 207–242. Cambridge University Press, Cambridge.

Roberts, Ian and Ur Shlonsky (1996) Pronominal Enclisis in VSO Languages. In Robert Borsley and Ian Roberts (eds.), *The Syntax of the Celtic Languages. A Comparative Perspective,* pp. 171–199. Cambridge University Press, Cambridge.

Robertson, Boyd and Iain Taylor (1993) *Gaelic.* Hodder and Stoughton, London.

Roeper, Thomas (1992) From the Initial State to V2: Acquisition Principles in Action. In Jürgen M. Meisel (ed.), *The Acquisition of Verb Placement: Functional Categories and V2 Phenomena in Language Acquisition,* pp. 333–370. Kluwer, Dordrecht.

Rouveret, Alain (1990) X-bar Theory, Minimality and Barrierhood in Welsh. In Randall Hendrick (ed.), *The Syntax of the Modern Celtic Languages. Syntax and Semantics* 23:27–79. Academic Press, San Diego.

—— (1991) Functional Categories and Agreement. *The Linguistics Review* 8:353–387.

—— (1994) *Syntaxe du gallois: Principles généraux et typologie.* CNRS Editions, Paris.

—— (1996) *Bod* in the Present Tense and in Other Tenses. In Robert Borsley and Ian Roberts (eds.), pp. 125–170. *The Syntax of the Celtic Languages. A Comparative Perspective.* Cambridge University Press.

Sadler, Louisa (1988) *Welsh Syntax: A Government-Binding Approach.* Croom Helm, London.

Sáinz, Kaldo (1994) Projections and Particles: V1, V2 and Agreement. Ms., University of the Basque Country, Spain.

Saito, Mamuro and Naoki Fukui (1998) Order in Phrase Structure and Movement. *Linguistic Inquiry* 29:439–474.

Schafer, Robin (1994) *Non-finite Predicate Initial Constructions in Modern Breton.* Ph.D. dissertation, University of California, Santa Cruz.

—— (1995) Negation and Verb Second in Breton, *Natural Language and Linguistic Theory* 13:135–172.

Schwartz, Arthur (1972) The VP Constituent of SVO Languages. *Syntax and Semantics* 1:213–235. Academic Press, San Diego.

Schwartz, Bonnie and Sten Vikner (1989) All Verb Second Clauses are CPs. *Working Papers in Scandinavian Syntax* 43:27–49.

—— (1996) The Verb Always Leaves IP in V2. In Adriana Belletti and Luigi Rizzi (eds.), *Parameters and Functional Heads: Essays in Comparative Syntax*, pp. 11–63. Oxford University Press, Oxford.

Seiter, William (1980) *Studies in Niuean Syntax*. Garland Press, New York.

Selkirk, Elisabeth (1984) *Phonology and Syntax: The Relation Between Sound and Structure*. MIT Press, Cambridge, MA.

Shlonsky, Ur (1987) *Null and Displaced Subjects*. Ph.D. dissertation, MIT, Cambridge, MA.

—— (1988) Complementizer-cliticization in Hebrew and the Empty Category Principle. *Natural Language and Linguistic Theory* 6:191–205.

—— (1991) Quantifiers as Functional Heads: A Study of Quantifier Float in Hebrew. *Lingua* 84:159–180.

Shlonsky, Ur and Edit Doron (1992) Verb-second in Hebrew. *Proceedings of WCCFL* 10:431–446. CSLI, Stanford University, Stanford, CA.

Smallwood, Caroline (1996) *A Minimalist Account of English Predication*. M.A. thesis, University of Toronto.

Speas, Margaret (1990) *Phrase Structure in Natural Language*. Kluwer, Dordrecht.

Sperlich, Wolfgang (1998) *Tohi Vagahau Niue: Niue Language Dictionary*. University of Hawaii Press and Government of Niue, Honolulu.

Sproat, Richard (1983) VSO Languages and Welsh Configurationality. *MIT Working Papers in Linguistics* 5:243–276.

—— (1985) Welsh Syntax and VSO structure. *Natural Language and Linguistic Theory* 3:173–216.

Stenson, Nancy (1981) *Studies in Irish Syntax*. Gunter Narr, Tübingen.

—— (1989) Irish Autonomous Impersonals. *Natural Language and Linguistic Theory* 7:379–406.

Stephens, Janig (1982) *Word Order in Breton*. Ph.D. dissertation, University of London.

—— (1993) Breton. In Martin J. Ball and James Fife (eds.), *The Celtic Languages*, pp. 349–409. Routledge, London.

Steuart, Shanley (1996) The Structure of the Verb Complex in Niuean. *Toronto Working Papers in Linguistics* 14:127–158.

Stowell, Timothy (1981) *Origins of Phrase Structure*. Ph.D. dissertation, MIT, Cambridge, MA.

—— (1989) Raising in Irish and the Projection Principle. *Natural Language and Linguistic Theory* 7:317–359.

Strachan, James (1949) *Old Irish Paradigms and Glosses*. 4th edition. Royal Irish Academy, Dublin.

Stump, Gregory (1985) Agreement vs. Incorporation in Breton. *Natural Language and Linguistic Theory* 2:289–348.

—— (1989) Further Remarks on Breton Agreement. *Natural Language and Linguistic Theory* 7:429–472.

Szabolcsi, Anna (1981) The Possessive Construction in Hungarian: A Configurational Category in a Non-configurational Language. *Acta Linguistica Academiae Scientiarum Hungaricae* 31:261–289.

Tabossi, Patrizia, Michael J. Spivey-Knowlton, Ken McRae, and Michael Tanenhaus (1994) Semantic Effects on Syntactic Ambiguity Resolution; Evidence for a Constraint-based Resolution Process. *Attention and Performance* 15:589–615.

Tallerman, Maggie (1990) VSO Word Order and Consonantal Mutation in Welsh. *Linguistics* 28:398–416.

—— (1996) Fronting Constructions in Welsh. In Robert Borsley and Ian Roberts (eds.), *The Syntax of the Celtic Languages: A Comparative Perspective*, pp. 97–124. Cambridge University Press, Cambridge.

Taraldsen, Tarald (1986) On Verb Second and the Functional Content of Syntactic Categories, in Hubert Haider and Martin Prinzhorn (eds.) *Verb Second Phenomena in Germanic Languages*. Foris, Dordrecht. pp. 7–25.

Thorne, David A. (1993) *A Comprehensive Welsh Grammar. Gramadeg Cymraeg Cynhwysfawr*. Blackwell, Oxford.

Thurneysen, Rudolf (1946) *A Grammar of Old Irish: An Enlarged Edition with Supplement*. Translated by Daniel A. Binchy and Osborn Bergin. Dublin Institute for Advanced Studies, Dublin.

Travis, Lisa (1984) *Parameters and Effects of Word Order Variation*. Ph.D dissertation, MIT, Cambridge, MA.

—— (1988) The Syntax of Adverbs. *McGill Working Papers in Linguistics: Special Issue on Comparative Germanic Syntax*, pp. 280–310.

—— (1991) Inner Aspect and the Structure of VP. Presented at *NELS 22*

—— (in press) T-positions and Binding in Balinese and Malagasy. *Canadian Journal of Linguistics*.

Trechsel, Frank (1995) Binding and Coreference in Jakaltek. In Clifford Burgess, Katarzyna Dziwirek, and Donna Gerdts (eds.), *Grammatical relations. Theoretical approaches to empirical questions,* pp. 449–471. CSLI, Stanford.

Trépos, Pierre (1980) *Grammaire bretonne*. Ouest France, Rennes.

Trueswell, John C., Michael K. Tanenhaus, and Susan M. Garnsey (1994). Semantic Influences on Parsing: Use of Thematic Role Information in Syntactic Ambiguity Resolution. *Journal of Memory and Language* 33:285–318.

Van Voorst, Jan (1988) *Event Structure*. John Benjamins, Amsterdam.

Vikner, Sten (1991) *Verb Movement and the Licensing of NP-Positions in the Germanic Language*. Ph.D. dissertation, University of Geneva.

—— (1994) *Verb Movement and Expletive Subjects in the Germanic Languages*. Oxford University Press, Oxford.

Visser, Fredericus Theodorus (1963) *An Historical Syntax of the English Language,* vol 1. E.J. Brill, Leiden.

Wackernagel, Jakob (1892) Über ein Gesetz der indogermanischen Wortstellung. *Indogermanische Forschungen* 1:333–436.

Waite, Jeffrey (1987) Negatives in Māori: A Lexical-Functional Approach. *Te Reo* 30:79–100.

—— (1994) Determiner Phrases in Māori. *Te Reo* 37:5–70.

Wallace, Charles (1992) *An Analysis of Jakaltek Phrase Structure*. M.A. thesis, Linguistics Department, University of California, Santa Cruz.

Watanabe, Akira (1993*) Agr Based Case Theory and Its Interaction With the A-bar System*. Ph.D. dissertation, MIT, Cambridge, MA.

Watkins, Calvert (1963) Preliminaries to a Historical and Comparative Syntax of the Old Irish Verb. *Celtica* 6:1–49.

Watkins, T. Arwyn (1993) Welsh. In Martin J. Ball and James Fife (eds.), *The Celtic Languages*. pp. 289–348, Routledge, London.

Wechsler, Stephen and Wayan Arka (1998) Syntactic Ergativity in Balinese. *Natural Language and Linguistic Theory* 16:387–441.

Weerman, Fred (1989). Prolog. In *The V2 Conspiracy*. Foris, Dordrecht.

Wexler, Kenneth. (1994). Finiteness and Head Movement in Early Child Grammar. In David Lightfoot and Norbert Hornstein (eds.), *Verb Movement*, pp. 305–351. Cambridge University Press, Cambridge.

Whittaker, Graeme (1982) *The Niuean Language: An Elementary Grammar and Basic Vocabulary*. University of the South Pacific, Niue Centre, Alofi, Niue.

Willie, Mary and Eloise Jelinek (in press) Navajo as a Discourse Configurational Language. In Ted Fernald and Paul Platero (eds.), *Athabaskan Languages and Linguistics*, Oxford University Press, Oxford.

Willis, Penny (1988) Is the Welsh Verbal Noun a Verb or a Noun? *Word* 39:201–224.

Witherspoon, Gary (1977). *Language and Art in the Navajo Universe*. University of Michigan Press, Ann Arbor.

Woolford, Ellen. (1991) VP-Internal Subjects in VSO and Nonconfigurational Languages. *Linguistic Inquiry* 22:503–540.

Zec, Draga and Sharon Inkelas (1990) Prosodically Constrained Syntax. In Sharon Inkelas and Draga Zec (eds.), *The phonology-syntax connection,* pp. 365–378. University of Chicago Press, Chicago.

Zribi-Hertz, Anne and Liliane Mbolatianavalona (1999) Towards a Modular Theory of Linguistic Deficiency: Evidence from Malagasy Personal Pronouns. *Natural Language and Linguistic Theory* 17.1:161–218..

Zwart, Jan-Wouter (1993a). *Dutch Syntax: A Minimalist Approach*. Gröningen Dissertations in Linguistics 10.

—— (1993b) Verb Movement and Complementizer Agreement. In Jonathan Bobaljik and Colin Phillips (eds.) *Paper on Case and Agreement I, MIT Working Papers in Linguistics* 18:296–341.

Index